GROWING UP MINNEAPOLIS
& MINNETONKA

"He was merely one of a thousand Americans of his time who were trying to fathom the significance of things: the explorers, the machinists, the agriculturalists, the boatbuilders, the men and women who were starting universities, the newspaper editors, the ministers. They had one thing in common: somewhere, somehow, they had learned to read, and the demands of frontier life had encouraged them to think. From this yeasty combination would spring all the developments that would make America great, all the inventions and the radical new ways of doing things and the germinal ideas which would remake the world."

James A. Michener, CHESAPEAKE

GROWING UP MINNEAPOLIS & MINNETONKA

A City, A Lake, A Family

ROSS FRUEN

Brule, Wisconsin

GROWING UP MINNEAPOLIS & MINNETONKA
A CITY, A LAKE, A FAMILY

First Edition

Published by:
  Cable Publishing, Inc.
  14090 E Keinenen Rd
  Brule, WI 54820
  Website: cablepublishing.com
  E-mail: nan@cablepublishing.com

Soft cover: ISBN 978-1-934980-89-7

Library of Congress Control Number: 2022947857

Cover design by Lverkeyn@gmail.com
Interior design by Jackie Pechin of Barebonz Design

COVER
  Top photo: Fruen Chalet-Crown Point, Big Island, Lake Minnetonka, May 2021
  Bottom photo: William and Henrietta Fruen family, Circa 1890

OPPOSITE PAGE
  The obelisk was erected in Lakewood Cemetery to honor my Great-great-grandmother Harriet White Fruen in 1887. The initial Fruen plot also includes Great-grandparents, William and Henrietta Bergquist Fruen and most of their children starting with infant Freddy in 1874.

Printed in the United States of America

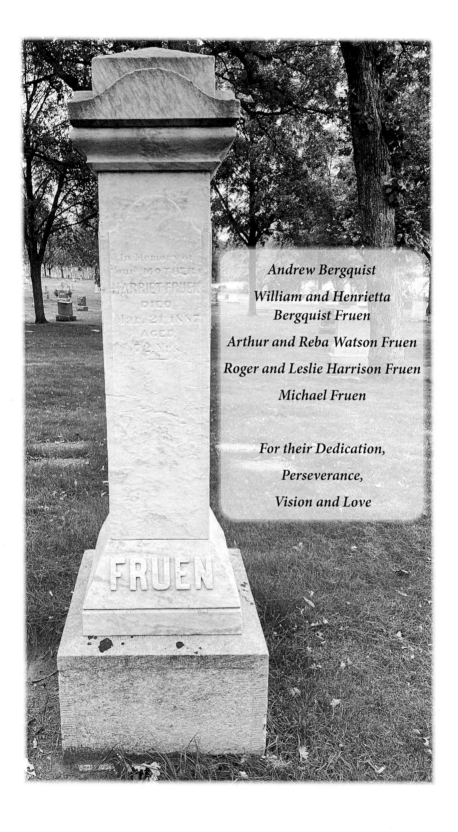

Andrew Bergquist

William and Henrietta
Bergquist Fruen

Arthur and Reba Watson Fruen

Roger and Leslie Harrison Fruen

Michael Fruen

For their Dedication,

Perseverance,

Vision and Love

Timeline

1852	Andrew Bergquist settles in Mdewankonton Dakota hunting grounds in today's Carver County, north of the Minnesota River, after escaping religious tyranny in Sweden.
1870	William Henry Fruen arrives in Minneapolis from England at age 19.
1871	Henrietta Bergquist marries William. They settle in the Bryn Mawr area of Minneapolis on Bassett's Creek at the western fringes of the fledging city.
1874	William dams the creek to power his screw manufacturing operation.
1878	William invents and patents the Fruen Water Wheel Governor in the wake of the Washburn A Mill explosion and sells it worldwide.
1884	William begins bottling and delivering spring water from his property and starts what becomes Glenwood Inglewood Spring Water.
1884	William invents and patents the Automatic Liquid Drawing Device – the first liquid vending machine.
1885	Arthur Bernard Fruen born.
1887	Harriet White Fruen dies.
1890	Reba Mary Watson born.
1894	William starts milling grain and produces the first packaged breakfast cereal.
1909	Arthur Fruen becomes president of Fruen Milling Company.
1912	Henrietta Bergquist Fruen dies.
1913	Reba Watson and Arthur Fruen marry.
1917	William Henry Fruen dies.
1919	Roger Fruen born.
1920	Arthur is elected to the Minneapolis City Council, becoming president his first term.
1923	Leslie Fruen born.
1928	Arthur and Reba acquire Big Island's Crown Point on Lake Minnetonka.
1957	Henrietta Braden Emerson dies.
1970	Arthur Bernard Fruen dies.
1971	Fruen Milling Company sold to Conagra.
1987	Reba Fruen dies.
	Roger Fruen dies.
2004	Glenwood-Inglewood sold to Deep Rock Water.
	Leslie Fruen dies.

Prologue

"If there was water, we were in it."

Tracy Fruen Bregman

MY NIECE TRACY'S DESCRIPTION of our family's relationship with water is precise. She may have been speaking of summers on Lake Minnetonka's Big Island, her Great-great- grandfather's Glenwood Spring or adventures on Minnehaha Creek. In a larger sense it distills the Minneapolis Fruen's reliance on water, which provided freedom, travel, sustenance, livelihood and, eventually, recreation and family gatherings at our island haven.

This story is uniquely American and Minnesotan. Two immigrants, a Swedish woman and a British man, met in church and continued our family's one-hundred-and-seventy-year journey in the pioneer years of Minneapolis and later, on a magnificent lake just west of downtown.

It is a narrative of the significance of place as locations take on a palpable, large-as-life importance. Our family places are infused with emotions and memories that seep into our thoughts and dreams. We are tethered to these touchstones and moorings and connected to the *genii locorum,* the spirit of place, as are the Dakota Native Americans who came before.

Growing up Minneapolis and Minnetonka… is a tale of sacrifice and escape to the Upper Midwest to forge a new life. Great amounts of courage and fortitude were required, and my ancestors were motivated by the ambition, adventure, opportunity and wanderlust that drive the pioneer spirit.

The family history dovetails with that of nascent Minneapolis and Minnetonka. My goal is not merely to resurrect the ghosts of family past, but to shine a light on the Mill City and the Big Water as well.

We all grew up together – the city, the lake and the family – through triumphs and setbacks, celebration and tragedy. The Fruens were there. In Minneapolis and on Lake Minnetonka.

> *"The power of place is undeniable. Many of us have experienced in different ways during our lifetimes – returning to ancestral homelands or family burial sites, visiting spectacular places of worship or historic battlefields, or standing in awe of remarkable natural beauty. These places tell us stories and provide us with long-lasting memories. It is through stories and experiences that we understand the power of place."*
>
> Gwen Westerman & Bruce White,
> *MNI SOTA MAKOCE: THE LAND OF THE DAKOTA*

Todd Fruen (R) and Tracy Fruen (L) fending off
Princess, the Old English water dog.
Fruen family photo

Contents

My mother after a long day on the water, 1973.
Fruen family photo

My father at the helm of our boat, the *Queen Merrie*, 1973.
Fruen family photo

Introduction

"A lake is the landscape's most beautiful and expressive feature, It is earth's eye looking into which the beholder measures the depth of his own nature."

Henry David Thoreau

IT SEEMED NORMAL TO me. After all, it was all I knew. Mom, Dad, sister Martha and I, plus a dog or two, piled into our station wagon at our South Minneapolis home. Forty-five minutes later, after driving to the landing in Tonka Bay and a short boat ride, we arrived at the family cabin on an island in the middle of Lake Minnetonka, the most heralded of the many thousand islands within the borders of Minnesota. The car ride was so short I barely had time to pick on my sister or develop back sweat from the vinyl seat. Dad always rolled his window down and rested his forearm on the chrome frame. I called him *"the man with the left-arm tan."*

The Lower Lake boat leg of our trip was even shorter than the car ride. My father Roger wore his trademark summer, red Ascot-style cap. Mother Leslie expertly fastened a hair net to protect her coiffure from the elements. The dogs jockeyed for position to nip at the spray off each side of the Alumacraft's stern. When the lake was calm, we cruised by Gale's Island at wide-open throttle on the way to our dock on Big Island's Crown Point. On days when Minnetonka's surface was choppy, Dad slowed the 50-horsepower Johnson outboard and angled the bow to minimize the impact of the jarring waves.

Summer weekends on the point were not for the weak of heart. Aunt Bunny, who did not grow up with the cabin culture, found Big Island life to be rather primitive, which meant that family branch did not visit very often. It was too bad as my cousin Debbie, one year and one day older than I, was a pal. One can sympathize a little regarding

1

the reticence of the uninitiated to embrace the Big Island element of the
Fruen Family lifestyle.

The noise was constant and loud. The incessant high-pitched whine
of outboard motors, the screeching children, the slap of hand on skin
as one more mosquito bit the dust. The barking dogs, the dueling tran-
sistor radios blaring the Twins baseball game and perhaps the Everly
Brothers combined to create a decibel level so high and discordant that
it made your ears hurt. Fruens are prone to deafness. There may be a
correlation.

The smells were visceral. Wet dogs rolled in sun-ripened dead fish.
Small puddles of multi-colored, mixed gasoline and motor oil floated
on the water's surface and snuck up on the unsuspecting swimmer.
Lighter fluid, combined with the smoke of charcoal briquettes, wafted
along the waterfront with an occasional vapor trail of Old Spice if an
uncle were in the vicinity.

Our summer version of snowball fights often ended abruptly with
strands of seaweed clinging to the face of a small, bawling cousin whose
breaths between sobs sucked the gamey green tendrils back into his nos-
trils. Pungent bug spray and oily sun block were slathered on squirming
young boys and girls who knew it would all be washed away during the
next painful belly flop.

After wriggling from our mothers' attentive grasps, there was a mad
dash to the boathouse to find the biggest, most inflated inner tubes.
There was generally a casualty or two due to the wet, slippery terrain of
the rock and cement as a cousin fell by the wayside. On occasion there
were opportunities to grab multiple tubes and stack them in the water,
creating a watery fortress: a hybrid of a bumper car and a Playskool
baby-ring nesting toy.

Our bodies took a beating. Splashing was the least of our concerns
as huge cabin cruisers piloted by people with more money than common sense motored by, too fast and too close to our dock, creating
huge waves that battered the shoreline and pitched the smaller children
sprawling backwards against the large stones and cement in front of the
terra firma. Bigger waves lifted the metal sections off the dock's frame,
which settled back into position when the disruption subsided. The
more experienced Fruens sensed the approaching tsunami and scrambled quickly from the dock with paperback books, towels, radios and
chairs in hand.

Feet took a pounding running up and down the 90 stone steps from the shore to the top of the hill where the Brick House and the Cottage stood. The indestructible, pimpled surface of the old white metal dock was unforgiving. We had no beach. The stone walkway covered the shore, giving way to large stones placed as a break.

Arms were strained and palms burned by the water-ski towrope as the braided yellow nylon whizzed through hands until the slack was taken up with a jerk when the speedboat captain gunned it. Lung capacity was crucial to our survival. I spent my 8th summer submerged in Lake Minnetonka with an older cousin's hand firmly palming the stubble on top of my head.

My older brothers Dave and Mike usually joined us. Mike and cousin Rick Fruen were close friends, and another generation arrived on Big Island when Dave and his wife Lael brought their children, David Jr. and Tracy. I was an uncle at ten.

My young cousin Ricky Barnett was the same age as Junior and, when he was visiting from Ohio with his parents Uncle Dick and Aunt Louise and siblings, we constructed a huge play pen with chicken wire. We tossed in some toys, and the toddlers had a great time staggering around the corral in their diapers, isolated from the dangers of a steep hill and a big lake.

The food was classic summer fare: hot dogs and hamburgers, corn on the cob, cole slaw and potato salad. The adults drank sun tea steeped outside in large containers. I drank milk or sometimes a purloined Royal Crown Cola from Aunt Margaret's stash in the ancient Norge chalet refrigerator, old enough to be called an "ice box."

The bottles were on the top shelf under the ice-encrusted freezer compartment, and crystals formed at the top, giving a slushy introduction to the first few gulps. The Dakota call Big Island *Wetutanku*, "The Great Sugaring Camp," but I can't imagine the springtime tapping of sugar maples produced an elixir as delicious as my aunt's RCs.

The best thing about watermelon for dessert was the opportunity to spit the seeds. Expectorating for pleasure was otherwise forbidden. When finished, the boys headed to the lookout and flung the rinds as far as we could out into the lake. Boomerangs that did not return. Soon, what appeared to be a fleet of small submarines headed for the point. Hungry carp were on the move.

Shirts were mandatory for all meals and, of course, we waited an hour before we could swim again, a practice since proven unnecessary. We played games in the hollow between the houses and the outbuildings to kill the inexorable hour before heading down to the waterfront. Volleyball and badminton were favorites, but we outgrew softball when balls launched into the Big Woods from the bats of our more prodigious sluggers.

Dad spent all afternoon driving the boat as his children, nieces and nephews – and later his grandchildren – took turns skiing. Mom spent much of her time perched on her webbed chair at the end of the dock in her sleeveless white shirt and a skirt and, with a beatific expression on her face, listened serenely to the ball game and worked on her tan, oblivious to the surrounding mayhem.

The adult dress code was "Fruen Casual." The women wore skirts and tops and perhaps the occasional muumuu while the men wore polo shirts from Munsingwear, a Minneapolis-based company, with the trademark small penguin logo over the left chest, or perhaps some style of Ban-Lon, made with a wrinkle-resistant fiber not known to nature. The dads wore trousers that were the precursor to Dockers. They looked like golfers who had lost their way. Aunt Margaret almost always wore shorts.

When the parents needed a break, they retired to the chalet to smoke a cigarette or use their pop-up bar to fix a drink. This was done out of respect for my grandparents' values and, more importantly, to avoid the inevitable lecture. Uncle Bruce liked his Manhattans while my parents preferred bourbon. It amused us to no end to see the grown-ups tiptoeing around and misbehaving. The visual images are vivid to this day: sails billowing in the breeze and the bright sun reflecting off the water.

People were part of the tableau. My father's generation did not produce many "characters," but Aunt Betty Fruen O'Connor's husband Charles was certainly one. I became a connoisseur of uncles at an early age. Sub-categories include mentors, glad-handers, the mean, the indifferent and ones you were happy to see. Usually the jolliest and friendliest of my uncles, Charles, was deathly afraid of water. He looked like the Michelin Tire Man as numerous inner tubes encircled his life jacket.

He teetered down the dock until he could be lowered into the boat in eager anticipation of reaching the mainland. I tip my hat to him for overcoming his very real anxieties. As the last boats departed in the early evening, my grandparents, Arthur and Reba, stood on the lookout waving goodbye, likely relishing the prospect of some quiet until the next weekend.

The raucous day of swimming, skiing and picnicking with grandparents, parents, siblings, cousins and aunts and uncles wound down, and we headed back to Minneapolis – tired, disheveled, sunburned, wind-burned and sometimes a bit cranky. I know things were not always idyllic in my father's generation as the siblings shared not only Crown Point but ownership of the family business. No matter the issues, they were put aside on the island. The children were not to be exposed to dissention.

Martha and I tried to enhance the car ride home by chanting, "*We want Dairy Queen!*" Dilly Bars were our go-to choices, but I estimate we only succeeded in scoring about a third of the time. Dad tried to distract us with his sing-along, bleating atonal renditions of his favorite childhood ditties such as "Riding on a Dummy Line" and "The Boys from the Institute." We often joined him.

The Cabin Culture is ingrained in Minnesota life. Most weekend cabin dwellers fight hours of frustrating traffic returning from the northern lake country to the Twin Cities. For us it was just a hop, skip and a jump. I could be a city boy at breakfast, a cabin kid in the afternoon and back home again at night listening to planes flying low over our house in their final descent to nearby Wold-Chamberlain Field. It was my Southwest Minneapolis lullaby.

Sculpted by ice, Lake Minnetonka
Photo by Ed Kohler, courtesy of Wikimedia

The Glaciers Recede and Humans Arrive

"Down a well of time only twice as deep as the pyramids of Egypt, a continental glacier was receding from Minnesota. It left a blasted landscape of bedrock, boulders, gravel, sand, silt, and water. A land made by ice. Plants, animals, and eventually Lutherans colonized and scratched at the surface of the land, but the power of the glaciers still dominates our physical environment and profoundly shapes our work lives and our recreation."

David Borchert as told to Kate Roberts,
MINNESOTA 150

THE GLACIERS OF THE most recent ice age sculpted the majority of ancient Minnesota and Wisconsin; gouging, scraping and polishing the landscape on their advance and depositing debris during their retreat. The massive Laurentide ice sheet, at its zenith 21,000 years ago, smothered almost all of Canada and much of the Northern U.S. from Maine to Washington State.

The Wisconsin Glacial Episode was the swan song of this era, lasting from 110,000 years ago to about 10,000 years ago. After the ice retreated north, the modern form of Lake Minnetonka began to take shape. Previous glacial events touched the Big Water, and the till deposited accounts for the wide variety of bottom material found including soils, hard sand, gravel, mud, small stones and boulders.

"Some claim the upper and lower portions of Lake Minnetonka are different. The lower contains more pebbles, sand and is deeper. The upper contains finer textured rock, is weedier and more shallow. Some claim water chemistry varies. Did the two glaciers from differing sources give us

two different lakes?" (Richard Etten, "A look at the geologic history of the Wayzata area," *swnewsmedia*)

■ ■ ■

*Mni Tanka (*Big Water*),* as the Dakota called Minnetonka, consists of approximately twenty-nine bays (depending on who is counting) connected by channels and marshes forming a 14,500-acre body of water eleven miles long and six miles wide. Its shape is so irregular that it is difficult to measure the shoreline, but a good estimate is 125 miles. The lake has eighteen islands, once again, open to debate.

"*The huge dirty blocks of highly compressed crystals of glacial ice melted over a period of 2,000 years or so. The drift dropped out and became the soil of the lakes and the land around them. The uneven shapes of these blocks of ice determined the basins of the lakes, the depths of lake beds, the irregularity of shorelines, presence of channels and islands and left a connected major imprint of 15 interconnected ice-block lakes that are labeled Lake Minnetonka.*" (Dick Gray, "Icy Origin Determines Lake Minnetonka Character")

The series of glaciers over the Americas created opportunities for migration of humans and other mammals. While there are many conflicting theories on the timing and methods of human migration from Asia, Polynesia and other possibilities to North and South America, it is probable that a combination of different waves, means and routes were in play.

The causes of the migrations are not totally clear but may have included population pressures, hunting opportunities, conflict and perhaps even curiosity. The dates of the early migrations are estimated to be between 50,000 and 15,000 years ago but with new discoveries, the earlier date continues to be pushed back.

The massive land bridge between Siberia and Alaska, Beringia, was created by low ocean levels. Migrants from the Pacific Islands and Asians following the western coast of the Americas by boat are now thought to have been early travelers. Many followed the "Kelp Highway" south, sustained by the extensive edible marine life ranging from seaweed, shellfish, fish, birds and the sea mammals such as seals and walruses that fed on the cornucopia of food sources.

The highway stretched, with a few interruptions in the tropics, from

Beringia to the Andean coast of South America. Previously most of the migration hypotheses relied on the land bridge explanation, but maritime routes bolster the theory of multiple means of migration as well as help to answer the confounding questions regarding the dates of human habitation in sites like Paisley Caves in Oregon and Monte Verde in Chile. Archaeologists have been aware of ancient footsteps in a dry New Mexico lakebed for many years. Recently, radiocarbon tests on tiny seeds near the footprints revealed a human presence 23,000 years ago, during the height of glacial activity, which would preclude the use of the Bering Strait route.

Paleo Indians in small nomadic groups arrived in today's Upper Midwest stalking the huge mammals. They used spears to kill mammoths, mastodons, as well as giant bison and 200-pound beavers.

The Paleo era evolved into the Archaic period when temperatures moderated, lakes and rivers began to transform into current shapes, and the tundra gave way to coniferous forests. As the mega mammals started to disappear, deer and smaller mammals became the primary source of food as well as fish, plants and nuts. The natives toppled trees for canoes, fires, containers and tools. In some locations copper was mined to create tools, hooks, spear points, beads and other decorative items. The Woodland group was the final culture before contact with Europeans in the Upper Midwest.

"To conjure the canvas of this world of the north country, try first to imagine forests alive with game, the trees so dense that a man on horseback could find no way through: lakes and rivers, teeming with fish, the primary pathways of travel...." (Mary Lethert Wingerd, *North Country*)

■ ■ ■

The Ojibwe and Dakota began their intense period of warfare in the 1730s, and the battles continued for decades. The westward push by the fur trade and the intrusion of the Iroquois precipitated a crowding of the various tribes and competition for the resources of northern Wisconsin, not the least of which were the beds of wild rice located in the shallows of lakes and rivers. The Dakota word is *Psin*, and the grain is an excellent source of proteins and minerals. A major cultural breakthrough in food storage occurred about 1,200 years ago when they learned how to parch (dry) wild rice.

Parching wild rice enabled them to stave off starvation during severe winters and gave them more mobility since they were not limited to a specific harvesting location anymore. The annual aquatic grass grows best on water moved by wind or water current, is the only grain indigenous to North America and is more nutritious than either oats or wheat. Wild rice was an excellent dietary alternative when deer and other game were scarce. It was a staple of the Dakota diet and was especially flavorful when served as a porridge with maple syrup, blueberries and cranberries.

The Dakota hid *Mni Tanka* from the Europeans for many decades. It was a gift from the Great Manitou, the esteemed head of the Dakota spirit-beings. The ancient Mound Builders left visible evidence of their religious ties to the Big Water during latter part of the Woodland Era. They occupied a large portion of the Upper Midwest and built large earthen structures between 350 BCE and 150CE used for ceremony, burial, and perhaps residences for the elite.

In the 1880s, 524 mounds were mapped on the shores of Lake Minnetonka and its islands. Big Island is the site of eighteen mounds. Sadly, almost all have been plundered or plowed under to make room for home construction. The Mound Builders chose sites similar to today's suburban gentry, mostly high, dry locations with beautiful vistas.

Not all mounds were round or conical in shape. The Upper Lake was home to many mounds, particularly near Mound City (known now as simply Mound) where 69 were catalogued on the north side of Halstead's Bay and 30 more in the vicinity. There was a variety of shapes and sizes. One grouping consisted of nine mounds, seven of which were circular and two others long and narrow.

The largest in the Upper Lake was fifty-two feet wide and eight feet high on Cook's Bay. Early looters discovered skeletons, scorched bones, shells, arrowheads and red pipes made from the catlinite extracted from the sacred quarries in southwestern Minnesota.

Sixty-nine mounds were in a low-lying meadow in today's Excelsior, suggesting the presence of a village. One contained thirty-five skulls arranged in a circle. The Dakota respected the mounds and did not disturb them as they valued Lake Minnetonka as a source of energy and power. As a child my father told me about the eighteen mounds on Big Island, and I immediately set out to find one. I returned tired and disappointed. I could not find them.

The early human history of Lake Minnetonka is murky; however, it has been established that the first people arrived about 8,000 BCE. There are gaps in habitation, but it is thought that sub-tribes of the Algonquins, including the Iowa, Cheyenne, Arapaho and Cree, arrived by 500 BCE and left a few centuries before the Dakota migrated there about 1500 CE.

■ ■ ■

The Dakota Creation Story has two prongs. Initially, Lake Mille Lacs was the spiritual nexus with the *Cancu Wanabi*, the spirit road, being the path to earth. When forced south and west from the original location by the Ojibwe, the Dakota shifted their genesis theory to *Bdote* (Mendota) at the confluence of the Minnesota and Mississippi Rivers.

"*Two bluffs were formed from the earth…The earth opened herself in that way, and from the mud the Creator made the first Dakota man and woman.*" (Mni Sota: *The Land of the Dakota*, Bruce White and Gwen Westerman)

The Big Water remained a source of sustenance and religious significance for approximately one hundred years before significant regularity of European incursion. "*We found on the shore a stone, shaped like an egg, standing on the small end, painted red and all the rocks around were sprinkled with a paint resembling blood. On the top of the stone was placed some Indian tobacco, ready for smoking; and about a rod from the stone was a grave. The bark with which it had been covered was rotten, so that hardly any traces of the grave were left except the mound…It is probably the grave of a Chief, who was killed with the others across the lake, but the warriors out of respect buried him here, and everyone who passes this way paints the stone, and leaves some tobacco, in memory of the departed chief.*" (Arthur Mills and Lucien Parker, *St. Anthony Express*, October 1, 1852)

Spirit Knob, then a sixty-foot-high hill, was situated on the tip of a peninsula at the outlet of Wayzata Bay where the trail circumnavigating the lake ends. The Dakota called the point *Wakon*, "the place of spirits." It was of great import and thought to possess great strength as the receptacle of power from the other sacred spots around the lake. It was the home of the Great Manitou, ageless master of the whitecaps and tempests of the Big Water.

Ceremonies were performed and scalps placed on an altar-like stone at the pinnacle. Other altars and rocks decorated the base of the hill. The Dakota sporadically returned to Spirit Knob after white settlement, and in 1859 some warriors arrived to offer the scalp of an Ojibwe victim. "...*the heathen orgies of a great and powerful race, for whose ancient homes we have just bartered a pittance of our trashy gold, were celebrated long before the world seeking Genoese* [Columbus] *reared the*

Indian Mound Park, St. Paul, MN., ca. 1900.
Photo courtesy of Minnesota Historical Society

Spirit Knob, 1867
Photo courtesy of Wayzata Historical Society

flaunting standard of Castile and Aragon upon the shores of the Haytian seas. The appearance of the ground; the marks upon the trees; the ruins of rude altars; remnants of old scalp hoops; the painted stone, and all such implements of savage rites, prove this theory to be correct." (*The Weekly Minnesotian*)

The stone was removed from its perch by a St. Louis physician, known only as Dr. S, to be examined by experts, but the trail ends with only a piece residing at the Smithsonian Institute. When the top of the knob was displaced, the hill began to disintegrate and was totally razed when it became a desirable site for home building. The view from the peak must have been glorious with The Big Woods, the expanse of the lake and the prairie to the West all in sight.

■ ■ ■

The Mdewakanton Sioux, "people of the water," is the Dakota band most strongly associated with Lake Minnetonka. In addition to hunting, fishing and ceremonial purposes, they used a path skirting the most northeastern bay, now Gray's Bay, to head north from their encampment south of the Minnesota River. This route offered mostly dry terrain and an easy ford across Minnehaha Creek. The Big Water was often a camping spot between sacred Lake Mille Lacs and the village south of the Minnesota River. Chief Shakopee's band used the northeast corner of Mni Tanka as a winter camp after spending the bison-hunting season roaming the prairies to the west.

■ ■ ■

Sporadic skirmishes between the Ojibwe and Dakota continued for several decades. On May 27, 1858, Ojibwe warriors hid in the woods south of the Big Water, waiting to ambush Dakota camped on the banks of the Minnesota River near the village of Shakopee. The U.S. treaties separated the two tribes, but this did not prevent conflict. The Ojibwe were eager to avenge an April attack near Crow Wing that had killed eleven women and children in their sleep.

In the pre-dawn hours, an Ojibwe shot a Dakota fishing from his canoe. A group of Dakota warriors responded to the gun fire and commandeered Murphy's Ferry to cross the river and engage the enemy war party.

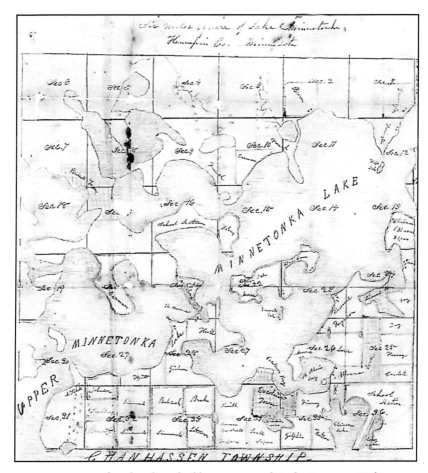

1856 map colored and marked by a young girl, Lydia Ferguson Holtz.
Photo courtesy of Excelsior Lake Minnetonka Historical Society

The commotion piqued the interest of white settlers, who rushed to the river to watch the battle much as the citizens of Washington, D.C. had ventured twenty miles to observe the First Battle of Bull Run when they thought it would be the initial skirmish of a short dust-up between the North and South.

"The townspeople hurried to the riverbank for ringside seats, undeterred by the occasional bullets whizzing by. When the ammunition of the Sioux [Dakota] *began to run out, the citizens of Shakopee furnished more so that the show could be continued."* (Ellen Wilson Meyer, *Tales from Tonka*)

The fighting ceased about 10 AM with no clear-cut winner in the "Battle of Shakopee." The Ojibwe retreated to Lake Minnetonka and the Dakota to their river camp. A group of about 200 Ojibwe approached Minnetonka Mills from the south, then broke into smaller groups and went house to house looking for food. Frank Butterfield was just shy of eight years old when five braves visited the family home: "*They came out of the brush behind our house firing off their guns and giving the war whoop as only an Indian can give it. Luckily they meant no harm. …Mother gave them a piece of pork and some flour. Before they left they saw my father's rifle hanging on some wooden pegs driven into the wall… They took it down and each one tried it out by taking a sight, but luckily they did not shoot… That night the Indians had their war dance… They jumped around, clapping their hands and slapping their sides at the same time keeping in step with their music, which was really a one-piece orchestra … a rawhide drawn over some sort of frame…that one Indian pounded with a club as hard and fast as he could.*" (Frank Butterfield, as told to his grandson, Avery Stubbs)

After midnight, the Ojibwe persuaded the settlers to carry the eight or nine wounded warriors to St. Paul for medical help in the Mills' four-horse carriage usually used to deliver finished furniture to market.

The Battle of the Broom is thought to be the final skirmish between the enemies, fought near present-day Harwick, Minnesota. An Ojibwe hunting sortie was attacked by Dakota who were protecting their traditional territory. The interlopers suffered some casualties and were pursued to a white settler's cabin, seeking sanctuary. The Ojibwe had no quarrel with the Anglos but were chased away by a woman brandishing a broom.

Now the Dakota turned their attention to European encroachment. The conflict boiled over in 1862 when skirmishes turned into open warfare. Throughout the five-week conflagration the Mdewakanton Sioux managed to protect Lake Minnetonka, their nearby spiritual hub, from the warfare.

A 1910 photo of the 20' X 26' white clapboard Scandia
Baptist Church, built in 1857 by Swedish settlers.
Photo courtesy of Carver County Historical Society

The Escape to Religious Freedom

"They stood crowded together on deck like a herd of cattle, shackled in the narrow stalls of the byre during a whole long winter, and at last stretching their necks and turning to the door when it began to smell of spring and fresh grass and meadows... The life at sea had undermined their bodies and souls. The land-frenzy was bringing them new strength. They had again seen the green earth. As seekers of new homes they had come sailing from the earth – now they were back on the earth, and felt life returning."

Vilhelm Moberg,
The Emigrants

MY GREAT-GREAT-GRANDFATHER, Swedish immigrant Andrew Bergquist, stepped from the steamboat in early 1852. He had traveled north from Illinois on the Mississippi, then west a few miles up the Minnesota River before disembarking near the modern town of Carver, Minnesota. Andrew was a trumpeter in the Swedish Army and a farmer, but when the barbarity against Swedish Baptists escalated, crops failed and political unrest ran rampant, he ventured from his home in Kristianstad. With him traveled his wife, Nilla Eliasdotter, and daughters Nilla, Henrietta and Katherine Marie to set sail on the *Gotha* from Goteberg to Boston, landing on September 11, 1849.

It was an example of the "push" dynamic of immigration. It was a dangerous time for Swedish Baptists who were subjected to violence and the kidnapping of their babies by Lutherans who then baptized them in their churches. There were economic opportunities for immigrants in America. The dream of religious freedom and the lack of class and social hierarchy at the time were also strong motivators to leave for America.

Andrew Bergquist.
*Photo courtesy of Carver County
Historical Society*

The mass Swedish immigration to the U.S. started in earnest during the mid-1840s, but the ocean voyage was fraught with danger and deplorable conditions. The ships were small and in poor repair. The Bergquist family was quartered in the cargo hold. Conditions were wretched, and sea sickness was the least of their worries.

Sensory assault and deprivation alternately ruled the day. There was precious little light or fresh air, and the fetid odor emanating from the hold was gag-inducing. Passengers waited in line to cook their meager rations, which were likely already infested with vermin. By the time the ship landed in Massachusetts, four of the seventy-six on board had died, and three babies had been born during the voyage.

Despite the ordeal Andrew, his family and their surviving shipmates were the lucky ones. Other ships sailing from Sweden suffered worse fates. Some wrecked, others were waylaid for months for repairs and one vanished into thin air.

Many of the newcomers headed for the verdant farmlands of Illinois and Iowa. Young men preferring city life flocked to cities like Chicago and Minneapolis to take advantage of the plethora of manufacturing jobs. Young women took jobs as domestic servants and laundresses. The Bergquists settled in Knoxville, Illinois, but discovered the same kind of interdenominational discord that had led them to leave their home in southern Sweden.

While the family lived in Illinois, Andrew heard about a wondrous lake in Minnesota named "Lake Minnetonka" from territorial Governor Alexander Ramsey. It offered some of the world's most fertile farmland just inland from its shores and a bounty of food from venison to waterfowl, fish, fruit and wild rice.

■ ■ ■

During the winter of 1776-1767, English map-maker Jonathan Carver made a foray into Dakota Territory and described the verdant Minnesota River basin as, "*a most delightful country, abounding with all the necessaries of life... Every part is filled with trees bending under their loads of fruits, such as plums, grapes and apples...*[with] *amazing quantities of maples, that would produce sugar sufficient of any number of inhabitants.*"

Wild rice beds hid thousands of ducks that flew away when approached, darkening the sky in seemingly infinite numbers.

■ ■ ■

The Paleo Indians were the first humans to arrive in what is now Carver County. They ranged far and wide stalking giant bison, mastodon and 200-pound beaver, spearing them with fluted stone points. The heavily forested area was sporadically occupied. Starting in 5,500 BCE and lasting for approximately 2,500 years, the climate turned arid. Lakes and rivers disappeared, making the territory uninhabitable.

Great fires spread west, turning forest into prairie. The precipitation and wildlife returned about 3,000 BCE, attracting hunters now using axes and other stone tools in addition to spears. The Mound Builders left their mark in the vicinity beginning around 1200 BCE and ending about 1500 CE. Once again, a pause in human activity ensued for approximately one thousand more years. The Dakota bands arrived around 1750 and enjoyed a period of one hundred years before the Euros appeared in earnest.

There were no permanent villages in the vicinity, but Dakota settlements dotted the southern banks of the Minnesota River consisting of dwellings made of tree bark and the more portable tipis. They ate what was available during the various seasons ranging from many varieties of fruit, plants and roots to cultivated vegetables including squash, corn and beans.

The Dakota ventured across the river to hunt and, when a deer or smaller mammals were killed, the meat was almost always boiled. This is the culture Andrew Bergquist encountered while trying to eke out a sustainable existence of his own in the area he shared with the eastern branch of the Dakota.

"Scandia was a name remembered,
By the ones who love that land,
But who had their home surrendered,
Here to work with heart and hand.
And the ground so hard and tangled,
With its roots grown deep and strong,
They must now though torn and mangled
Yield the power they held so long."

Henrietta Bergquist Fruen,
RECOLLECTIONS OF A PIONEER

The densely wooded, hilly location Andrew chose was unique for its topographical significance. A heavy band of deciduous forest, called *Chantonka* by the Dakota, *Le Grand Bois* by the French and The Big Woods by the English, skirted his site. It acted as a rough north-east to south-west line of demarcation, 100 miles long and 40 miles wide between the woodlands of the east and the tall grass prairie to the west.

The 5,000-square-mile temperate hardwood forest consisted of tightly spaced red oak, burr oak, aspen, American elm, sugar maple, ironwood, green ash and basswood. The Big Woods was an island of forest before European settlement. It provided logs for cabin-building and sap for making sugar. Today only two percent remains.

In 1852 Colonel Owens of the U.S. Army described The Big Woods area around Lake Minnetonka, a few miles north of the lake Great-great grandfather Bergquist named *Clearwater*: *"They went ashore and walked through pea vine, nettles and ginseng. There they saw a sugar maple tree which was three feet in diameter—also, there were white oak, white hickory, white ash and hardwood trees... The belt of timber is at least two miles wide all around the lake, having for its outer margin a heavy growth of very large white oak, sugar maple being secondary growth... We have taken the entire circuit of the lake* [and found] *as far a timber land as the great West affords, 100 miles in extent and two miles in width, with navigable lake in its center, and the best prairie from its outer boundary... What an enviable home for the thrifty and affluent agriculturists!"* (Quoted in *Living Waters*)

By mid-18th century, the Dakota had driven the Iowa and Cheyenne out after being pushed south and west by the Ojibwe. They battled sporadically with their enemies, most notably in a clash over hunting grounds on the northwest shore of Lake Clearwater on September 7, 1852, not long before Bergquist arrived. The contested land was a favored hunting ground for both bands. Burials, including Wild Buffalo and Chief Chaska, are located on the lakeshore and on Paradise Island (now Coney Island).

■ ■ ■

Great-great-grandfather set out on foot to find Lake Minnetonka but took the wrong trail and encountered another large lake. Andrew made camp at the south-east shore of what is now called Lake Waconia, west and slightly south of Lake Minnetonka and twelve miles north of the river. Bergquist sensed it was the place his family would call home. He staked out a one hundred-sixty-acre claim and headed back to Illinois to retrieve his family.

He arrived to find his wife and daughter Nilla dead from the cholera epidemic that had swept the region. Shaken but undeterred, he married a widow named Elenor Nilson. With her three young children and his daughters Henrietta and Katherine Marie, the newly created family headed back to what is now called Scandia and their new life.

Once the blended Bergquist family staked their claim on the southeastern shore of then Lake Clearwater, Andrew began a campaign to attract other Swedish Baptists. He wrote many letters championing the benefits of the recently opened territory and was successful in drawing fellow countrymen from Iowa and Illinois. He extolled its virtues in a submission to Chicago's Swedish American newspaper, the *Hemlandet*, soon after Minnesota acquired statehood: "*This settlement is in my opinion the best and most beautiful in Carver County. It is situated on one of the most beautiful—if not the most beautiful—lakes in the whole State. This is also the consensus of opinion of all travelers who have visited it. The lake is twelve square miles, surrounded by a rich growth of sugar maple, and the soil is extremely fertile. The Swedes own most of the land contingent on the lake, and fourteen lakes border* [within several miles] *on its shores. The price of land here at present is $6 an acre. The Swedes who have settled here came from different provinces of Sweden. And most of them have embraced the Baptist faith...Some Swedish Lutheran families, who had settled here, did not like to mingle with the Baptists, wherefore* *they sold their land to Germans who bought large tracts of land south of the lake."*

He may have lost his way to Lake Minnetonka, but Bergquist was an ardent champion of his serendipitously found new home and became a civic-minded citizen and booster. He was Scandia's first postmaster and community clerk. He also donated land for the settlement's cemetery – God's Acre – in 1855, which is one of the few vestiges of Scandia that remains.

Andrew's letters struck a chord with a Swedish group from Burlington, Iowa, and Andrew Peterson and his brother-in-law, John Anderson, headed to Scandia in 1853 to assess the prospects of cheap, fecund farmland for themselves. According to historians R.I. Holcombe and William H. Bingham, the men navigated their way through the woods and *"found him* [Bergquist] *living in the wilderness and the home that sheltered him, an improvised tent formed of blankets spread over the branches of trees."*

Despite the austere atmosphere, the two Iowans were suitably impressed by Scandia's potential and upon his return to Burlington, Peterson worked in a nursery to save money for the tools, supplies and equipment needed to establish his farm in Minnesota. Concurrently, Rev. Frederick Olaus Nilsson settled in Burlington to serve as a pastor to the Swedish Baptists. He was exiled from Sweden for forming the first Baptist church there contrary to the laws enforced to ensure the purity of the country's national denomination, Lutheranism.

Rev. Nilsson led many of the Burlington Baptists to Scandia in 1853, helping to stabilize the fledgling community. Most of the settlers chose the densely forested land surrounding the east side of Lake Clearwater over the less fertile, adjacent meadowland. This meant felling trees and spending years "grubbing," the arduous task of extracting roots and stumps. Neighbors helped each other clear fields, sharing labor, horses and food.

The back-breaking work critical to starting a farm was exacerbated by harsh weather extremes including tornados, blizzards, bitter cold, scorching heat and suffocating humidity. Adding to the misery were hostile bands of Dakota, plagues of grasshoppers, abject poverty, homesickness and crushing loneliness. Great-great-grandfather Andrew, quite the salesman, neglected to mention the less pleasant elements of the Minnesota Territory.

■ ■ ■

Only superseded by sustenance and survival, religion was a vital priority in the settlers' lives. Rev. Nilsson presided over the first church service held in John Anderson's bark claim shanty. Subsequent services were held in settlers' homes until 1856 when a wooden church building, The Swedish Baptist Church, was erected on Lake Clearwater's eastern shore. The church dominated even the private lives of the parishioners, acting as judge and jury when its members strayed from accepted norms of behavior such as adultery and dereliction of family obligations.

Rev. Carl Tideman succinctly stated, "*Discipline was carried out with a Puritan severity*" with expulsion being one of the consequences. Biblical quotes were used to rationalize the church's intercession in legal matters. As is too often the case, internal strife among the worshippers eventually caused a dwindling membership.

> "*And when the wintry winds were blowing*
> *And the lake with ice was bound,*
> *Younger ones their true faith showing,*
> *Sought the peace their friends had found.*
> *So the ice was cut and lifted,*
> *In its place the pastor stood.*
> *And they baptized them, ere they drifted.*"

Henrietta Bergquist Fruen
RECOLLECTIONS OF A PIONEER

Baptism by total immersion was a ceremony inexplicably performed in February. A hole was made by sawing through two feet of ice, and the frigid dip into Lake Clearwater tested one's religious fervor. Andrew and Elenor were baptized in this manner, as were many others. Rev. Tideman put a positive spin on the ordeal, writing "*there is no report of any disastrous effect or cases of pneumonia.*"

My great-grandmother Henrietta and her sister Katherine Marie were baptized in the Mississippi River. Religious life in Scandia was stern and unforgiving, which seems ironic given the Baptists' dedication to Christ and His teachings. There was precious little peace, joy or tolerance, echoing the unforgiving climate and landscape. "*The difference*

Above Left: My great-grandparents in New Smyrna, Florida. Henrietta in the fronds, William holding his hat.
Fruen family photo

Above Right: Scandia Baptist Cemetery land donated by Andrew Bergquist.
Photo courtesy of Scandia Baptist Cemetery Association

Below: Map indicating planned Scandia township. The settlement was never incorporated. *Photo ourtesy of Carver County Historical Society*

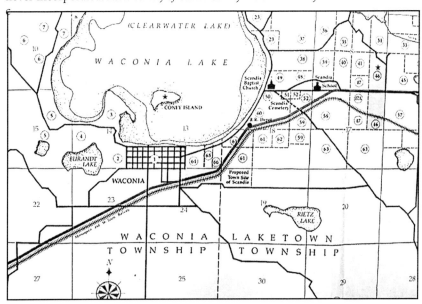

between Indigenous people and settlers is that Indigenous people have origin stories and creation stories, and settlers have colonization stories. That is the stark difference...that relationship to land and being of the land, coming from the land versus coming to it in a process of settling." (Dr. Adrienne Keene, *All My Relations* podcast)

■ ■ ■

Decisions made in Washington reverberated across the frontier, and no one was affected more than the Dakota. The promised annual payments often ended up in the hands of white agents rather than the tribes, and settlers continued to encroach on the fertile land, hunting grounds and waterways of the Minnesota River Valley. The Dakota were boxed in, relegated to two stretches of river each seventy-five miles long and twenty miles wide.

The Dakota did not understand the European concept of land ownership. They believed land could be occupied but not owned. When food was scarce and the terms of the treaties were ignored, the hunters ventured across the Minnesota River into their traditional grounds in search of badly needed protein provided by larger mammals.

The stressors that caused the financial Panic of 1857 were felt internationally, creating the first world-wide recession. Taoyatedduta (Little Crow) spokesman for the Mdewakanton and Wahpekute bands, traveled to Washington, DC, to plead their case.

Young Dakota men were angered by the whites' condescension, unethical trading practices and the broken promises. Mdewakanton Chief Big Eagle explained, *"Many of the whites always seemed to say by their manner when they saw an Indian, 'I am much better than you,' and Indians did not like this."* Despite pleas from the elders to moderate their actions, they took out their frustrations on the white farmers by killing their livestock.

The settlers were unnerved by Dakota customs and curiosity when the natives would peer through windows, walk into a cabin uninvited or stare silently when addressed. In turn, the Dakota considered the whites' refusal to offer food to be rude. The breaking point occurred after crops failed in 1861 and the severe winter of 1861-1862 left the Minnesota River bands on the brink of starvation.

Little Crow, Dakota leader and reluctant war chief
during the uprising of 1862.
Photo courtesy of Minnesota Historical Society

Adding to the misery, the government defaulted on the annual payments to the bands guaranteed by treaty and cut off credit at the Upper and Lower Sioux Agencies. The Dakota were starving. The delicate equilibrium of the "middle ground" engendered by the fur trade had unraveled.

Conflict was inevitable. The fuse was lit by a chance meeting near Acton, Minnesota, on a Sunday morning. Four Dakota hunters – Breaking Up, Killing Ghost, Brown Wing and Runs Against Something When Crawling – were returning from an unsuccessful hunting trip when they came upon the home of the Jones family. One of the Dakotas grabbed some eggs and was scolded by another. This caused a dispute accompanied by accusations of cowardice.

The offending brave insisted on proving his maligned bravery by heading back to the Jones' store to kill the proprietor. The owner headed to his brother-in-law Howard Baker's home where they were joined by a man named Webster.

After what appeared to be a friendly contest of target shooting, the Dakota turned and opened fire, killing Jones first and then turning their attention to the women. Baker lunged in front of the volley of bullets, taking one in the chest. Webster and Mrs. Jones were the next fatalities. As the Indians fled the scene, they noticed the Jones' adopted daughter Clara and shot her too, preferring to leave no witnesses. The calamity to come was triggered by a young brave's pride and a handful of eggs.

The more bellicose younger band members lobbied their reluctant leader, Little Crow. He walked in both worlds, wearing white man's clothing, building a house, tending a farm and joining the Episcopal Church while still trying to lead his tribe. This duality did not sit well with his more restless members.

Tribal elders stripped him of his title, but the band still considered him their war chief. Little Crow was torn. His dying father had told him to "*be honest…make yourself respected by the white people,*" but he also bristled at being considered a weakling. Little Crow gave his impatient warriors a blistering lecture on August 18, 1862: "*Braves, you are like little children; you know not what you are doing. You are full of the white man's devil-water. You are like dogs in the Hot Moon when they run mad and snap at their own shadows… See! The white men are like the locusts when they fly so thick that the whole sky is a snowstorm. Count your fingers all day long and white men with guns in their hands will come faster than you can count. Yes; they fight among themselves* [Civil War] *but if you strike at them they will all turn on you and devour you and your women and your little children just as the locusts in their time fall on the trees and devour all leaves in one day… Braves, you are fools. You will die like the rabbits when the hungry wolves hunt them down in the Hard Moon* [January]."

When Little Crow realized his speech fell on deaf ears, he reluctantly agreed to lead them into battle. At first, when Little Crow and his men descended on the Lower Agency their vengeance was systematic, attacking only the employees and sparing those they deemed innocent.

But that strategy was soon abandoned. Eighty whites lay dead at the conclusion of the battle. War parties spread out, attacking farms, settlements and even towns such as Hutchinson and Forest City.

No one was immune to the killing spree. The marauders initially focused on the German-settled town of New Ulm, striking twice on August 18th and 19th. The Dakota referred to the residents as "*bad speakers*," likely because of their unfamiliar accents. In addition to the grievances held toward the new regulations concerning confinement to reservations, which they usually ignored, the Dakota resented the price-gouging practiced by New Ulm merchants.

The battle on August 19th was the most intense of the entire conflict. After the hostilities had momentarily ceased, New Ulm was nearly deserted except for smoldering wooden buildings and the bodies of the German dead. In late August many Swedes living in Scandia, including the Bergquists, hastily buried their valuables and retreated to Paradise Island, giving them a 360- degree view of the proceedings on shore.

"*A twelve foot high wall of logs was built with a trench on the outside of the stockade. Holes were made through which the settlers could fire on their attackers, and arms, ammunition, food and water were brought inside. The men kept watch in the stockade at night, and all were prepared to take refuge there in the case of an attack on the town.*" (Waconia Heritage Association, *WACONIA: Paradise of the Northwest*)

Those who stayed on shore retreated to the fledgling town of Waconia and barricaded themselves in a log cabin surrounded by a hastily erected stockade slapped together by old men and boys. The wall offered little protection but was never tested by the marauders. The evacuees on the heavily forested island pitched tents, hunted for food and remained for fourteen days.

An excerpt from Andrew Peterson's diary explains the ordeal in his typically succinct style: "*We were scared of the Indians so we fled to the island in Klairwater Lake and stayed there until the evening of the 21st when we fared home.*" Although the Dakota attacked towns and villages up and down the river basin, some warriors ventured away from the stream to raid in south-central Minnesota with no apparent plan. Fort Ridgely, Big Stone Lake, Milford, Slaughter Slough and other communities along the Minnesota and Cottonwood rivers and Sacred Heart, Beaver and LaCroix creeks fell victim to the Dakota depredations, but the warriors were stopped at Hutchinson before reaching Scandia.

"And the neighbors start in terror
When they hear that awful cry,
And to each one, life seems dearer,
When around them others die
And not far from Lake Clearwater,
Many dreadful deeds were done;
Through those days and nights of slaughter.
Man or child, they cared for none."

Henrietta Bergquist Fruen,
RECOLLECTIONS OF A PIONEER

My great-grandmother Henrietta was traumatized by the attacks, and her vengeful attitude toward the Dakota is obvious throughout the stanzas. The venom notwithstanding, her writing skills and imagery were strong.

Over the many decades following the establishment of Fort Snelling, the Dakota had managed to keep their sacred Lake Minnetonka a secret from the white settlers, but eventually it became a destination for the newcomers after the Treaty of 1851. The rush was on for prime plots.

By mid-August 1862, pioneer settlers around Lake Minnetonka were in panic mode. Rumors were rampant and exaggeration ruled the day. The most frightening gossip was that *"all the tribes clear to the mountains are moving."* Many whites exited the area for good while some risked the dangerous trek to the relative safety of Fort Snelling or the fast-growing community of St. Anthony, soon to become known as part of Minneapolis.

Other outlying pioneers came to the town of Excelsior on the southeastern shore of Lake Minnetonka where a stockade was built around the school. The school's cupola became the lookout's perch. Some armed Civil War veterans kept their weapons loaded as they waited out the danger in their cabins.

The small, crowded side-wheel steamboat, *Governor Ramsey,* was enlisted to carry townspeople to tiny Gooseberry Island (now Gale's Island) just south of what was to become the Fruen family's Crown Point location, but the boiler failed, and the boat finally drifted to the shore at Tonka Bay. Some of the passengers finally reached the island while others went home.

Reverend Charles Galpin planned an escape to Big Island from Excelsior in case the hostilities reached the lake. The location would become our family's summer haven, but not for sixty-six more years. The war raged in the vicinity of Minnetonka for a month but never reached its shores. Some 30,000 residents of twenty-four Minnesota counties fled their homes in terror, leaving towns nearly deserted.

The whites' fears were allayed when the forces of ex-Governor Henry Sibley turned the tide. The final engagement of the uprising, the Battle of Wood Lake on September 26, 1862, was not much of a contest. Sibley had no military experience, but he vastly outnumbered his enemy with 1,600 troops against about 300, killing fourteen and losing seven. While atrocities were committed by both sides, the pioneers wanted swift retribution for the deaths of up to 800 white Minnesotans. Trials were hastily held, and frontier justice prevailed when 303 Dakota were sentenced to death by hanging.

After much delay, which only served to fan the flames, President Lincoln studied the 303 individual cases and initially authorized the hanging of those convicted of atrocities. When only two Dakota were confirmed rapists, Lincoln reconsidered, expecting considerable backlash from white Minnesotans if only two were executed. He added those who had murdered civilians, bringing thirty-eight prisoners destined to wear a noose. Dakota warriors, known as *akicita,* who had fought U.S. soldiers in battle, were exonerated.

Predictably, the public outcry was deafening, and the condemned were attacked by a mob as they marched to Mankato for the hangings scheduled on December 26, 1862. The day after Christmas, thirty-eight Dakota were hung by U.S. soldiers in what remains the largest mass execution in U.S. history. As many as 4,000 onlookers cheered the proceedings. A large platform was built so all the prisoners could be executed simultaneously.

The bodies were buried in a shallow mass grave on the sandy beach of the Minnesota River near Mankato, but not before souvenir locks of hair and patches of skin were taken. In the dark of night a group of doctors, including Dr. William W. Mayo, unearthed the corpses to use in anatomy studies. Spring flooding in 1863 erased the last vestiges of the executions.

■ ■ ■

On May 2, 1866, the Bergquists moved to Minneapolis, likely due to dissention in the Scandia church, They left the farm in the hands of son Frans, who had joined the family in America after initially staying in Sweden. In addition to working the land, Frans started a school in the Scandia Baptist Church and delivered the mail. The local congregants paid his wages. Andrew and Elenor initially joined the First Baptist Church of Minneapolis but soon requested and received permission to leave and found a new congregation of fellow countrymen and women.

The Bergquists and twenty-two others consecrated the Swedish Baptist Church of Minneapolis by holding hands in a circle and praying. In 1886, pastor Dr. Frank Peterson praised the Scandinavian parishioners as the best possible Baptists since they were "*Protestants, religious, weren't communists or socialists, and very few of them were peddlers, organ grinders, or beggars.*" My forebears remained friendly with the Petersons and the rest of the Scandia community, returning often to visit Frans.

Henrietta Bergquist and William Henry Fruen met through the church and were married in October 1871. Andrew died on February 21, 1896, and is buried with his second wife Elenor in Hillside Cemetery in Minneapolis. In addition to his birth and death dates, his tombstone reads "*A. Bergquist, 'Gone Before.'*"

Great-grandfather Fruen, a strong personality and a devoted Anglophile, erased the influences of the Swedish culture from his family. A look at the first names of the eleven children confirms it: nary an Oscar or an Ebba can be found. The Bergquists exhibited tremendous bravery and fortitude in facing the array of risks they took while gaining a foothold in their new, challenging home. We are poorer for the loss of this legacy.

Bassett's Creek dammed by William Fruen in 1874 to power his screw factory.
Fruen family photo

William Fruen Charts his Course

"In 1872 Minneapolis annexed St. Anthony on the east bank [of the Mississippi]. Men with New England roots...moved in to build the new city. The early movers and shakers included men named Washburn, Phelps, Lowry, Peavy, Bull, Welles, Kingman, Bovey and Crosby. Donaldson and Loring, Brackett and Salisbury, Heffelfinger and Wells, Atwater and Walker, Fruen and Gluek were there too."

Barbara Flanagan,
MINNEAPOLIS

DISEMBARKING FROM THE SHIP after crossing the Atlantic in April 1865, nineteen-year- old William Henry Fruen walked up the hill from Boston Harbor to the din of church bells tolling for the fallen President, Abraham Lincoln. The independent, ambitious young man arrived with few belongings and the clothes on his back after abandoning his position as a machinist's apprentice at New Castle on Tyne, England. He was a prime example of the "pull" dynamic of immigration and was lured across the Atlantic by the prospect of forging his own destiny and the desire to escape the rigid strictures of his lowly status in class-conscious England.

He was born to John Henry and Harriet White Fruen in Fisherton Anger Parish, Wiltshire on the Salisbury Plain west of London, on the banks of the Avon River and in the shadow of Stonehenge. John Henry was a boot maker, shopkeeper and refreshment room proprietor on Fisherton Street.

Being in the right place at the right time was one of William's

A photo of John H. and Harriet White Fruen's family in England. William was already in America. Standing in the back row are Julia, Kate, Bessie, and Fannie. In the front row are daughter Harriet, and Harriet W., John, Beatrice (seated in front of John) and Emma. *Fruen family photo*

innate traits confirmed by his arrival in Massachusetts amid a social and economic maelstrom fueled by mass immigration and the rapid expansion of the railroad. Large cities grew exponentially, and the myriad of small communities dotting the map were drawn closer as time and space shrunk. This growth spawned many innovations, inventions and life-extending improvement of diet and health care. The expansion was prevalent in the Northeast, Midwest and the Plains. The west was still wild and untamed, and the South was reeling from the indignities of Reconstruction.

In Boston, William began his own version of the American Dream when it was more easily achieved and soon found employment with the Boston Screw Company, learning all the facets of screw manufacturing as well as the making and repairing of the machinery. Soon my great-grandfather was designing new machines and became a shareholder of the company.

On January 26, 1867, William married Elizabeth "Lizzie" Caverly of Fitchburg, and they settled in East Boston. They had a daughter, Minnie Beatrice, and a son, William Franklin. Lizzie died in 1869 from complications caused by her son's delivery and, at the age of 23, Great-grandfather was a widow with two children. At the same time, the American Screw Company began acquiring smaller entities including the Boston Screw Company, the sale of which gave William capital to start his own venture. This was always his goal.

■ ■ ■

Great-grandfather heard of the burgeoning region along the Upper Mississippi where the stream widens, and the powerful falls of St. Anthony stretched from side to side. The falls were the largest source of waterpower between Niagara Falls and the Sierra Nevada Mountains in California, and Minneapolis was on its way to becoming the grain milling capital of the world. The lumber industry's use of the Father of Waters was at its peak, but as Minnesota's prime stands of pine disappeared, the timber trade began to head west. Flour mills started to crowd their lumber counterparts from the riverfront.

Leaving the children in the care of Lizzie's family, Great-grandfather headed west to Minnesota in 1870 to investigate. He first visited St. Paul and then decided to open his machinery building and repair shop on the west side of St. Anthony Falls at 2nd and Cataract, now 6th Street in Minneapolis. This was an early example of William's uncanny habit of being in the right place at the right time. Great-grandfather began studying the mills and machinery and perceived a need for the updating and upgrading of industry safety. *"An inventive man, Fruen developed a water-wheel governor, an elaborate device to regulate the speed of the wheels that powered the mills...."* (Sharon Parker, "Down by the Old Fruen Mill: The graffiti on these walls mask stories of ingenuity and enterprise," *Minneapolis Observer Quarterly*)

Once he was settled in Minnesota in 1871, William sent for his parents and youngest sister, 13-year-old Beatrice, who came to America to visit the place he had written about so enthusiastically. Father John Henry preferred England and returned. Mother Harriet, however, not only stayed but called for her other unmarried daughters – Fanny, Emma and Harriet – to join the rest of the family in the Upper Midwest. Great-grandfather's children from his first marriage, Minnie and William Franklin, also moved to Minneapolis.

Particularly impressive considering the time, William's mother and sister, the two Harriets, became successful Minneapolis businesswomen. Great-great grandmother Harriet researched business opportunities in the city and opened a dry goods store at 705 Washington Avenue South named Mrs. H. Fruen's Notions, which operated for many years in the flour milling district on the Mississippi River. William's sister Harriet owned a dress shop on Talmadge Street and speculated in real estate, specializing along Lake Street where the rapidly growing city was expanding south.

■ ■ ■

William Fruen met Andrew Bergquist's daughter, Henrietta, through the First Baptist Church of Minneapolis. They married in 1871, purchased land and built their home, Glenwood Springs, overlooking Bassett's Creek at the western edge of Minneapolis. The neighborhood was to be called *Bryn Mawr*, "Great Hill" in Welsh. It was undeveloped, occupied only by John Oswald, a Swiss immigrant, and his 160-acre tobacco and fruit farm. The fruit was converted to "J. C. Oswald's Native Wines" and marketed as "medicinal." Soon he added distilled liquor to the product line and started the J.C. Oswald & Co., the first wholesale liquor and wine distributer in the Mill City. My abstemious Baptist great-grandparents were the unlikeliest neighbors.

The Fruens lived in their beloved Bryn Mawr for over 110 years. William and Henrietta raised eleven children there. My grandparents, Reba and Arthur, and their six sons and daughters purchased a home at 56 Russell Avenue on top of the hill above Glenwood Inglewood and the Fruen Milling Company.

In 1874, Great-grandfather incorporated the Northwestern Manufacturing Company, dammed the stream and constructed a water-driven screw factory with an annual output of 8,000 gross. The effects of the financial Panic of 1873 were late in arriving in the Upper Midwest, but Great-grandfather's investors were insolvent, and he plugged along for a few years despite a dearth of capital. In early 1878, the price of screws plunged from 90 cents per gross to 19 cents. The American Screw Company bought William's operation, and he agreed "*not to engage in the manufacture nor teach others how to make screw machinery.*"

■ ■ ■

William made a habit of using his intelligence, inventiveness and drive to succeed to great advantage. Just as the literary school of Naturalism was coming into vogue, my great- grandfather was a living symbol of what can happen when the forces of nature, ambition, environment, economics and serendipity collide.

On May 2, 1878, a spark ignited from friction caused by millstones rubbing together ignited and destroyed the largest grain processor in the world, the Washburn "A" Mill, a six-story, limestone leviathan located at St. Anthony Falls. Eighteen people were killed and one-third of the city's milling capacity disappeared overnight as well as nearby houses, businesses, a machine shop, lumberyards, a railroad roundhouse, and other types of storage buildings. Windows were blown out as far away as St. Paul's Summit Avenue, and chunks of limestone were found eight blocks away. The ruins belched smoke and cinders for a month.

William Fruen went to work immediately, designing and patenting an alarm system that sounded when the flow of grain between millstones became dangerously low and stopped the machinery before damage could occur. He had earlier converted his screw factory to manufacture the Minneapolis Water Wheel Governor, also known as the Fruen Water Wheel Governor, designed to control the speed of the water wheels powering the mills. With the new safety precautions in place and an even larger capacity, the Washburn "A" Mill recaptured its status as the largest in the world when it reopened in 1880.

The invention was sold around the world to countries such as Japan, England and Argentina, and Great-grandfather's innovations were instrumental in the recovery of Minneapolis' milling industry. The city led the country in flour production for the next fifty years, and the income generated by his inventions made Great-grandfather Fruen a

William and Henrietta Fruen family Grandfather Fruen is standing
with the bow on his chest, ca. 1894. *Fruen Family Photo*

Artist's enhancement of mill explosion, March 2, 1878.
Photo courtesy of MinnPostcom

William H. Fruen's Water Wheel Governor in production, 1890.
Fruen family photo

prominent Minneapolis businessman. The city was now called the "*Budapest of North America*" for its milling capacity.

■ ■ ■

In the 1870s, the *Minneapolis Journal* sang the praises of Bassett's Creek in a flowery, hyperbolic style, calling it "*one of the finest streams on this continent…from Medicine Lake to the River flows…a fairylike scene of sylvan loveliness.*"

The creek is a narrow and rather shallow stream that flows eastward through hills and marshes from Medicine Lake to the Father of Waters. The Dakota named it *Hawa Wakpadan* (Little Falls River) and used it as part of their serpentine path to the Mississippi. Early European settlers called it The Brook, and it became known as Bassett's Creek when Joel Bean Bassett established a farm at the confluence of the creek and the river in 1852. The stream was used recreationally for fishing, swimming and skating.

Sadly, as the population of Minneapolis grew, the brook became a dumping ground, particularly on the eastern half, for all sorts of refuse including tires, animal carcasses, garbage and ashes. Since much of the creek valley was marshy and not conducive to building, it continued to resemble a large gutter. Adding to the pollution, the three-story North Star Shingle Mill and a steam-powered linseed oil operation were built along the waterway. In May 1867, Minneapolis Mayor Albert Ames referred to it as "*that mammoth sewer called Bassett's Creek.*"

The arrival of railroad lines cut lead times and a line ran west from St. Paul, crossing the Mississippi and following the course of Bassett's Creek, eventually providing a spur for the yet-to-be-founded Fruen Cereal Company. It also created an informal border between the Minneapolis Northside and the rest of the city. The stream separates Bryn Mawr from the Harrison neighborhood except for a protuberance jutting north that includes the glen, the abandoned mill and the Glenwood Inglewood/Brewery operation, keeping them in Bryn Mawr.

The spot Great-grandfather Fruen chose at the small falls west of the fringes of downtown to relocate his business was upstream from the pollution and, despite its proximity to the city proper, was still in the wilderness. The site was a wooded glen in the creek valley. William constructed his bare-bones workshop next to the creek.

The neighborhood of Bryn Mawr expanded on the higher ground south of the stream. In a sterling example how random occurrences can change the trajectory of one's life, Great- grandfather happened upon another profitable business. While digging through a layer of blue clay, he uncovered a spring that produced pristine, natural waters. The clay filtered impurities and added just the right amount of minerals. Great-grandfather saw an urgent need for potable, good-tasting drinking water and began selling the spring water at his property in 1882.

Initially the business consisted of a wagon, a horse and a driver who delivered two-gallon crockery jugs to downtown hotels and businesses at the price of 5 cents each. As the enterprise grew, a fleet of wagons carried five-gallon glass jars called "*carboys*." Soon the newly christened Glenwood Company filled customers' coolers from five-hundred-gallon horse-drawn tanks.

William soon owned a six-wagon operation with tandems of double-hitched horses pulling the heavy loads. The sawdust-strewn icehouse kept the bottles of water chilled. Every February, ice was cut from the nearby Twin Lakes in Robbinsdale and loaded into the building. In the 1970s, long-time Bryn Mawr resident Edna Stolt recalled an incident that crystallized the clash between the old ways and the new technology.

Glenwood-Inglewood adds more wagons and horses to the supply side of the business. Logistics were a priority. *Fruen family photo*

In the early 1920s just before the transition to trucks, a wagon was returning to the glen. The horses were giddy with excitement to get home to eat and rest and accelerated to cross the railroad tracks just as the Great Northern came barreling through, crushing everything in its path. According to witnesses, the wagon driver had fallen asleep.

■ ■ ■

"An hour's inspection of the area in the neighborhood of these springs satisfied me that no place in the neighborhood of the city, except the vicinity of Minnehaha Falls, was so well adapted by nature for the construction of a park, comprising rarely attractive topographical features – while the distance from the center of business was less than half that to Minnehaha, and the apparently unlimited capacity of the springs, which gushed from the hillsides at various points over a widely extended area, seemed to offer every possible opportunity for the ornamental use of water." (H.W.S. Cleveland quoted by David A. Smith, "Glenwood Spring: A Premier Park – and Water Supply?" *Minneapolis Park History*)

Cleveland is considered second only to Frederick Law Olmstead in the pantheon of American landscape architects and was hired to design the world-renowned Minneapolis park system. His template for parks and parkways was gospel for many decades. Horace moved his family from Chicago to Minneapolis after blaming their "winter cholera" on the local tap water.

After switching to the much more "palatable" Glenwood spring water, their symptoms disappeared. Enamored with the spring water and the *"hills and valleys of graceful form,"* he wondered, *"whether it is worth our while to ascertain the character and capacity of the springs"* to determine if they could handle the city's volume and, if so, *"the city should secure them, and enough land around them to preserve them from contamination, and then enclose the area as an ornamental reservoir as had been done in Philadelphia, New York and Boston."*

■ ■ ■

Meanwhile, William Fruen was hard at work while the concept was being considered and, on December 16, 1884, he was granted a patent for a "Liquid Drawing Device," the precursor to the modern coin-operated vending machine. After a penny was inserted into the slot, spring water was dispensed. Form and function were both advanced, as the design resembled a four-sided office building with small indentations acting as the windows. A larger depression was the doorway to the edifice containing the water tap and drinking glass.

The mechanism was activated by the weight of the coin, and the water was measured and poured. The vending machine and the water it dispensed were sold to many hotels including the West in Minneapolis,

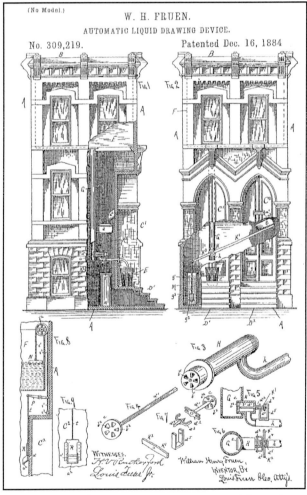

Fruen's Automatic Liquid Drawing Device was patented December 16, 1884. It is the first coin-operated vending machine.
Photo courtesy of U.S. Patent Office

considered to be the first grand hotel in the city, where it was placed in the large, elegant lobby. The invention was a bit before its time.

At the same time, Great-grandfather was pursuing Cleveland's suggestion to use Glenwood Spring to deliver potable water through aqueducts. The Mississippi's pollution was growing at an alarming rate, and William suggested the city allow him to pipe spring water two miles to the downtown area, supplying homes and restaurants along the route. His partners were attorney and real estate magnate Thomas Lowry and hotelier Joseph West. The City Council approved the plan with only one dissenting vote, but it was vetoed by Mayor George Pillsbury, who thought the cost to be prohibitive.

Great-grandfather Fruen was a focused and determined man and regrouped with Alderman Phillip Winston as a partner but failed to garner the needed votes. A third and final effort was made but, by this time, Winston was mayor and vetoed the project. The Mill City finally was forced to use his spring water in 1913 during the typhoid epidemic. The business diversified to produce distilled water for druggists, seltzer water, and expanded its reach to offer delivery to homes and businesses.

In the spring of 1885 Great-grandfather placed ads in the *Minneapolis Tribune*, praising the purity of his spring water. He quoted an analysis by University of Minnesota Professor James Dodge who agreed, "*This water is extremely pure, being almost entirely free from organic matter.*" The ads suggested readers to "*Drive out and see as fine a spring as you ever looked upon.*" William also warned readers about his competition: "*Do not confound this spring with the Inglewood. Ours is the Glenwood.*"

William acquired the nearby Inglewood Company, named the merged entity Glenwood- Inglewood and installed Inglewood's ex-proprietor Arthur Holbrook as president and his oldest son, William Franklin, as secretary of the enterprise. This became a Fruen philosophy. Jobs and titles were not handed out to the offspring without education, a proclivity for business and a predilection for hard work.

The merger had its growing pains and Great-grandfather wrote from Florida to my grandfather, Arthur, regarding some friction with the combined firm's president. William Fruen Sr. had no problem putting the hammer down when necessary. "*I am very sorry to hear that Will is having trouble with Arthur Holbrook. It must be a terrible strain on him. What does Holbrook want? I think that Will had better come*

*down here and let Art H. run the business alone. He would soon be crying
like the baby he is for Will to come back. It will do no good to quarrel with
him: better to separate than fight. Tell him so."*

Had I been Great-uncle Will, I would have accepted the invitation of
a free Florida vacation during a frigid Minnesota winter. Great-grandfather bought out Holbrook and handed the reins of Glenwood-Inglewood to William Franklin.

Great-grandfather was never inclined to idleness and, stepping
back from the water business, he used his knowledge of grain milling
to start a new venture. Utilizing the water power of Bassett's Creek, he
milled whole grains and developed ready-to-eat packaged breakfast cereal in 1890 using rolled wheat. It was first private-labeled for the Pettijohn Company. William acquired the breakfast cereal rights, which
he subsequently sold to the Quaker Oats Company. Great-grandfather
also packaged his own cereal called, "Fruen's Best Wheat Wafers" and
"Fruen's Rolled Wheat."

Minnesota was fast becoming the leader in wheat production, and
the state's economy was booming. Reverend George Briscoe lamented,
*"Men work in wheat all day…lounge round talking about wheat when it's
wet, dream about wheat at night, and I fear go to meeting Sabbath Day to
think about wheat."*

William's efforts were innovative for two reasons. His plant was not
located in the main milling district along the Mississippi, and he was
the first to market packaged goods rather than sell in bulk. Bags of Fru-
en flour were featured in the Sears Catalog for decades.

■ ■ ■

Great-grandfather and thirteen-year-old Great-uncle Ben visited
Great-great-grandfather John Henry in 1892, traveling by train to Montreal where they boarded a ship heading to Liverpool, England. After
landing, they headed to Fisherton Anger to join John Henry. Ben kept
a detailed diary of their trip to London and the sites they saw such as
the infamous Tower of London and the mammoth Crystal Palace in
Sydenham Hill.

The cast-iron-and-plate-glass edifice covering 990,000 square feet
was built to house the Great Exhibition of 1851, which showcased the
manifold inventions of the Industrial Revolution on the eight miles

of displays. Ben likely preferred the dioramas including the first dinosaur sculptures in the world based on mid-19th century research, which was still in its early phases. (Fossils had just been identified as a distinct entity of huge animals a few decades earlier.) The dinosaur models at the Crystal Palace resembled Claymation cartoon characters more than the actual gargantuan creatures.

They visited relatives and headed to the country to see Stonehenge and the High Tor in Derbyshire, a beautiful park area with limestone cliffs towering over the River Derwent Gorge. William and Ben returned to the U.S. in late September 1892 after a ten-week absence.

In 1909 William stepped back from the grain business and my 24-year-old Grandfather Arthur, a graduate of the University of Minnesota School of Engineering, took over what was then called the Fruen Cereal Company. His calculated concentrations in Cement Construction and Waterpower Development were the perfect fit. William and Henrietta spent their winters in New Smyrna, Florida, but kept in close contact with the family in Minnesota.

The March 9, 1912, *Minneapolis Tribune* confirmed a shocking telegram from Florida a few days before:

"MRS. H. FRUEN FUNERAL SATURDAY: ONCE FLED TO ISLAND TO ESCAPE INDIANS

Mrs. Henrietta Bergquist Fruen of Minneapolis who died suddenly of apoplexy at New Smyrna, Florida Monday, came to Minnesota as a child fifty-eight years ago...They settled near what is now the town of Waconia and were the first settlers in that vicinity, where they encountered most of the experiences incident to pioneer life.

Once they were driven from their home by fear of an Indian uprising [Dakota War of 1862] *and sought safety on an island in the lake near their home... She was married about forty years ago to William H. Fruen in Minneapolis and had lived in this city ever since, occupying the family residence at Glenwood Springs for twenty-seven years... She seemed to be in at least her usual good health until her sudden illness and death last Monday."*

On March 12, the *Waconia Patriot* added, *"Mrs. Fruen wrote several poems, one of which* [Recollections of a Pioneer] *is of considerable interest to the inhabitants hereabouts. The poem covers a space of fourteen pages and almost 100 stanzas of the early history of Waconia."*

William H. Fruen's first grain milling building, 1894. *Fruen family photo*

Early days of the Fruen Cereal Company. *Fruen family photo*

■ ■ ■

It may seem as if the Fruens lived a fairy-tale life in their wooded glen, but they suffered the same trials as many families of that era. Newborn Freddy died in 1874 and was buried in the newly purchased family monument plot in Lakewood Cemetery just two years after its dedication. It is the final resting place for six generations of Fruens. *"That Walter J. Fruen, thirty-six years old, vice president of the Fruen Cereal Company of Minneapolis, committed suicide after brooding over a love affair is the belief of relatives, following an investigation by the coroner when Fruen's body was discovered in the basement of the company's mill at Minneapolis. The body was found by Harriet Fruen, seventeen years old...when she stopped at the mill on the way to school.* ("Business Man Ends Life," *Morris Tribune,* March 6, 1909)

Bassett's Creek claimed the life of four-year-old Katie Fruen in November 1879 when she broke through the ice and drowned. Thomas Benjamin's asthma was so serious that he was sent to live in San Diego to escape the frigid Minneapolis winter air. The younger Henrietta went overboard on religion, did missionary work for the Apostolic Church in South Africa and suffered a nervous breakdown. She recuperated in Torquay, England, *"the English Riviera,"* staying with the Dyers, British Fruen cousins.

Despite the family's business success, William and Henrietta were not part of the Minneapolis social elite. Great-grandfather, although British, did not have an old New England Yankee pedigree, and Great-grandmother's Swedish heritage was not acceptable to the Grande Dames of Minneapolis. No Baptists were listed on the Minneapolis Social Register, I presume. This likely was not an issue as they were consumed with family, business and church as well as reading and writing.

Great-grandfather Fruen has a reputation in family lore of being a tough, strict taskmaster who thought curtains in the house to be an unnecessary affectation. But he had a gentler side, too, as he closed his February 17th letter to Grandpa, *"My best regards to Reba* [my grandmother], *a kiss for little Elizabeth* [my aunt] *and love for yourself. Your Father."*

William lived for five years after Henrietta's death, dying on October 17, 1918. He spent much of his time writing about business, political,

Wm. H. Fruen, Here Since 1870, Is Dead

Funeral of Early Minneapolis Business Man Will Be Held Monday Afternoon.

William Fruen obituary headline, 1917.
Photo courtesy of Minneapolis newspaper

Promotional material

religious and philosophical matters. He was an ardent supporter of free trade, probably influenced by his experience in exporting his inventions to Asia, South America and Europe. He believed the absence of tariffs and other types of protectionism led to peace and economic growth.

A *History of Hennepin County* reports that the English immigrant William *"loved this country so much that he would often break out in patriotic song."* By the turn of the century the trajectory of his life and that of his adopted city had dovetailed through the synergy of grain and water. William and Minneapolis were firing on all cylinders.

■ ■ ■

William Fruen's Glenwood Springs home burned to the ground sometime after his death. For many years, a plaque rested on a boulder marking the location and describing his life's work. The metal was appropriated in 1942 to support the country's World War II efforts. I believe Great-grandfather William would not only have approved but also would have been proud and honored to help his adopted nation.

He was a chameleon, adapting to shifting business environments as well as swiftly capitalizing on opportunities. William was able to frequently reinvent himself. He evolved from machinist apprentice to screw manufacturer to milling safety inventor to marketer of spring water and finally to grain miller without skipping a beat. He was a good citizen and raised a family that not only benefitted from his dreams but would also continue to leave an imprint on the city of Minneapolis.

The Fruen family has not forgotten its Bassett's Creek legacy. One hundred fifty years after William settled on the stream, a family member was a commissioner for the organization dedicated to bringing back the faded glory of the watershed. The creek and its valley provided a freshly minted immigrant and his family not only the opportunity to gain a foothold in Minneapolis but to thrive.

An early 1900s photo of the confluence of the Minnesota and Mississippi Rivers. Called "Bdote" by the Dakota bands in southern Minnesota and is considered the site of their origin and the center of their universe.

Photo by Harry Emerson

It Started as a Lark

"I remember a hundred lovely lakes, and recall the fragrant breath of pine and fir and cedar and poplar trees. The trail has strung upon it, as upon a thread of silk opalescent dawns and saffron sunsets. It has given me blessed release from the troubled thinking of our modern days."

Hamlin Garland,
McClure's Magazine

AFTER THE END OF the War of 1812, the United States turned its attention to western expansion. As part of the plan for frontier defense between Lake Michigan and the Missouri River, one of the commissioned military fortifications was Fort St. Anthony, later renamed Fort Snelling, strategically situated at the confluence of the Mississippi and Minnesota rivers. The site became available after the 1805 Treaty of St. Peter, or Pike's Purchase.

Zebulon Pike negotiated a nine-square-mile parcel with the Dakota. The fort, built between 1820 and 1824, was located high on the bluffs overlooking the rivers. It served as a buffer between the Ojibwe and Dakota and kept the rivers safe for American traders.

In May 1822, two seventeen-year-old boys, Joseph Renshaw Brown and William Joseph Snelling, their imaginations stoked by stories told by the Dakota about a large lake west of Fort St. Anthony, ventured west. It was *"towards the setting sun, in the big woods."* Brown was a drummer boy and Snelling the son of fort commander Colonel Josiah Snelling. The two could not have had more different backgrounds.

Brown was a self-sufficient teenager who skipped out on his printer's apprenticeship and ran away from home after his mother's death, escaping the severe and suffocating treatment doled out by his minister father. He joined the Army and was sent to the later-to-be-named

Fort Snelling, still under construction. Young Snelling had washed out
of West Point after two difficult years and joined his father at the fort
where he chafed under Josiah's stern discipline. Joe often escaped to
camp with Dakota friends nearby, learned their language and served as
a translator.

The boys, accompanied by soldiers named Watkins and Stewart, set
out on their adventure by canoe, although some historians believed they
hiked, ascending a small tributary of the Mississippi called *Wapka Cis-
tina* (Little River). The stream would later be called Brown's Creek and
Little Falls Creek until it was christened Minnehaha after Longfellow's
Song of Hiawatha was published. After portaging past the 53-foot falls,
the party entered Dakota Territory where reports of previous European
visitors are largely unsubstantiated.

■ ■ ■

*"For thirty years after her discovery in 1822...Sioux-owned and Sioux-
loved Minnetonka slept in peace on the very doorstep of the white man's
world. While Minnesota was making history all around her, Minnetonka napped on, undisturbed by the white man's fuss and flurry. For those
thirty years more Minnetonka's red children trod her shores or gracefully
plied her waters with canoe and paddle. Indian life continued to follow
its age-old conservation pattern: enough game and fish for food; enough
pelts and skins for clothing; enough porcupine quills for ornament; 'down
wood' for fire; crowded saplings for tent poles."* (Blanche Nichols Wilson,
Minnetonka Story)

The abundance of wildlife included geese, ducks and turkeys and
a variety of mammals. Beaver, fox, muskrat, deer and bears flourished
around Lake Minnetonka.

It is probable that French trappers, traders, explorers and perhaps
missionaries like Father Louis Hennepin saw Lake Minnetonka in the
past, but the Minnesota River bands of Dakota zealously protected
their revered body of water, keeping it secret for decade after decade.
The geography of the area helped keep the lake hidden. The shoreline
was thickly forested, and sightlines to the Big Water were also obscured
by the uneven topography and marshland. Minnetonka was advanta-
geously tucked between the two major trading routes along the Minnesota and Mississippi Rivers. The Dakota only used the lake seasonally

for hunting, fishing and religious ceremonies.

The creek contained a few smaller rapids and cascades, and the party camped the first night on the banks of the stream just past what is now Penn Avenue in Minneapolis after passing the future site of our home on Clinton Avenue. Hordes of swarming mosquitoes filled the air, and sometime during the second day Joseph called it quits and walked back to the fort. The rest of the expedition continued.

After one last portage near the source of the creek, the remaining members of the party entered Outlet Bay (now Gray's Bay) near the northeast end of the impressive lake known to the Dakota as *Mni Tanka* (Big Water), interpreted by the whites as Minnetonka.

Paddling through patches of wild rice waving in the wind and yellow water lilies floating on green pads, the group entered *Wayzata* (North Shore) Bay. They dipped their paddles in clear water, passing the sacred Spirit Knob peninsula and gliding over large schools of fish as they entered the wide-open expanse of the Lower Lake. After two days had passed, Colonel Snelling became concerned about the boys' safety, conjuring visions of hostile Dakota, bears and wolves, and dispatched a search party. The adventurers were located dining on fish and fruit. Had they explored the lake further they would have found plums, grapes and a variety of berries. The search party and their quarry returned to the fort in one day, canoeing downstream.

■ ■ ■

The Big Water returned to its clandestine status for almost thirty more years. Even the soldiers at Fort Snelling seemed disinterested. It did not appear on European or American maps until the 1850s. The most accepted traditional "re-discovery" version involves Governor Alexander Ramsay's party camping on Big Island in late June 1852 and naming the body of water "*Minnetonka.*"

Benjamin Richards, however, provided perhaps the most thorough history in 1957 with *The Early Background of Minnetonka Beach*, crediting the rough and tumble, grizzly frontier man Eli Pettijohn with the "discovery" of Lake Minnetonka. Richards arrived in the region in 1841 to teach the finer points of agriculture to the Dakota, who had very little interest in adapting to the culture and society of the white interlopers. He married a mixed-blood woman by the name of Lucy Prescott and, as a government employee, he was allowed access to lands west of the Mississippi River.

"*Pettijohn asserts he and Willis Moffett set out from Fort Snelling in October 1850 to 'find a lake spoken of by the Indians.' They traveled along the Minnesota River to present day Chaska where they camped. Next morning the men turned due north and reached the lake 'near the present site of Excelsior.' Continuing they traced the lake shore to the outlet of Minnehaha Creek. Pettijohn claimed a tract of land along the creek by chiseling his name, date and the words 'mill site' into a big oak.*" (Frederick L. Johnson, *The Big Water: Lake Minnetonka and Its Place in Minnesota History*)

Eli had boundless energy and tackled every undertaking with enthusiasm. He built two mills on Minnehaha Creek and initially produced Pettijohn's All Wheat Good to Eat there until William Fruen took over production, which served not only as an early connection between our family and Lake Minnetonka but also a harbinger of the Fruen Cereal Company, incorporated in 1890.

Like many pioneers he combined physical strength with an outsized personality. The burly frontiersman met an ignominious end at the hands of Minnehaha Creek. At the age of 96 he ventured down to the water, slipped and fell into the stream. He managed to pull himself to safety, but the inadvertent bath left him weak and chilled to the bone. The Minnetonka trail- blazer died a few days later.

■ ■ ■

In addition to the occasional trappers and traders that may have stumbled upon the lake, there were a handful of hermits and a few others who jumped the gun before the Mendota Treaty of 1851 ceded two million acres of Dakota land to the U.S. government. Chief Honkakaduta pled with the federal negotiators to exclude Minnetonka from the agreement, but his request was denied and the scramble for land began.

Early settler life around the lake was less than Arcadian: "*The early white settlers had a terrible time; their horses sank out of sight in mud pits and feral pigs ran loose through the villages. Dinner often was squirrel stew, baked raccoon, or dried beaver tail, apparently a delicacy at the time. Far from idyllic, the earliest cabins often had only a blanket for a door and no windows – and the gaps between the rough-hewn logs allowed wolves to try to snatch babies from their cradles. Really."* (Eric Dregni, *By the Waters of Minnetonka*)

In August 1852, a group of New Yorkers visited Fort Snelling to experience first-hand the newly opened territory on the Mississippi. Mrs. W. H. Elet was a writer looking for material for her next project. She was the adventurous, driving force of the excursion, and soon they headed to the place a Dakota woman had referred to as "Big Water."

The party traveled to *Bde Maka Ska* (White Banks Lake) – previously named Lake Calhoun – by horse and wagon where they reached the old Dakota farming site of *Mahiya Wicasta* (Cloud Man) and his band, called *Heyate Oturjwe* (Village at the Side). They followed a trail to the source of Little Falls Creek at Gray's Bay, which they called Lake Browning in a nod to British literature.

"The waters were so clear we could often see the sandy bottom, and numbers of fish sporting around us. The white and yellow water lilies grew profusely near the banks which were now marshy, now rising to an elevated ridge of oak land. Then we entered the woods where the uplands rose to considerable elevation. A long peninsula was rounded, and...we found ourselves in a clear and beautiful lake...." (Elizabeth Fries Elet, *Summer Rambles in the West*)

■ ■ ■

Most historians agree that Simon Stevens and his family were the first whites to settle on the creek near what is now known as Minnetonka Mills. Simon, wife Sarah and son Eldridge arrived at the 160-acre site on November 8, 1852. They traveled by "mud wagon," a customized stagecoach with iron tires and wide wheels suited to ride through the slippery muck.

The twelve-foot dam at Minnetonka Mills, two miles east of outlet into Gray's Bay, was first used to power the saws that cut timber floated from Lake Minnetonka. Soon a factory turned the wood into chairs and beds. It was Hennepin County's largest business and, more ignominiously, one of the first polluters in the watershed producing blizzards of sawdust and clouds of noxious varnish fumes. The mill burned in 1868, but a new one was built to mill grain in 1869.

Jim Shaver arrived and helped build the dam at Minnetonka Mills. He and his wife Sarah built a home and boarding house there in 1853.

Men like Stevens, Jim Shaver and Calvin Tuttle were early movers and shakers interested in the timber surrounding Lake Minnetonka. Many of those looking for farmland were turned into lumbermen as they began the arduous process of clearing the land they claimed. Many planted crops around tree stumps.

Cloud Man *(standing center)* and his lieutenants. Mrs W. E. Ellet and her party passed "Cloud Man Village" in August, 1952, after it was abandoned. *Photo courtesy of Minnesota Historical Society*

Hezekiah Brake of Excelsior, before buying land in northwestern Hennepin County, had a crisis of confidence in his aptitude for wilderness life when his party was stranded on Big Island in 1853 during one of those springtime storms when winter refuses to release its grip on the Northland. He had an overly active imagination: "*There were noises of all sorts about us. Besides the roaring waters, wolves howled, and the woods seemed full of sounds, as I sat smoking by the blazing fire, brooding over our danger, and my wife's fears for my safety, I wished heartily that I had never undertaken the life of a pioneer.*" (The "howling wolves" that terrified Brake were likely a chorus of bullfrogs.)

Simon Steven's brother John courted a group of prospective investors from New York City, and his efforts were effective as a contingent of New Yorkers, led by tailor George Bertram, formed the Excelsior Pioneer Association. The first house was completed in 1853, and the town blossomed into arguably the best preserved and most quaint neighborhood on Lake Minnetonka. The southwestern settlements of Excelsior, Minnetonka and Minnetrista were the first to be surveyed and organized, and Wayzata came close behind. Land was available for sale in 1854. By 1855, nary a foot of shoreline remained unclaimed.

The Minnesota Territory was a hot real-estate market for those interested in investment or business opportunities, with Lake Minnetonka being particularly attractive for its vast stands of hardwood. Although investors were rewarded, they also amassed debt.

What goes up comes down, and bank failures led to the Panic of 1857. The lengthy period of expansion came to a screeching halt. The defaulting of loans given to the railroad industry was a major factor.

Unemployment rose and banks closed their doors. Grain prices plunged. Demand for manufactured goods evaporated and land values plummeted, leaving planned settlements on Lake Minnetonka, such as Island City, St. Albans, Tazaska and others, languishing on the drawing board.

Hapless Hezekiah Brake of Excelsior was getting hammered by his now-worthless real estate foray in northwest Hennepin County and his unhappy wife, Charlotte, who did not care for lake life in the least, expressed her dissatisfaction in a letter: "*Do let us leave this terrible lake country... The crisis so long talked about and dreaded is here. I can see you are making no money. Your thousands brought from New York are almost gone... I cannot stand this life any longer.*" Defeated by frontier life, Hezekiah and Charlotte Brake left Excelsior.

After the Civil War, uses of the Big Water shifted from subsistence farming and lumber milling to the era of recreation and luxury hotels catering to the well-heeled. Lake Minnetonka was evolving as the Fruens were putting down roots and working hard and smart in Minneapolis towards the chance to purchase a seasonal home on the lake and enjoy some relaxation while writing a new chapter in the hand in glove relationship between the family and water.

Lake Minnetonka Poster
Courtesy of Excelsior-Lake Minnetonka Historical Society

Big Island Myth and Reality

"Island living was no luxury; it was plain hard work. There was wood to be gathered, chopped, stacked and carried to the wood box; there were fires to be made in the kitchen range, and ashes to be taken out. Laundry was done with washboard and tub, after the water was carried and heated and carried again. Later there was a rotating washing machine and a hand wringer... For ironing, heavy irons were heated on the range and each changed for another when one cooled off. When the heavy work was done, there were lamp and lantern chimneys to clean. The long grass was cut with a scythe, and trimming was done with the sickle."

Scriver family,
BIG ISLAND REMEMBRANCES, FRUEN FAMILY NEIGHBORS

IT WAS CALLED *WETUTANKA* , the Great Sugaring Camp, long before the white man arrived and eventually renamed it Big Island. They found what may have been the remnants of a Dakota fortification. This was extremely rare as the band usually dug defensive trenches rather than built forts.

"*While crossing the lake, the wind and waves drove our boat up on a strip of land...which was known* [after] *as Meeker's Island. An old Indian fort on the island attracted our attention. It was built of slender logs set in a semi-circle as a screen against arrows, and had formerly been used by the Sioux* [Dakota] *as a protection against the Chippewa* [Ojibwe]." (Hezekiah Brake, June 1852)

Only a handful of similar structures have ever been found, and other theories include a windbreak for sugaring, a chute for channeling deer for hunting or some sort of edifice for ceremonies. Big Island is known to have been a wild-ricing and maple-sugaring camp. Recent archaeological discoveries include bits of pottery dating from 800 BCE to 200 CE, and stone chips indicating the 1-1/2-mile long and 3/4-mile wide island was also used as a tool maintenance and finishing center.

In late summer 1852 a group of territorial government officials took a boat tour of the Big Water accompanied by journalist Col. John P. Owens from *The Weekly Minnesotan,* who reported passing a large island with a Dakota camp in residence. His September 11, 1852, article is believed to be the first published account of the lake from a white man's perspective. The name Owens Island was used for a brief period.

Associate Justice Bradley B. Meeker* was part of the Minnetonka tour and claimed land on the Point Comfort and Crown Point south end of Wetutanka across from Brightwood (now Gale's) Island, forcing the encamped Dakota to leave. Judge Meeker sold Big Island to William and John Morse** (uncles of the infamous Lizzie Borden) in 1856, just before the Panic of 1857.

■ ■ ■

"Many springs, many moons, and many leaves of the forest have come and gone, says the Ancient Legend of Mahpiyata, since a daring party of young Ojibway warriors and hunters…came down from the north, in the moon that geese lay, to rid the favorite Minnetonka hunting and fishing ground of their hereditary enemy, the 'Mighty Dahkota'… They skirted the shore of Smith's Bay to Huntington's Point whence, at the waning of the moon before the dawn, they stealthily crossed to Big Island." (Bergman Richards, *The Early Background of Minnetonka Beach*)

Special places such as Big Island have their share of myths and legends, which are often embellished after starting with a kernel of truth. The chronicle of the beautiful Dakota young woman, Mahpiyata, and

---

* Our family's future home was known as Meeker's Island for four short years before the Morse brothers became the owner.

** Many people believed John Morse was the actual hatchet murderer of Lizzie Borden's father and step-mother in August 1892. Morse, a large man of considerable strength, was a trained butcher and was known to carry his tools with him. He was a guest of the Bordens at Fall River, Massachusetts, on August 3 and stayed in the guest room where Lizzie's step-mother was slain. Lizzie was acquitted of the murders that made her famous. (Could Morse have honed his hatchet skills while clearing land on Big Island's Crown Point?)

the Ojibwe war party leader, Tayandwada, *(I Esteem Him Well)* is an example. Dakota Chief Wakanyeya, *(He Who Towers Among Men)*, was protective of his daughter, the *Celestial Peace Maiden,* and deterred the young warriors bearing gifts as he deemed them unfit for the maiden, except Ksapa, the brave selected to marry her.

When the Ojibwe attacked the Dakota on Big Island, Mahpiyata watched from the safety of the dense Big Woods of Crown Point, across from Gales' Island. The Dakota were being dominated by the enemy when she emerged from her hiding place to inspire her braves. The Ojibwe were so awed by her fearlessness that Tayandwada ran the gauntlet of Dakota, took her captive and brought her to the Ojibwe encampment in the Turtle Mountains near the North Dakota-Manitoba border.

After a wary introduction to and reception from the Ojibwe people, Mahpiyata became an accepted member of the community, learning their culture and traditions while imparting her knowledge of Dakota customs. She eventually married Tayandwada and, while happy, she yearned for peace and finally persuaded her husband to accompany her to her settlement between Lake Minnetonka and the Minnesota River as a prologue to harmony.

Inroads were made and a call went out to neighboring bands of Ojibwe and Dakota to gather on Big Island for a celebration of feasting and ceremony. The revelry continued for days, and the bond was solidified by many inter-tribal marriages. Mahpiyata and Tayandwada are said to be buried on the north end of Big Island as an example of solidarity between the Dakota and Ojibwe. "*With the red wand they passed the bad spirits, with the blue wand they passed the tempting spirits, with the white wand they passed into the beginning of a higher life. Thus ends the legend of Mahpiyata.*" (Bergmann Richards, *The Early Background of Minnetonka Beach*)

■ ■ ■

In the rapid-fire world of pioneer real estate, the Big Island went through multiple name changes in its first years after appearing on the white man's radar. By 1855, Cottage Island and Morse Island were added to list. Brothers William and John Morse bought the 275-acre island using military bounty claims and built the first house there in 1856.

By May, Minnewashta carpenter Henry R. Eddy reported, "*Worked for W.B. Morse on the island putting in window frames*" and "*setting glass.*"

After surveying their land, the brothers started selling lots for summer homes and rented tents to campers. Summer cottages began appearing, mostly situated on the isle's southern end including Crown Point and Point Comfort. For many years maps continued to list the name as "Morse or Big Island," but the marketing of the Big Island Amusement Park eventually eliminated "Morse."

An enclave of Scandinavians appeared on the western side of the island in the early 20th century. "*One notable person who built a cottage on the island was David Clough, who was illiterate until his wife taught him to read and write. He was elected to the Minnesota Senate in 1887 and became Minnesota's Governor in 1895. By the 1910s, part of West Big Island was populated by Swedish immigrants. Residents fished, swam, played music and card games. They spoke Swedish amongst themselves until the 1940s. Most families were gone by the 1960s.*" (Lydia Christianson, "Glimpses into West Big Island," *Sun Sailor*)

Entrance to the Big Island Amusement Park.
Courtesy of Minnesota Historical Society

An inventive use of the island was the makeshift brewery that served beer when much of the Lake Minnetonka citizenry professed to practice sobriety. When a new keg was being tapped, a horn sounded the alert that could be heard as far as the nearest shore in Deephaven. While much of the 275-acre island was considered a sanctuary for the bibulous, the residents of Crown and Comfort Points, including the Fruen family, were more abstemious.

■ ■ ■

One could not write a better version of a Gilded Age American Dream story of success and failure than that of Olaf O. Searle, a Norwegian immigrant who came to Minnesota in 1881 with nothing to his name but his work ethic and determination to be a success. Olaf went to work for the St. Paul, Minneapolis and Manitoba Railway and was a quick study, soon creating the A.E. Johnson and Co. with partner Aleck Johnson, a Swede. The two men sold steamship passage and farmland to a mostly Scandinavian, Finnish and German market.

In one year alone, they sold 150,000 acres of land along the Northern Pacific Railroad right of way in Central Minnesota worth $950,000. Olaf also dabbled in banking and real estate. The ventures were hugely successful and, in 1891, Searle plowed some of his profits into an opulent 125-acre estate for his wife, Dagmar, son Ralph and himself on the side of Big Island facing Lafayette Bay. The neo-classical style would have fit in an upscale Minneapolis neighborhood seamlessly. It was a stark contrast from the ramshackle cabins that still dotted the Lower Lake shoreline.

He sank $250,000 into his yellow, white-trimmed, three-story masterpiece which included 21 rooms, marble baths, hand-carved woodwork, multiple verandas, murals created by artisans; a library stocked with $25,000 worth of books, a massive furnace, porcelain stoves, marble-accented bathrooms, steam heat and gaslights. The basement housed a wide assortment of wines and liquors. A large painted rendering of a Valkyrie dominated one room.

The meticulously manicured lawn featured ornamental plantings, which led to a Japanese garden with fruit trees, a Koi Pond, a footbridge and a gazebo. Russian olive trees and shrubbery were added to the thick forest. The ostentation was incredible, and I am sure the old guard in

Opulence and Tragedy. The Big Island Olaf Searle Mansion. Trying to "*keep up with the Joneses*", an unwise marital choice and an economic turndown led to his demise. The Gilded Age novel material all burned down, including his island dream. *Courtesy of Big Island Legacy*

Orono and Wayzata held up their noses in condescension.

Olaf had a channel, now known as "Big Island Channel" or "Alligator Alley," dredged without asking anyone's permission. Scores of years later it caused confusion due to a governmental error. There is a spit of land on Searle's old property, a peninsula really, that at some point was named Mahpiyata Island. Given Searle's proclivity for ornamental landscaping, it is possible the channel was carved simply for decorative purposes.*

Searle erected a mammoth boathouse with a tower adjacent to a dock large enough to handle one of the large steamboats that ferried passengers from the shore and could accommodate a full orchestra for a summer concert. In the spring the servants moved the Searle

---

* Until recently, this was news to me. I often fished there and never considered it an island. Perhaps in periods of heavy rain it is. In 1964, maps were issued misplacing Mahpiyata Island from its proper place (if it is indeed an island) to the western, bisected part of Big Island created by the channel. Confused? Join the club.

family from Minneapolis with one of them swimming a cow across to the island. Olaf and Dagmar often entertained their guests with music and expensive wine and lived what appeared to be the perfect bucolic existence.

A combination of forces such as the economy and perhaps heredity and environment converged to cause Olaf Searle's financial empire to come tumbling down. The 1893 depression hit him hard as he suffered bank failures, defaulted on North Dakota farmland and, for a period, saw his Big Island property fall into foreclosure.

He continued to spend summers on Lake Minnetonka where Dagmar retreated into a life dominated by alcohol and died in 1905. It appears that Olaf also had his struggles with the Demon Rum. In 1916 he campaigned for a bridge connecting Big Island to the mainland which would have significantly increased the value of his holdings, but the project failed to win approval.

In 1913 Searle married a twenty-year-old fortune hunter who he soon divorced, but the damage had been done as she fleeced him of almost all his assets. Later, he left Big Island for good and lived in a Minneapolis boarding house. Olaf died in 1926, and his beloved, abandoned island estate went up in flames a few years later, leaving just the foundation.

■ ■ ■

"Big Island Park is an island of majestic trees, rolling lawns, knolls and numerous beautiful vantage points from which may be enjoyed a variety of vistas of water and sky, and altogether it is a most unusual resort from a natural beauty standpoint." (*Street Car Journal*, Volume XXXI, No. 4)

In 1905, the Twin City Rapid Transit Company acquired 65 acres on the north end of Big Island where they built a $1.5 million amusement park, which was operational by the summer of 1906 as a destination and source of revenue for their streetcars. Suggestions for a name included Whooperup and Uneedagoodtime, but a less whimsical one was selected. The Park featured a honeycomb of concrete and gravel paths for walking and extensive ground for picnics. A 1,500-capacity music casino offered dancing. In the beginning, national acts like Frederick Innes and Eugenio Sorrentino's Banda Rossa Orchestra performed, but usually local acts entertained.

Postcard of the Wharves on Beautiful Big Island Park

Among the attractions were a carousel, a figure-eight roller coaster, the Magic Chute, a baseball park, a "Trip Through Yellowstone Park" ride and an "Old Mill," where a couple could steal a kiss while riding in the dark in a small "boat." The trench for the moat is visible still. There were also smaller rides including one interestingly named the "Hooligan Slide." Other diversions included a moving picture house, a carousel, the Merry Maze, the Laughing Gallery and a Penny Arcade. For couples seeking some privacy without the customary chaperone, rowboats were available to rent.

Three paddle-wheel ferry boats were built to transport people back and forth from Excelsior to the Park. The boats could accommodate 1,000 passengers at a time and ran every 20 minutes. At any time on any given weekend over 10,000 visitors could be walking the grounds of the Park. A 186-foot-high beacon resembling the Tower of Seville glowed brightly every night and could be seen all over the lake. It also served as the water tower supplying the amusement park. Grandmother Reba visited the Park in her teens, not realizing she would spend much of the rest of her life on Big Island.

While still popular, the Park closed in 1911 due to debt, over expansion and the cost of accessing and operating a venture in a relatively remote location. The introduction of the Model T provided many more options and extended the range of travel for most Americans to pursue leisure activities. Before lodging in the West was common, people slept in their cars. The term *"auto-camping"* was coined to make it sound more upscale.

By 1917, many of the Park's Spanish-Mission-style buildings were torn down with most of the metal stripped for the World War I effort. The Tower of Seville was toppled by a team of horses. One hundred years later, the Park lives on at The Minnesota State Fair in St. Paul where the bumper boats of the Big Island Old Mill ride still navigate the dark Tunnel of Love, which provided privacy for clandestine kisses I shared with my first girlfriend, Marilyn. It took me two bus transfers to reach the fairgrounds, but young love prevailed.

During the early 1920s, the state of Minnesota bought the land formerly housing the Park and developed it as a vacation camp for veterans of "the Great War." The camp consisted of 30 cabins, campsites, a swimming beach, showers and a mess hall. It operated for 80 years. The land is now a 56-acre *"passive recreation park"* managed by the city of Orono but is underutilized with few visitors except for the occasional vandal.

LAKE MINNETONKA FROM ZUMBRA HEIGHTS, AT VAN DUSEN HOME, LAKE MINNETONKA, MINN.

View from the Van Dusen Estate
Old postcard

Lake Minnetonka Goes Upscale: The First Wave

"You better come out here and see My Lake for yourselves. You can't imagine how she glows in the sunshine and glitters in the moonlight. On grey days, she looks sad and lonely, just like I feel sometimes, but in no time at all, she can kick up her heels and treat you to a first-class squall. Yes, sir, she's tricky all right, but I'm never leaving her, never!

Hezekiah Hotchkiss,
LETTER TO FAMILY IN BOSTON, OCTOBER 1852

WHEN GREAT-GREAT-GRANDFATHER Andrew Bergquist was getting his family situated in Scandia, a scant 14 miles south of the Big Water on Lake Clearwater, Mni Tanka was no longer a secret. The Mendota Treaty of 1851 opened the floodgates. Although many Dakota leaders refused to sign the document, the U.S. government declared it ratified anyway – opening the door for white settlement.

Opportunists staked claims on the lake before the ink was dry, and the parcels needed constant monitoring as claim-jumping was rampant. It was a difficult choice: stay in a slapdash dwelling and suffer the brutal winter or leave until spring, hoping the crude structure still stood and the squatters had stayed away.

It was nearly impossible to build a sturdy, air-tight structure as transportation issues, scarcity of materials and the short season precluded producing much more than a small shack. Before the building began the parcel of land had to be cleared of the dense, deciduous forest. Soon the hermits, loners, farmers and speculators were being invaded by settlers and commerce. Fledgling communities evolved into

small towns. The Big Water was undergoing another character change.

Lake Minnetonka was now on the public's radar although, getting there was a formidable task. The "roads" – glorified cow paths – had three seasons: muddy, rutty and impassable. Many preferred to walk beside the wagon to eliminate the jaw-rattling vibrations. By the mid-1850s, a trail was carved through woods and vegetation to Wayzata from St. Anthony on the Mississippi. The trip took a day using oxcarts for transportation.

The nascent settlement of Wayzata had one street, a general store, a saw mill and three primitive hotels for the road weary. Ben Keesling's inn was so rudimentary and unsuccessful it was re-imagined as an ashery to turn byproducts from the saw mill into potash. It would take a long time before Wayzata acquired the cachet of today. (I half-expect a trendy bistro named "The Ashery" to debut soon.)

As haphazard and chaotic as much of the land rush seemed, one man, a tailor from upstate New York named George Bertram, was methodical in his efforts to build a settlement on the shores of the Big Water. He was driven not only by opportunity and the pioneering spirit, but other forces and events helped push him west.

The Industrial Revolution and Isaac Elis Howe's invention of the sewing machine made Bertram's vocation less lucrative. The expansion of railroad routes provided easier access to the frontier. Dakota treaties opened millions of acres. Vestiges of the Pilgrims' community vision remained and was bolstered by the Second Great Awakening during the first half of the 19th century.

Bertram made an exploratory trip west in 1852 and chose a site on the southern end of the Lower Lake where he met the Mdewakanton Dakota. He noted, "*Shockapi's braves were painted black, white, yellow and red, and the squaws, save for a sort of apron, were entirely nude.*"

After selecting the site he would call "Excelsior," named either for Longfellow's poem of the same name, or the Latin phrase "ever upward," he hustled to New York City where he hung his shingle advertising his passion project:

Go West!
Join the Excelsior Pioneer Association
Inquire – 268 Grand Street

With a fastidiousness perhaps informed by the precision demanded in tailoring, Bertram laid out his plan and wrote its constitution. The fee for joining the organization was $8 plus a fee of $1 weekly from November 12, 1852, to July 17, 1853. The payments entitled each Association family to a one-acre lot in settlement and the opportunity to acquire 160 acres outside Excelsior for $1.25 an acre. George commissioned a carpenter from Iowa, Robert McGrath, to build a two-story shingled log house. Upon receiving 350 commitments, the first wave of settlers arrived with Bertram in June 1853 and the Township of Excelsior was created in 1857.

The settlement thrived and, to this day, it is the lake community most familiar to the Fruen family. The city has done a good job maintaining the feel of old village times, but battles to keep developers at bay are continuous. The developers are determined to tear down older homes and replace them with large houses, taking almost every square foot on the lot and blocking the views of neighboring homeowners from all directions.

When Excelsior was platted, a prime thirteen-acre greenspace on the shore, described as a *"common pleasure ground,"* was protected from development. Excelsior Commons, preserved almost 170 years ago, is home to swimming beaches, a boat landing, baseball fields, picnic facilities and playgrounds. The band shell hosts a summer concert series. Platforms are erected for dancing.

Citizens of Excelsior during the first quarter of the 20th century recalled the four epic pageants heralding the town's history from the Dakota to white settlement. Throngs of spectators sat on the hill rising from the Commons toward Water Street as hundreds of actors played the multitude of characters. George Bertram and his colleagues had given Excelsior, and its visitors, a far-sighted, priceless gift. On a beautiful day one can lie on the grass, read a book and gaze at Crown Point in the distance.

One of Excelsior's most dynamic and fascinating characters was Peter Gideon; a talented, odd, driven and often contentious New Englander. He did not approve of alcohol, beards, horse racing and gambling but supported women's suffrage, spiritualism and a healthy lifestyle. Gideon was a self-educated horticulturalist who planted peach pits and, when they sprouted, moved them to his family's apple orchard. The trees produced fruit by the time Peter was nine.

Later, Gideon was in desperate straits with winter approaching, no money and no winter coat. While experimenting with hybrid seeds to produce apples sturdy enough to withstand the northern climate, he stitched some vests together to make outerwear to ward off the frigid winds blowing from the Lower Lake. The answer to his experimentation came in the form of Siberian crab apple seeds. Soon the Wealthy Apple, coined after his wife's first name, became the top-selling apple in the Upper Midwest. Though the Wealthy has disappeared, its descendants include the Haralson, the tart, firm apple perfect for eating and baking.

Lake Minnetonka was home to over 500 cone-shaped burial mounds with 98 on Gideon's land. At first, like many other curious seekers, Gideon took a shovel to a few mounds until he discovered a skull, which rendered him physically ill. He soon was contacted by the spirit world and advised to protect the work of the Woodland Period's Mound Builders.

According to *Happenings around Deephaven: The First Hundred Years,* Peter took his stand on the 4th of July in 1872 and declined to allow "*despoilers* [to] *set foot on his property*," believing the interlopers "*belonged to a group determined to open an Indian mound... The sparks which flew probably rivaled the evening's fireworks*." Most of the desecrated mounds revealed little save for some human bones, bits of pottery and a few stone arrowheads. Gideon never accumulated wealth despite his skill and innovation. In his last years he sold most of his land, dying alone in 1899.

As a precursor to their post-bellum affinity for Lake Minnetonka, southerners, many from St. Louis and New Orleans (including the author Samuel Clemens – better known as Mark Twain) boarded steamboats to see the upper reaches of the Mississippi and the mighty Falls of St. Anthony. "*...grand tours of the Upper Mississippi began to feature the lake on their itinerary. Indian lore added a mythical dimension to its appeal... an increasing number of curiosity seekers heard of the magnificent lake in the Northwest that had so recently been frequented by Indians*." (Paul Clifford Larson, *A Place at the Lake*)

This practice ceased when the Civil War erupted. Able men and even boys enlisted as Minnesota produced the first regiment for the Union. The Halstead brothers, Frank and George, are arguably the most well-known Lake Minnetonka Civil War veterans. Frank was an Upper

Lake trailblazer when most of the activity was concentrated on the Lower Lake. He arrived from New Jersey in 1855 and built a cabin he called Rough and Ready on the bay that now bears his surname.

Halstead immersed himself in the nascent lake community and was chosen to participate in the christening of Lake Minnetonka's first steamboat, the *Governor Ramsey*, in 1860 by smashing a bottle of water against the bow. Frank then joined other local dignitaries, including the governor, for an inaugural trip around Big Island: "*In his manners he was ever quiet and unassuming, and though sympathetic and approachable, he invited no confidence and gave none. A recluse, he was hospitable and affable, and when asked why he chose to live such a secluded life, he always replied in such a manner as would show the interrogator that it was not a question he cared to answer. Little is known of Captain Halstead for this reason.*" (*Minneapolis Tribune*, July 6, 1876)

Captain Frank Halstead returned from the Civil War to the Big Water and built a larger home on the Upper Lake known as The Hermitage. His naval expertise was tapped when he was consulted on dredging Hull's Narrows to accommodate larger boats. Now known simply as the Narrows, the boggy marshland was the only access point to the Upper Lake from the Lower.

Captain Halstead, as he was usually known, was determined to provide better steamboat service on Minnetonka and leveraged all his assets to build the seventy-eight-foot *Mary*. It was an ill-fated venture and left Halstead was penniless and despondent. The Captain jumped into the lake with a sack of rocks attached to his neck just before the observance of the nation's centennial in July 1876. His boat, with oars neatly stored, was soon found. His body bobbed to the surface near Crane Island. The local newspaper reported Excelsior's subdued centennial celebration.

The Captain was buried near his home, and brother George arrived in Minnesota on July 19th with his dog, Ring, and moved into The Hermitage. He decorated his new home, augmenting it with brother Franks's war mementos including firearms, medals, flags and canteens. He added a porch to receive his many callers.

For 25 cents, the curious could tour The Hermitage. A price-hike to 50 cents did not dampen demand. George encouraged this source of revenue and was pleased when the visitors brought a picnic lunch, which he was very happy to share. Many signed and sometimes left a message on the exterior of the 1-1/2-story building. The Major preserved the graffiti by framing it in glass if he found it worthy and paid the writer a small honorarium for their artwork.

The older brother adopted Frank's passion project, the steamboat *Mary*, the only remaining vessel on the lake with a defective Ames boiler. He had been warned of the danger but ignored the issue. The boat exploded at the Hotel St. Louis dock on July 1, 1880, and the senior Halstead was determined to be criminally negligent.

The Major was released due to a technicality, but he was reviled for the rest of his days for his carelessness and disregard for safety. In September 1901, the Hermitage burned to the ground while George slept. A young boy rummaged through the wreckage and brought a souvenir rib bone home. His horrified mother buried it post haste.

It took a cessation of hostilities, an outbreak of yellow fever, the summer climate, the ugliness of Reconstruction, and the arrival of the railroad to turn Lake Minnetonka into a tourist destination nationally and internationally. Boating and the scenic vistas were the attraction, but it took the train to deliver the vacationers to Wayzata, the only Big Water stop in 1867.

While towns like Wayzata and Excelsior were growing as year-round residences, Minneapolitans did not establish summer homes on Minnetonka until the mid-1870s. There were only two local families, the Guilds and the Gales, to live seasonally on the lake. Transportation from the city was still slow and intermittent.

A major impediment to attracting throngs to the lake was the crude living quarters available: "*Unfortunately, lodgings at Lake Minnetonka in the late 1870s were, according to a St. Louis Times correspondent, sadly lacking... '...there is probably no place in the United States where the accommodations are so inadequate or so poor.' He told of people arriving at Excelsior in the evening and leaving the following morning, 'disgusted with the beggarly accommodations and indigestible meals which are offered to them.'"* (Frederick L. Johnson, *The Big Water*)

Affluent tourists expected luxury, pampering, sophisticated menus, top drawer entertainment and service, not small, drafty boardinghouses serving delicacies like Muskrat Stew with a choice of sides: beans or a Swamp Potato.

Prominent attorney Charles S. Gibson of St. Louis was one of Lake Minnetonka's most ardent early boosters who first visited the Big Water in 1854 and returned year after year until his annual pilgrimages were interrupted by the Civil War.

After the Confederates surrendered, Gibson reappeared with a plan he executed with precision. He purchased a quarter-section of land in Deephaven and brought landscape architects from Boston to Minnetonka in 1870 to suggest the best location on his Breezy Point peninsula, a stone's throw from Big Island, to build his beloved North Home (later contracted to Northome). It was nestled in the deep woods with only a primitive, winding road cut through the maple trees to provide access.

Sir Charles, who claimed to be a British Knight, was not finished. He constructed the 200-room Hotel St. Louis on the rest of his property as an alternative to the primitive hostelry that existed at the time. It was beautifully appointed with marble top furniture, brass beds, plush carpeting and elegant window treatments.

"The St. Louis was a rectangular gray building with green trim overlooking Carson's Bay and Bay St. Louis. It had three floors with a veranda on each level and some 200 gas-lit rooms besides dining rooms, a parlor, smoking room—and a bath on every floor with 'plumbing of the highest quality.' Before long it had a telephone and electric lights and bells. Behind the hotel was a row of neat white cabins for Negro servants who worked at the hotel or had come with visitors from the South." (*Deephaven Historical Society Newsletter*, Summer Report 2004)

Gibson was a gifted proselytizer and champion of Lake Minnetonka. His disciples came from the South, mostly New Orleans, St. Louis and Kansas City. Some brought their horses, coachmen and carriages for touring around the Big Water. Nightly entertainment ranged from the carefree (dancing and musical productions) to the cerebral (plays and poetry).

Sir Charles was the trailblazer in the upscale niche, and the Lake Minnetonka hostelry industry and grand hotels began sprouting like mushrooms on the sylvan shores. They began developing their own niches to differentiate from the competition. One offered an all-white staff while another touted its healthy approach to its service.

The *National Health Journal* extolled the lake's "*climate made pure and health-giving by the rarefied air of a high altitude and cooled by the grateful winds of the North.*" The weather was advertised as an elixir for ailments ranging from hay fever and insomnia to the more serious

The grand St. Louis Hotel's opulence comes to Lake Minnetonka
via Charles Gibson's Health and Pleasure Resort.
Photo courtesy of Excelsior Lake Minnetonka Historical Society

yellow fever and tuberculosis. Others emphasized the scenic wonders
of the Big Water including Tonka Bay's Lake Park Hotel, which boasted
a veranda for every room. Fascination with Native American life was a
strong draw, and local Dakota band members would perform at some
hotels dressed in full regalia.

Billiard rooms, bowling alleys, roller-skating rinks, grass tennis
courts, swimming beaches, boats and baseball fields were available for
the sporting crowd. The locals viewed the Southern men with curiosity,
claiming they rarely ventured out of the shade, preferring to sit on a
porch smoking cigars and enjoying refreshing libations.

■ ■ ■

Sir Charles may have been the pioneer of upscale Minnetonka hotels,
but no one bested railroad baron James J. Hill for sheer opulence and
conspicuous consumption when his five-story, hybrid-styled, monolith-
ic Hotel Lafayette opened on July 4, 1882. The main building covered

five acres and featured hallways ten feet wide. The hotel was positioned strategically on a gently sloping hill to ensure that all the 300 rooms had a view of the Lower or Upper Lake.

Hill was a living example of the Horatio Alger stories popular during the Gilded Age. As the nation pushed westward, vast fortunes were made in real estate, agriculture, lumber, the railroads and manufacturing. The rags-to-riches stories were meant to show, with increasing difficulty, that the American dream was still achievable. Canadian-born Hill left school at 14 to help support his family and moved to the U.S., landing in St. Paul on the banks of the Mississippi as a 17-year-old shipping clerk for a steamboat company.

On his way to being known as the "Empire Builder," he worked diligently for 20 years for a variety of companies, digesting the aspects of the transportation business including bookkeeping, trading and freight handling. He had a knack for identifying and seizing opportunity and, in 1879, Hill and his partners acquired the bankrupt St. Paul & Pacific Railroad and transformed it into the lucrative St. Paul, Minnesota & Manitoba Railway Company.

Hill was made president and set his sights on expansion west. His foresight was instrumental in establishing communities and driving economic expansion along the route of his Great Northern Railroad which, linked with the St. Paul and Pacific, would eventually reach the Pacific Northwest.

"'Give me Swedes, snuff and whiskey, and I'll build a railroad through hell,' Hill proclaimed, since strong Scandinavian immigrants were his favorite beasts of burden – that is, until they organized into unions." (Eric Dregni, By the Waters of Minnetonka)

The railroad magnate did not rest on his laurels and never did things in a small way. To celebrate his railroad tracks reaching Washington State, he hosted a lavish banquet for 1,000 guests at his majestic hotel on Lake Minnetonka. The guest list included German and English nobility and monarchs, nine governors and generals each, architect Cass Gilbert and the father of the country's environmental movement, John Muir. Ex-President Ulysses S. Grant also attended. Many arrived at the Big Water on train cars commissioned for the occasion.

"Lake Minnetonka and the Hotel Lafayette will from this day on be renowned, for it is assembling about itself a company which attracts the gaze of the whole United States... And the tables, ach Himmel! Never shall

Hotel Lafayette, billed as "the finest hotel west of New York City," opened in 1882.
Photo courtesy of of Minnesota Historical Society

The four story, forty room Keeywadin Hotel in Deephaven was a five-minute
boat ride to Crown Point. Single rooms were $2.50 a night and doubles
went for $4.50. For a little extra, you could have a bathroom.
It burned to the ground in 1924, ca. 1910.
Photo courtesy of Minnesota Historical Society,

I see such long tables again during my life's span! My hand goes lame at the slightest endeavor to describe such a banquet." (Herr N. Mohr, *Streifzug durch den Nordwestern Amerika*) The evening went well until the serving staff sampled the ample supply of the finest liquor one could purchase.

The temperance movement reached Minnesota with great fervor, and Wayzata and Excelsior prohibited the sale and consumption of alcohol except for beer and wine. James J. Hill had no problem flouting convention, or laws for that matter, and soon a brawl ensued. Glasses and cups went airborne and the police tried to intercede. General Grant had survived the Civil War unscathed but caught some shrapnel when a pie plate glanced off his head.

W.E.B. du Bois, a civil rights activist and a future founder of the N.A.A.C.P., was a waiter that summer at the Hotel Lafayette while he was working his way through college. His feelings toward white privilege solidified through his experience serving some of the boorish, entitled, condescending guests.

The era of gracious summers in the luxurious hotels did not last and a variety of circumstances conspired to cause their demise. Yellow Fever had run its course in the South, and the economic downturn of 1893 contributed to a decrease in occupancy. The advent of automobile touring and the rails west opened other destinations, including the growing number of national parks.

The Minneapolis vacationers who frequented the grand hotels began building their own places on the Big Water. By 1898, Lake Minnetonka was connected to the Mississippi by horse-drawn wagons riding on rails from Stillwater to Excelsior. This transportation upgrade arrived too late to prolong the Hotel Era on the lake.

On October 4, 1897, the Hotel Lafayette burned to the ground after it had been put to bed for the season. One by one the other hotels closed or caught fire. The Hotel St. Louis was razed in 1907. The vacated locations soon became sites for individual cabins, cottages and year-round residences as the next wave of gracious living descended on the shores of Lake Minnetonka.

Arthur B. Fruen
Fruen family photo

The Glue

"Just in case we needed a roof over our head."

Grandfather Arthur Fruen explaining his rationale for
designing the Fruen Milling Company office building in
the style of a colonial-style house during the Depression.

THE SHORT PARADE UP the steep hill above the mill and the spring
to 56 Russell Avenue South started every day at lunch time when Grandpa and three of his sons were in town. Arthur walked to the office and
back into his late seventies. Grandmother Reba prepared the meal and
ate with her husband and boys.

Children of "self-made" parents have a difficult second act to perform.
Being born in the United States is an advantage, and although upward
mobility has become much more difficult to achieve, the opportunity is
virtually non-existent in other parts of the world. A self-made man or
woman often wrestles with the dichotomy of giving children every advantage and then resenting them for their head start in life.

Grandfather Arthur Fruen navigated these waters very well. He
enjoyed the benefits of a stable childhood, a large comfortable home,
healthy diet, nice clothes and a good education. Grandpa took it from
there. He was an excellent student but, because of his smaller stature,
athletics took a back seat to activities such as speech and debate at Minneapolis North High School. He inherited his parents' intelligence and
work ethic and merged that base of traits with great people-skills and,
by his early twenties, he was William's trusted confederate and business
confidante.

Arthur earned his father's respect and strove to maintain it. He was
brilliant, learned, personable, indefatigable, compassionate, insightful
and strong. Grandpa had an innate sense of fairness, a sense of humor
and a humble, self-effacing manner. He blended these personal attributes

with business acumen and commitment to his cherished city of Minneapolis, balancing them in harmony with his dedication to his family. His friends and colleagues called him "A.B."

Grandfather was naturally inclined to generosity. One of the nation's great entrepreneurs, Irwin Jacobs, once told my Uncle Doug that he appreciated Arthur's largesse for putting food on his family's table during the Depression. The Fourth Ward Alderman and president of the Minneapolis City Council took care of his constituents.

Art Fruen was an officer, board member or director of numerous civic organizations including the Minneapolis Park Board, the Glenwood Civic League, Minneapolis Taxpayers Association, Hennepin Federal Savings and Loan, the Grain Dealers national organization and Westminster Presbyterian Church. He also belonged to Rotary and the Minneapolis Athletic Club. He was a joiner, networker and leader par excellence. A.B. was the treasurer of the Automobile Club of Minneapolis, which had a social component at the time. During a period when anti-Semitism ran rampant in the city, Grandpa lobbied the membership to admit Jewish members. Journalist Eddie Schwartz recounts, *"I was accepted and Lou Gross at the same time, for membership, and it was deliberately put up by Arthur Fruen, the Alderman of the old 4th Ward, because he insisted at that time, in the '30s, the time had come to cut out this foolishness, and they'd better accept some other members. Lou Gross and I were the first two, and we accepted, and voted in, and joined."*

■ ■ ■

The 4th Ward ethnic mix consisted of Jews, blacks and whites. Grandfather served them all. Finntown was a neighborhood with a high concentration of immigrants from the Nordic country they called Suomi. The frame and stucco 1-1/2-story houses looked like many others in Minneapolis except for those with more than one chimney, denoting the presence of a summer kitchen in the back designed to keep the main living space cool during July and August. A sauna was often located in a basement corner.

My grandmother, Reba Mary Watson Fruen, more reserved and stricter than her husband, was largely left to handle the daily management of the household and her six children. At times she seemed a bit standoffish due to her proper bearing. Her father, John Watson, was an educator, and Reba was adamant her children and grandchildren spoke proper English.

If I asked her, "*Grandma, can I have some candy?*" she replied, "*You can, but you may not.*" Diction was also part of her focus. She insisted on proper pronunciation to the point of pronouncing the "h" in words such as "whether" and "who." I may be wrong, but it seemed to me that although she loved all her grandchildren, she favored the girls.

Great-grandfather Watson was born in Illinois after his grandfather Martin, a sailor, emigrated from Port Hope, Ontario, with his two brothers. The siblings joined the three Port Hope Reeves sisters in perfect marital symmetry.

After graduating from Minneapolis South High School, Grandmother worked for The Superior District of the American Baptist Mission Society. She was given a half-day off every Saturday afternoon. Arthur and Reba met in church, marrying in 1913 at Temple Baptist Church in front of 200 witnesses. The reception was held at the Watson home at 2917 Bloomington Avenue South, and the newlyweds headed west for a three-week camping honeymoon in the West.

My grandparents were founders of the Bryn Mawr Baptist Church but left after a schism caused by the hiring of a zealous evangelical-style pastor and a proposed building expansion, which divided the worshippers. The Fruens left the Baptist Church because they felt their rigid tenets were at odds with their values and felt the new minister in Bryn Mawr was a step backwards. They started attending services at Westminster Presbyterian Church in downtown Minneapolis. The congregation was formed in 1857 and the current stately, Romanesque-and-Gothic-designed landmark was finished in 1897.

Grandma often ceded a disagreement to her husband's point of view, preferring to lose the skirmishes in deference to the big picture. However, she held her own when provoked. Once when Grandpa tried to show her a more efficient way of sweeping the kitchen floor, she chased him from the room brandishing her broom. When he was too bossy for her tastes, she warned, "*Arthur, don't be so executive.*" She knew how to "manage" Grandfather in delicate situations.

When younger daughter Louise was inconsolable after cracking up her father's immaculate Cadillac, Grandma hustled her in to tell Grandpa while tears were still streaming down her face. My aunt was a well read, strong student and attended Mount Holyoke College in Massachusetts.

John Henry Watson
Fruen family photo

Reba Mary Watson on her
wedding day, June 18, 1913
Fruen family photo

She was the most urbane and sophisticated of the six children and lived in New York City, Santa Barbara and Phoenix before settling in Ohio. I remember being amused when Aunt Louise played a Barbra Streisand album that annoyed my father, who did not care for the singer's politics.

Reba was also close to her oldest child, Betty (Elizabeth) albeit with a mother's discerning eye. They read the same books and discussed them, but Grandma thought she spent too much time on hair and make-up. Aunt Betty was lovely in every way and carried herself in a peaceful centered manner. Another excellent student, she attended University High School and Carleton College.

■ ■ ■

In addition to her other obligations, Reba served as Arthur's personal secretary for his civic and city council business. Grandpa thought she might appreciate a respite from the children but also insisted on crisp, professionally written correspondence.

Grandmother and Grandfather headed down to the mill office after dinner many nights to work on correspondence both personal and political. I believe she was often A.B.'s ghostwriter, penning much of his written communication. Reba controlled his engagement calendar and accompanied him to most meetings, keeping her eye on the clock. She extricated him from long discussions in order to head to the next appointment.

I believe Grandma would have liked to participate in more social activities, but time was at a premium and Grandpa had little inclination to indulge in what he considered to be non-essential pursuits. Reba belonged to the Woman's Club of Minneapolis and enjoyed attending events such as a luncheon for Lady Halifax, wife of Lord Edward Frederick Lindley, the British Ambassador to the United States.

My grandparents often attended the Automobile Club of America conventions, and one in 1952 stands out. It was the Golden Jubilee event held in Washington, D.C., and Grandma was invited to have afternoon tea with First Lady Bess Truman and tour the White House. For the moment, Reba put aside any partisanship in deference to her Democratic hostess.

Despite appearances to the contrary, Grandmother ran the show in many ways at 56 Russell. At every major family event in the city, she

Bryn Mawr fashion show. Sitting: Aunt Betty (L), Grandma Fruen (R)
Standing: Uncle Dick (L) and father Roger (R), August, 1951
Fruen family photo

Fruen Family Portrait: Standing L to R Dick, Roger, Arthur
Sitting L to R Bruce, Doug, Reba, Betty, Louise
Fruen family photo

did the lion's share of cooking. After the meal she was escorted to the living room to rest and enjoy her grandchildren, but within minutes she was back in the kitchen, presumably to help with the clean-up. This was actually the time to gather intel on family inside information. She could dry the same plate for five minutes while listening intently to the chatter.

■ ■ ■

Arthur and Reba enjoyed touring the national parks, and Glacier National Park in Montana was a favorite. Grandfather's home movies from the late 1930s show bighorn sheep grazing on a rocky outcropping, yards away from the Lodge swimming pool. In August 1937, Uncle Bruce sent a postcard home from the Swift Current Auto Camp in Glacier National Park, reminding my 18-year-old father to take care of the *"kittens and chickens."* Bruce intimated he was feigning illness to avoid his father's strenuous hikes: *"Grinnell Lake is at the head of a chain of lakes. Louise, Doug, Mother and Dad went on a hike to the next one down, Lake Josephine. I was sick yesterday and the day before so I couldn't go. I didn't go on the hike this morning either. 13 miles today and 18 tomorrow."*

A.B.'s civil engineering background explains his love of gadgets, and cameras were at the top of his list. Every activity from daily mundanities to the majesty of national parks was chronicled with his movie camera or a small Kodak Bantam folding camera with a range finder. Reba described his artistic process: *"It is very painful to the family when he takes pictures, but we all enjoy them when they are finished. We have to wait for a cloud, or the sun to go through one. We have to wait for a car to go by, or some people to pass. Then he doesn't take just the view we think that he should, and we all tell him about it. The small children have gotten to the point where they run when they see the camera. But the pictures are always very fine...."*

■ ■ ■

Born in 1919, my father Roger was the third child of Reba and Arthur. From an early age he had an appealing, gregarious, energetic personality and was eager to join his older siblings in their activities. He was a happy, mischievous child and apparently charming, too. I was taken

Roger Alan Fruen
Fruen family photo

Leslie Harrison's 1948 engagement
photo at Lake of the Isles
Photo courtesy of Minneapolis Tribune

Roger Fruen at The Parade football field with the
Basilica of St. Mary in the background
Fruen family photo

aback when, at the age of ten, I attended the Bryn Mawr Elementary all-school reunion with my father. He was greeted effusively by his old teachers and friends like a visiting dignitary. I was impressed.

As he grew, he traveled in a rag-tag pack of neighborhood boys who explored their domain, played baseball and swam in nearby Cedar Lake which, of all the city lakes, most closely resembles a northern Minnesota body of water with a forested shoreline and three beaches. Dad matured into a handsome, well-mannered young man. He had confidence bordering on cockiness but not enough to be off-putting.

Roger enjoyed challenging himself physically with football, boxing and hockey being favorite sports. Long-distance swimming was his most rigorous activity. A swim to Gale's Island and back was a prelude to the vigorous test all the way to Excelsior. After high school, life kicked into high gear. In a period of eight years, he attended the University of Minnesota, joined a fraternity, married, had two sons and returned safely from serving in the Pacific Theater during World War II.

My father came home from the Pacific Theater to find his marriage in shambles. Dad tried to get custody of David and Michael but, in those days, the father rarely prevailed. Roger picked himself up and went to work in sales at the Fruen Milling Company. He was a part-owner and secretary of the corporation. Roger took agricultural courses at the University of Minnesota's St. Paul Farm Campus and, three years after marrying my mother, he was sent to Worthington, Minnesota – then the Turkey Capital of the World – to run the poultry feed division. He was given the opportunity but still had to prove himself.

An amusing quality of Dad's was his corny, faux impersonations of a gruff man who was irritated about virtually everything. His go-to phrase for the departure of a guest was, *"Come again when you can't stay so long."* After a long, late autumn and a crushing winter Roger would see a niece or nephew, turn to someone and exclaim, *"Such a cute baby and look at the damn thing now!"*

If an infant grandchild smiled, Roger dismissed the expression as *"gas pains,"* although sometimes his affection for a new-born boiled over and he referred to his granddaughter or grandson as a *"keeper."* One imitation was a jab, I think, at a folksy Upper Midwest accent. If a meal appealed to him, he would exclaim, *"pretty tasty!"* He poked his nose in the kitchen sometimes to see how dinner was progressing. He was very interested in gravy and interceded if it was too *"skinny,"* often

M♥M A

Minneapolis Internal Medicine Associates

1633 Medical Arts Building, 825 Nicollet Mall, Minneapolis, MN 55402
612-332-8314

Richard Adair, M. D.
James L. McKenna, M. D.
R. Charles Petersen, M. D.

Richard R. Sturgeon, M. D.
A. Boyd Thomes, M. D.
William B. Torp, M. D.

November 5, 1987

Mrs. Leslie Fruen
5232 Clinton Ave.
Mpls. MN 55419

Dear Leslie:

I am following the priest's suggestion in sending you a note about
Roger. He was one of the grandest men I have ever known. To sum it
all up, he was lovely.

Sincerely,

My father's oncologist, Dr. McKenna, sent this note to my mother.

Henrietta "Nettie" Braden
Watson Emerson
Fruen family photo

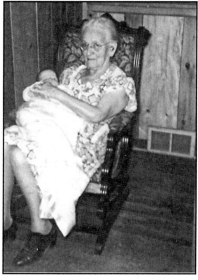

Ross Fruen's first Big Island visit. Great-
grandma Emerson is rocking him in
the "baby nook" in the brick house.
Fruen family photo

adding more floor to the mix.

During holiday season, Dad perused the day's haul of Christmas cards after dinner. I looked forward to his questions and comments. After looking at a card he frequently asked, "*Who the hell are Lucy and Paul* [etc.]*?*" Mom shook her head and responded, "That's your cousin and her husband!" Despite his protestations to the contrary and periodic episodes of churlishness, my father was an admired, respected and popular relative and friend.

My father died in October 1987 from complications arising from leukemia. His memorial service in the Lakewood Cemetery Chapel accommodated an overflow crowd with many shoehorned on a bench behind the altar. The exterior of the building is inspired by the Haghia Sophia, a Byzantine Romanesque masterpiece erected in Istanbul in 537 CE.

The two bronze doors open to display the kaleidoscope of Art Nouveau-stained glass and over ten million small mosaics of chromatic stone, marble, and glass accented with silver or gold. The tiles, inspired by the interior of the San Marco Cathedral in Venice, were imported from Italy.

Six artisans accompanied them to Minneapolis and carefully put them in place. The chapel is solemn to reflect the gravity of the occasion but colorful enough to be uplifting and celebratory. Dad was given the tribute he deserved.

■ ■ ■

Help for Grandma arrived in 1936 when her mother, Henrietta Braden Watson Emerson, moved into 56 Russell to better care for her husband Henry at the end of his life. She took the upstairs bedroom shared by Uncle Bruce and my father, and a room was added in the basement for the displaced brothers. Family lore suggests she did much of the disciplinary heavy-lifting. She is remembered for her admonition to her grandchildren, "*Nothing good happens after midnight.*" This may have been inspired by Roger's habit of sneaking out of the window to extend his curfew.

Great-grandma Emerson came with an extensive background in child-rearing. She married her first husband, Great-grandfather John Henry Watson, when she was eighteen. He was a widower with two

Four-year old
Roger Fruen on
the lap of Grandpa
Harry Emerson's
Hudson, 1923
Fruen family photo

Betty, Roger, and
Dick Fruen,
Christmas 1920
Fruen family photo

Bryn Mawr Boys Club newspaper caption, "More beans and pie,
they cried." Left to right; Sparky Seep, Roger Fruen, Arthur Fruen,
unknown, unknown, 1932. *Photo courtesy of Minneapolis Tribune*

children, seven and eight years old and his teenaged wife, barely ten years older than her stepchildren, had an instant family. Handling her grandchildren would be a comparative walk in the park.

I had my own little book club with Great-grandma. As a toddler I grabbed two or three of our "standards," handed them to her and climbed on her lap, assured she would not refuse. I have a favorite picture of her holding me as a newborn in a rocking chair in the "baby nook" of the Big Island Brick House's second-floor bedroom where a crib or chair resided. It was my first visit to Crown Point.

Great-grandma Emerson was extremely hard of hearing and wore an apparatus hanging from her neck that resembled a garage-door-opener transmitter. Wires from the device were connected to her earpieces. She also suffered from digestive issues, which she treated by drinking ginger ale. This produced tremendous belches she could feel but not hear. I was being taught the rudiments of the social graces and could not understand why I had to cover my mouth to stifle a burp, but Great-grandmother let it rip.

Until she died in March 1957, Great-grandmother Henrietta Emerson was a lovely woman and an integral part of the family. We all mourned her passing. The death of my maternal grandmother Margaret Harrison two months later caused my first existential crisis. My mother found me hiding, trying to deal with the news. I told her, *"Now I have only one Grandma left."* Then I asked, *"Am I going to die?"* She reassured me that I need not worry about that for a long time.

Christmas Card photo of 56 Russel South, Minneapolis
Fruen family photo

56 Russell Avenue South

"Included under the term 'Colonial Revival' are all of the styles inspired by old homes in every section of the U.S., whether settled by the English, the Spanish or the Dutch. Around 1925, the Spanish Colonial Revival style – associated with the romance of Old Spain and the glamour of new Hollywood – was particularly popular."

David A. Wood,

The Griswold-Fruen-Nordin House

LEADING UP TO THE Crash and the Great Depression, the 1920s' growing prosperity drove a great demand for housing that led to a more eclectic mix of styles than had previously existed across America.

Like William Fruen, Frank Griswold was an inventor of safety products. Griswold's specialty was traffic safety. He installed his first traffic light at 4th and Marquette in downtown Minneapolis and was soon selling his products to 55 locations around the country. His success enabled him to build his large, impressive home at 56 Russell Avenue South in 1926. Frank's business was booming, he expanded his factory and doubled his payroll just as the Depression brought the nation to its knees. The Griswold Signal Safety Company went bankrupt, the assets went to auction and Mr. Griswold was forced to sell his five-year-old home in 1931.

My grandparents struck an advantageous deal and the family moved into 56 Russell, which stayed in the family for 48 years. While not an exact example of Spanish Revival, some prominent exterior elements include white stucco, a wrought-iron balconet above the front door and round door entrances. *"The interior displays and even stronger Spanish Colonial influence, with its oak floors and woodwork, rounded doorways,*

56 Russel South, Minneapolis
Fruen family photo

rough-textured walls and wrought-iron stair rail and living room sconces. Overall, the house can perhaps be described as a restrained and dignified interpretation of Spanish Colonial style with element of other Colonial Revival styles." (David A. Wood, "The Griswold-Fruen-Nordin Home") The house would not stand out in San Antonio, but it was unique on top of the hill in the western edges of Minneapolis.

The Oriental rug runners in the large living room led to the sunroom. I spent time watching sports with Grandpa, sitting on the floor next to his easy chair. As a child I explored, venturing into the finished basement completely devoid of furniture. The workshop had been my father and younger brother Bruce's shared bedroom. Dad crawled out the window at night to meet his friends, and Bruce let him back in before breakfast. Little brother owed my father. Dad had spent a week in kindergarten instead of in his second-grade class, holding Uncle Bruce's hand to stop him from sobbing.

The dining room featured a long table to accommodate a large crowd, and the door behind the head of the table led outside. It was a Fruen rite-of-passage to graduate to the grown-up table.

I was preoccupied with Arthur's gizmos and contrivances. The front hall closet had lights that illuminated when the door opened and went dark when it closed. I shut myself inside and opened and closed it. I often went home smelling like mothballs.

Grandpa is credited with installing Minnesota's first automatic garage-door opener. This is inaccurate. The first owner, traffic safety guru Frank Griswold, devised the contraption, which was activated by inserting a key into the control box sitting on a pole. A small tunnel ran from the basement to the unattached, one-car garage and provided steam heat through the radiator. Another innovation ahead of its time was the half-bath powder room located on the first floor.

I did not often venture upstairs at 56 Russell, where the bedrooms were located, but I recall the master as being large with equally commodious closets. A sewing room claimed one of the children's previous berths. The only major structural change they made to the home was adding a small upstairs greenhouse for Grandmother. Most of the improvements made by the Fruens were of the landscaping variety.

A wrought-iron fence with a gate in front was added as was an impressive, terraced flagstone wall stretching down Russell past the empty lot Arthur and Reba also owned. It resembled a geological cutaway exposing shale-like strata accumulated throughout the eons. My grandparents purchased the lot to provide a larger yard for play and landscaping.

I do not remember the waterfall, pond and rock garden that once graced the far corner of the yard, perhaps as a nod to the Fruen's close association with water. It may have been removed to prevent grandchildren like me from riding home wet and dirty. Eventually, the next-door lot was sold and a house built. A cement bench remained. It was difficult to get into trouble on a bench.

Christmas was the main event at 56 Russell. All the local families gathered and, in the early 1960s, another generation joined us. Brother Dave and his wife Lael brought my niece and nephew, Tracy and David Jr. The tree was positioned in the corner of the living room and loaded with ornaments and old-style bubble lights.

After Christmas dinner, Grandma's progeny gathered at her feet to listen to her read a poem, "Little Orphan Annie," written by James Whitcomb Riley in 1885. It was a treasured, albeit an odd, one. In it, Annie told a cautionary tale for ill-mannered children with the key line – *"Er the gobble-uns'll git ya ef you don't watch out."* – repeated throughout. We looked forward to the recitation every year but, in retrospect, it was a bit creepy for the holiday season.

One year Grandfather Harrison fell asleep in his chair, and we draped the bows of his glasses with tinsel. The Major suffered a stroke a

Winter at 56 Russell
Fruen family photo

Arthur and Reba Fruen's 50th wedding anniversary celebration. The four young Barrett children stayed in Ohio but the others were present. I am standing on the left next to sister-in-law Lael, brother Dave, sister Martha is seated in front of me and brother Mike stands third from the right, niece and nephew Tracy and David are sitting on laps. *Fruen family photo*

few months after my birth in 1951 and walked with a cane, which doubled as a weapon. One moved quickly to avoid a hook from his curved handle or a parry from the cane's rubber tip.

It was a festive scene of mass mayhem like a Big Island Saturday but with a more formal dress code and nary a whiff of gas, oil or seaweed. Arthur and Reba gave each grandchild and great-grandchild a gift and a $25 U.S. Savings Bond.

One year Grandpa Fruen opened Hennepin Federal savings accounts for all of us with a $25 balance. The presents were appreciated and the Savings Bonds, while almost hypothetical to the younger, gave us money for the future. The best part of the account was the passbook in my name and the deposits stamped in ink. Still, the gifts were secondary to the gaiety: Kinship with cousins and the food took center stage. The parents received an extra gift as their offspring blew off some Christmas energy. All children were spent when it was time to leave.

The biggest family event at 56 Russell was Arthur and Reba's 50th wedding anniversary in 1963. Many friends and relatives came out of the woodwork. The grandchildren and two great-grandchildren were dressed in their best, and everyone behaved. Of all their accomplishments, my grandparents were most proud of their family that Grandpa called the "tribe."

Christmas 1970 was difficult. The date fell less than two months after Grandfather's death. At one point during the afternoon Grandma disappeared, and my father was dispatched to find her. She was upstairs in her bedroom, grieving the loss of her husband and our beloved family patriarch.

Grandmother lived alone for nine years after Arthur's death. Her children hired live-in help, but she promptly fired them. With dimming eyesight, she burned herself on the stovetop and agreed to move to the Presbyterian Home in 1979 at the age of 89, ending the Fruen family's 110-year Bryn Mawr residency.

The inhabitants of 56 Russell were the glue that held our large family together. I will be forever grateful for their love, the example they set, their dedication to the city of Minneapolis and their gift of Lake Minnetonka's Crown Point.

Wood plaque given to Arthur Fruen upon his retirement. The two gavels
represent his stints as president of the Minneapolis City Council.
The police badge also honors his service.

Photo courtesy Anica Fruen

Politics, Business, Riots and Gangsters

"I have always found Alderman Fruen working for the benefit of his ward and the city-at-large. He has been able to get many improvements for the Fourth Ward through his progressive work and his experience as an engineer. These projects have made it possible to put many unemployed men back to work. I have always found him honest and hard-working for his constituents and the city...."

1941 endorsement from 6th Ward
Alderman John Peterson

ARTHUR BERNARD FRUEN'S FIRST political foray in 1921 was one for the record books. He won his 4th Ward Alderman contest, but the city council could not decide on a president. The 176 rounds of deadlocked votes of 13-13 along liberal and conservative lines wore the Council down. On the next ballot Grandfather was a compromise choice and, without even starting his alderman duties, he was President of the Minneapolis City Council. Equally rare was his serving not only his first two years as Council leader but also his last year, 1945, when Hubert H. Humphrey was elected mayor.

Grandpa's first race was contentious and even litigious. His opponent suggested a Fruen-related organization distributed leaflets accusing him of socialism and being a member of the Non-Partisan League, a rural organization of small farmers and local business people with links to the Socialist Party of America, rather than the *"Republican in good standing"* that he was. A judge upheld Arthur's win, finding *"no evidence of deliberate, serious and material violations of the corrupt practices act."*

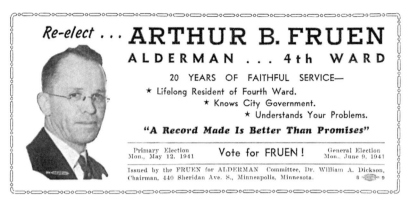

Fruen for Alderman campaign handout.
Fruen family photo

Grandfather ran on a platform denouncing "Townleyism, the Non-Partisan League, hate, class privilege and socialism while supporting established governmental unity and Americanism." In 1926, he sought the Republican nomination for U.S. Congress, running against freshman Congressman Godfrey Goodwin, born Alfred Gustafson to a Swedish immigrant and single-mother Cecilia Carlson.

When he moved to St. Paul from St. Peter, Gustafson changed his name to a more Yankee-sounding one, perhaps thinking that it gave him more gravitas. What made the primary unique is the long list of Goodwin challengers, five in total – a long-time record for Congressional primaries in Minnesota. Arthur reached double digits in vote percentages, but Goodwin prevailed.

■ ■ ■

The Fruens were not immune to nasty politics. The family dog, a Llewelyn Setter named Skeets, was poisoned when someone threw a strychnine-laced piece of meat over the backyard fence separating the lawn from the alley. The perpetrator of the despicable, politically or gangster-motivated act was never apprehended but, according to a Minneapolis newspaper, many neighbors and friends stopped by 56 Russell to offer their sympathies.

Labor issues had long simmered in Minneapolis and in 1934, Grandpa faced a challenging year when business and politics collided to create a predicament. Minneapolis had historically been a "closed" city and kept attempts by workers to unionize largely at bay through the efforts of the Citizens' Alliance. The General Truck Drivers Union Local 574 was well schooled by national labor leaders, who saw a great opportunity to grow its membership.

The Teamsters continued to gain strength, and the local issued a strike order. Violence erupted in the Market District with strikers and police escalating the conflict until two deputies were killed on May 22 during the "Battle of Deputies Run." Governor Floyd B. Olson presided over an agreement on May 31, but some companies broke it trying to sneak a convoy of non-union drivers through the gauntlet under the ruse of delivering essential hospital supplies.

Convinced the employers were not following the agreement, another strike was called on June 16. Governor Olson announced martial law and brought the National Guard to Minneapolis. On Black Friday, July 20, the police fired on the strikers, killing two and wounding 67. Now, my maternal grandfather, Major Edward S. Harrison, entered the fray. Nicknamed "Cleve" after President Grover Cleveland, he had retired from the Army when he married my grandmother, Margaret Noyes Bagley, in 1922 and perhaps was anxious to see action again.

His friend Totton Heffelfinger, leader of the Citizens' Alliance and part of the Peavey grain family, sent out the call for his "deputies" to help quell the protest. Margaret and my 11-year-old mother Leslie pleaded with Grandfather to stay away from the fighting. Cleve prevailed and headed downtown to crack some heads and returned home unscathed. One of Heffelfinger's "deputies" ludicrously wore his polo helmet for protection, sending an inadvertent elitist message.

The local union had direction from the National Teamsters and input from Marxist and Trotskyist influences, and all together they were well-organized and formed an impressive negotiating team. They were looking for fair wages, an "open" city, union recognition, better working conditions and shorter work weeks.

This was A.B. Fruen's dilemma. The family companies would be adversely affected by unionization, but he did not tolerate violence at the hands of the police or the Communist and Socialist elements of the Teamsters. Governor Olson and his administration dealt with most of the strike negotiations, but pressure had been on the Minneapolis City Council during the early Depression years to provide financial relief to the hordes of jobless citizens.

Minneapolis labor riots, 1934
Photo courtesy of National Archives

Glenwood-Inglewood delivery truck. From horses to internal combustion.
Fruen family photo

This issue proved just as rancorous as the truckers' strike. Private charities increased budgets and the Council issued $2 million worth of bonds for direct relief, but frustration was approaching desperation. *"Left-wing dissidents intensified their activities in 1932, further compounding the tense situation. By summer large members of the unemployed were appearing at City Hall, invading council meetings and heckling aldermen whose proposals dissatisfied them, particularly those who suggested a work relief program. Objecting vigorously to any work arrangement, they favored direct relief only and that preferably in cash."* (Raymond L. Koch, *Politics and Relief: Minneapolis during the 1930s*)

The Depression deepened in 1934, but the local Minneapolis chapter of transportation workers union, 3,000 strong and growing, ended the strike when it was recognized and various other demands were met. Glenwood-Inglewood had more to lose by unionization than Fruen Milling due to its home and business deliveries. Its drivers finally joined the local in 1936.

The headline in the Teamsters newspaper read:

"Glenwood Drivers Are Joining Union."

"Glenwood-Inglewood drivers, who have been joining the Union at a rapid pace, will soon be covered by a Union agreement according to the latest advices. When this company is brought under a Union contract it will complete the unionization of the bottled water companies in this city." (*The Northwest Organizer*, August 19, 1936)

■ ■ ■

When someone rhapsodizes about the glories of the good old days, tell them about Minneapolis in 1934. As if the Depression and labor riots were not enough to manage, gangsters found the Twin Cities attractive hideouts when the heat was on in Chicago. And inevitably, one of the Fruens had a mobster encounter. *"Why do these dangerous gangsters all head for St. Paul when they hide out from authorities or take a rest? Why is this city the happy hunting ground for kidnappers, thugs, thieves and machine gunners?"* (*St. Paul Pioneer Press* Editorial Board)

The answer is simple. Ma Barker's Gang, Alvin "Creepy" Karpis, John Dillinger and others had a deal with St. Paul Chief John "the Big Fellow" O'Connor, offering refuge for mobsters if they adhered to three different stipulations: no bad behavior in the Capital City, mandatory check-in with police when they arrived, and a bribe. The deal was known as the *"layover agreement."* This arrangement drove FBI Chief J. Edgar Hoover to distraction, and he was bound and determined to eradicate the gangster element.

John Dillinger had a "safe house" at the Charlou Apartments at 33nd and Fremont in Minneapolis and used it as a staging location for bank robberies in Sioux Falls, South Dakota, and Mason City, Iowa. When the Feds broke into the Fremont residence in April 1934, the official report included a snarky comment. The list of weapons included: *"one bullet-proof vest, one loaded 50-round machine gun, one Thompson sub-machine gun, one .45 automatic pistol and one high-powered rifle (nice people)."*

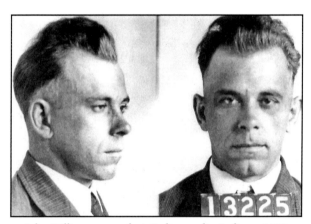

John Dillinger mug shot, Indianapolis, Indiana, 1933
Photo courtesy of FBI

Grandpa Arthur was on a train from Chicago to Minneapolis in the mid-1930s when he met an FBI agent in the club car. The man said, *"'Fruen... Fruen... That name is familiar. We had occasion to look up a Mr. Fruen quite carefully a few months ago.' 'Why,' Art said, 'I never heard of it – it couldn't have been me. Tell me about it.' The F.B.I. man went on to tell Art that this Fruen lived at the Athletic Club, drove a maroon Buick, and kept his car at a garage on the corner of Sixth Street and Fourth Avenue South operated by a man named Harry Dafoe. One dark night a drizzly rain was falling when Mr. Fruen drove up to the Dafoe garage and called out, 'Harry, have you a man you could spare for a few minutes to drive me up to the Athletic Club and bring my car back, because I have no raincoat or umbrella?' Before Harry had a chance to reply, a man stepped up to Harry and said, 'Say, I'm in a hurry. I'll be glad to drive this gentleman up to the club and bring his car back. You get my car ready while I'm gone.' Mr. Fruen asked the man if he knew where the Athletic Club was, and he said he did. The man got in the front seat with Mr. Fruen and they drove off. In about ten minutes he was back at the garage, paid his bill, and drove away in his own car. THE MAN WAS [JOHN] DILLINGER. The F.B.I. man told Art they had three men shadowing Dillinger at that time and the gentleman who took Dillinger for a ride to the Athletic Club was [Grandpa's brother] Will Fruen. They had to investigate him very thoroughly to make sure he was not an accomplice. Will says he remembers the occasion, but the first he knew about the Dillinger ride was when his brother related the story to him."* (A.B. Fruen as told to the Rotary Club of Minneapolis *Journalette*)

Isadore Blumenfield grew up on the north side of Minneapolis. He claimed his nickname, "Kid Cann," was in reference to his boxing prowess. Others suggested the genesis of the moniker came from his habit of hiding in the outhouse when conflict broke out. He was drawn to the seamy side of life and began bootlegging, handing the proceeds to his brothers Harry and Yiddy, who invested it in legitimate businesses.

Soon Isadore dabbled in prostitution, money laundering, extortion, illegal gambling, mail, stock and wire fraud and racketeering with interests in Las Vegas, Cuba and Florida. He owned 16 percent of the Twin Cities Rapid Transit Company. He and his cronies fleeced the company of millions during the conversion of streetcars to buses, even making a small fortune by selling the scrap metal from the tracks. Kid also controlled liquor stores and licenses, bars and nightclubs.

Blumenfield was accused of juror tampering, bribing politicians, three murders, kidnapping and violating the Mann Act. His tactic of threatening witnesses and jurors was effective, but he ran out of luck when finally convicted of transporting hookers across state lines and sentenced to two years in prison. In the early 1960s, Isadore served four years in Leavenworth for malfeasance in his liquor businesses. He moved to Miami Beach where he reconnected with crime boss Meyer Lansky and continued his criminal dealings until his death at age 80.

Kid Cann moved frequently but usually lived near the old Minneapolis neighborhood, close to his Northside roots. He bought a home on Glenhurst Avenue, the same street where Uncle Bruce lived. Close by, my father's and Uncle Dick's families resided a short walk away on Cedar Lake Parkway. (The Glenhurst neighborhood has a fairy-tale atmosphere, and a hint of gingerbread in the air would not seem out of place.)

Blumenfield preferred quiet, nice but modest, well-kept neighborhoods. No extravagances. In the fifties, much to the chagrin of his new neighbors, he moved to south Minneapolis. His home, at 5900 Oakland Avenue, is one block west and a few houses south of where I resided for six years with my wife and our young family. His sister lived directly across the street at 5901, and it is rumored that a tunnel ran under Oakland Avenue and connected the two homes.

■ ■ ■

I do not understand how an even-keeled, straight-arrow like my grandfather was embroiled in so many hotly contested elections, but in 1936 another protracted dispute reared its head over the vote for president of the city council. Once again, multiple votes were taken with the council continually deadlocked in a 13-13 tie. At one-point A.B. won the vote 13-12 with one member absent. For a moment everyone thought the ordeal was over, but the city attorney pointed out that while Arthur had a majority, 14 votes were necessary to win. The voting continued, and Grandfather finally lost.

It took another trip to court to resolve the tie vote in 1943. In a compromise agreement the current council president, W. Glen Wallace, would serve the first year of the term and Grandpa the second. Alderman Fruen achieved a great deal improving the city he lived in his whole life and living up to his campaign slogan, "*A Record Made Is Better Than Promises.*" Much of his work involved handling mundane complaints like missing manhole covers, pothole-filled streets and the addition of bus routes to satisfy his constituents. Once Arthur had achieved some of his goals he added, "*He Has Proven Himself Capable and Honest*" to his campaign slogan.

Grandfather also captained projects to serve the city beyond his ward. Perhaps his proudest achievement was the building of a convention center and auditorium that housed the Minnesota's first major league-sports-title winner. The Minneapolis Lakers captured the NBA

Championship in 1949 and 1950, the only NBA franchise to win in its first two seasons of existence.

Grandpa also spearheaded the drive to improve the Parade Grounds, adding baseball, diamondball and tennis facilities. He would now be proud to see the addition of an ice arena for figure skating and hockey. At a time when Minneapolis was growing its infrastructure by leaps and bounds, A.B.'s engineering education and experience was invaluable to the council and city.

In 1939, Grandpa testified before Congress as an industry expert regarding the proposed Federal Seed Act. Grain shipments had little regulation, and the quality of the commodities was inconsistent as suppliers, both domestic and foreign, often shipped goods interspersed with weed seed and other ingredients not consistent with the advertised product. Arthur Fruen vigorously pushed for more stringent quality standards, labeling and enforcement. The Federal Seed Act of 1939 was signed into law by President Franklin D. Roosevelt. It took effective on February 4, 1940.

One wonders where Arthur got the energy and the ability to proficiently keep so many balls in the air at once. He was inexhaustible. Dedicated to his family, business and civic duties, he achieved so much while appearing to not even break a sweat.

Grandpa retired from the council in 1945 when his year of serving as president expired. He was 55 years old and wanted to defer to younger hopefuls. World War II was ending, and he wanted to travel. A.B. was honored for his years of service and presented with a shield-shaped wooden plaque with a pair of gavels representing his two terms as city council president and a police badge with his name.

Minnesota Lieutenant Governor Gottfrid Lindsten summed up A.B.'s years of service: "*May I imaginatively reconstruct somewhat, in episodical recapitulation, Alderman Arthur Fruen rising to his feet, submitting a motion to the chair. Clean cut, a fair man, courteous to his colleagues and respected by them, an honor to have his friendship, in analytical discussion of the subject matter, with the ability of a Bob Taft, Alderman Fruen presents his viewpoint, understandable to all, projected with exemplary clarity, so typical of his ability.*"

In 1949, Grandpa visited a city council session along with another 4th Ward alumnus, the 93 year-old, cantankerous and vocal William Currie. The Minneapolis Journal reported, "*Minneapolis aldermen were*

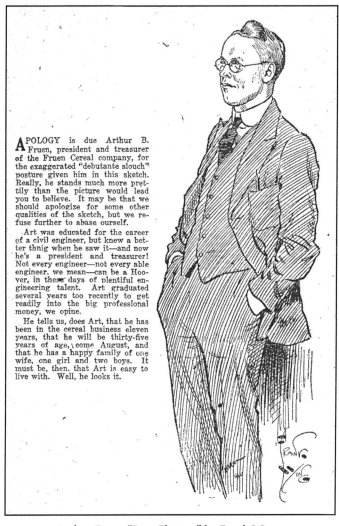

APOLOGY is due Arthur B. Fruen, president and treasurer of the Fruen Cereal company, for the exaggerated "debutante slouch" posture given him in this sketch. Really, he stands much more prettily than the picture would lead you to believe. It may be that we should apologize for some other qualities of the sketch, but we refuse further to abase ourself.

Art was educated for the career of a civil engineer, but knew a better thnig when he saw it—and now he's a president and treasurer! Not every engineer—not every able engineer. we mean—can be a Hoover, in these days of plentiful engineering talent. Art graduated several years too recently to get readily into the big professional money, we opine.

He tells us, does Art, that he has been in the cereal business eleven years, that he will be thirty-five years of age, come August, and that he has a happy family of one wife, one girl and two boys. It must be, then. that Art is easy to live with. Well, he looks it.

Arthur Fruen "Base Flattery" by Frank Wing.
Published in the *Minneapolis Tribune* on July 12, 1920.
Photo courtesy of Minneapolis Tribune

insulted by a former colleague Friday – and seemed to love it. Said former Alderman William A. Currie, 'We had a good council in those days – then they chose them for their brain matter. Now it's different I guess.' Currie, short, white-haired, and spry, attended the council meeting with another former council member, Arthur B. Fruen, who served from 1921-1945... Fruen greeted the present council and said he followed its doings with interest, 'though we may not always agree with all of you.' 'All of you!

None of you!' interposed Currie."

■ ■ ■

My grandparents traveled overseas in 1945, spending two months in western Europe and northern Africa, including Egypt and Morocco. They mixed pleasure with business as Arthur was eager to observe the various countries' post-war economies. Upon their return, the *Minneapolis Tribune* interviewed Grandfather. Interested in all things British, Grandpa was intrigued by the nationalization of industry. He commented, *"The older men in the grain trade feel that there is not a bright future for England. Trade is pretty much restricted to the sterling countries, and the excess of imports over exports is continuing with high taxes and increasing national debt."*

A.B. was a quick study. At the age of 24, he was named president of the Fruen Cereal Company. Soon the rapidly growing corporation was rechristened the Fruen Milling Company. He innovated quickly broadening the product line to include feed for livestock. A 25,000-bushel concrete square-bin elevator was added in 1912, and the operation became diesel-powered in 1916.

In addition to diversification, Grandpa expanded and consolidated. He understood that being nimble and making quick decisions after thoughtful analysis were traits to be valued. Three fires that plagued the mill in the early 20s destroyed Great-grandfather William's original workshop and other buildings but also provided the opportunity to improve and modernize. *"As flour milling reached its peak in the early 20th century, a revolution in marketing and advertising arose out of a need for flour manufacturers to differentiate products that were essentially the same: the grain came from the same fields..., and it was milled on the same types of machines using the same techniques."* (Mill City Museum, Minnesota Historical Society)

An army marches on its stomach, and this axiom kept the Mill City mills humming. Military security forces guarded the operations from sabotage. The demand for foodstuffs peaked during World War I as Minneapolis fed U.S. troops, their allies and the nation. After the cessation of hostilities, Minnesota experienced an economic downturn. Crop prices fell just as farmers accumulated loans and demand dropped. The mills shared their pain.

Aerial view of the milling and spring water facilities
Fruen family photo

The milling center of the U.S. moved east to Buffalo, New York, and many of the 20-plus operations along the canal adjacent to the Falls of St. Anthony on the Mississippi were shuttered, abandoned and dismantled. (The Pillsbury Mill A was the last to close in 2003.) The Fruen Milling Company had packaged cereal since the late 1800s and was poised to broaden its product line, however Grandfather was ready and persevered.

"The mill was completely electrified, a quarter mile of railroad trackage was installed in and around the mill, and a complete new elevator erected along with new machinery that would make it possible to turn out a variety of grain products, for both humans and animals." ("Ancient Fruen's Mill Still Rolling," Lake Area Explorer)

■ ■ ■

Sons Dick, Roger and Bruce joined the company after their educations were completed. Uncle Dick handled all the marketing and advertising materials while my father and Uncle Bruce shared sales duties and eventually were named vice-presidents. Grandpa installed a non-family member, Sheldon Johnson, as president to mitigate potential sibling rivalry.

Rolled oats were a specialty almost from the start with daily capacity reaching 750 tons by the late 1960s. The customer base was expanded to include Malt-O-Meal, Kellogg's, General Mills and Pillsbury. The Fruen Milling Company celebrated its 60th anniversary in 1954 by adding new equipment and more storage facilities. A Minneapolis newspaper article called the company, "*One of the largest millers of diversified cereals and farm feeds in the Upper Midwest. The lofty elevator tower is a landmark of the Glenwood area of Minneapolis.*"

In the 1960s the Fruen Milling Company introduced its most successful program since the firm's inception: a premium line of branded equine products for performance horses, principally thoroughbreds and standardbreds. The feed featured minerals, vitamins, supplements and the first steam-rolled racehorse oats.

Fruen products could be found at breeding farms and racetracks from Belmont to Santa Anita and, internationally, mostly in Japan, South America and the Caribbean. Different blends were sold in burlap bags with names such as "*Bridle*," "*Apache*" and "*North Star.*" In 1973 I had the opportunity to visit the stables at the Saratoga Springs track and was impressed to find a pervasive presence of Fruen racehorse feed.

Grandfather was a life-long Minneapolis and Bryn Mawr resident and attended Harrison Elementary, Sumner Junior High and North High before graduating from the University of Minnesota. He stepped away from the milling business in 1962 at the age of 77, perhaps holding on a bit too long, reluctant to surrender the reins. The editorial in the Minneapolis Tribune read, "*A Good Citizen Retires,*" "*Art Fruen has always been a modest man, though that didn't keep other people from recognizing his valuable contributions to his city and his beloved Glenwood neighborhood. Fruen will long be remembered for his fair-mindedness, for his willingness to listen to others, for his careful approach to problems, for his fine devotion to his friends, his family and his business. A mighty good citizen.*"

A.B. Fruen was a "*compassionate conservative*" fifty years before the term was coined.

Fruen family chalet, Crown Point, Big Island, Lake Minnetonka
Fruen family photo

The Fruens Join the Cabin Culture

"Once upon a time, a long time ago – in 1878 to be exact – three young men took a boat trip from Northfield down to the Cannon River to Red Wing, up the Mississippi to Hastings, and then to St. Paul, where they found a drayman to transport the boat to Lake Minnetonka. One young man got sick and went home, and then there were two. Those two sailed, rowed, camped, weathered the weather and the mosquitoes and remembered the clear water and beautiful islands of Lake Minnetonka."

Scriver family memories

ONE OF THE BOYS was Hiram Scriver and, by the turn of the century, he was president of the St. Anthony Falls Bank. When a foreclosure occurred on some Big Island property, he acquired the acreage for himself. In the 1920s, Eugene Scriver was a realtor, friend and Bryn Mawr neighbor of the Fruens and introduced my grandparents to the beautiful Crown Point location high on a hill with arguably the best view on the Lower Lake towards Gale's Island, Tonka Bay and Excelsior.

It was not an upscale lake home. It was rustic, and conveniences were non-existent. There was no telephone. Electricity did not reach the point until 1940. The hill was steep, and trees reached all the way to the shoreline.

The Big Woods still occupy much of the island's southwest half with the trees packed so tightly a hiker would be hard pressed to find a path. The forest reaches almost to the tip of the point with just enough space cleared for cottages, a front yard, a hollow in the back and room beyond for outbuildings before the property surrenders to the timber.

115

The cottage, Crown Point
Fruen family photo

■ ■ ■

There was a great deal of work ahead to realize the plans Grandpa Arthur conceived but, in 1928, the Fruens became owners of what was to become an iconic site on the Big Water. Just in time for the stock market crash, the Great Depression and the drought years... The purchase included a cottage that was just large enough to snugly house my grandparents and their six children. When Great-grandmother Emerson joined the household in 1936, she was given the master bedroom in the back of the house. A bathroom was attached to her room, ending trips to the outhouse nestled in the woods west of the cottage.

Arthur and Reba used the bedroom between the master and the front porch. The room had two entrances, one led into the atrium and the staircase while the other had a Dutch door that provided access to the front porch and a view of the lake. The bottom half of the door kept the dogs and children out, and the top opened to allow the breezes of the Lower Lake inside.

The two oldest children, Betty and Dick, had their own rooms upstairs; my father Roger and his younger brother Bruce shared the open loft sleeping quarters. The two youngest, Louise and Doug, slept on swinging beds chained to the ceiling on each end of the front porch. I am certain the two little ones headed inside if one of the lake's quick-striking, violent thunderstorms percolated over the Lower Lake. No matter how large the house, the Fruens always seemed to fill it, both on the island and in the city.

The original cottage gave the family a base of operations to expand and complete the Crown Point domicile. The Shingle Style of architecture arrived in the U.S. in the late 19th century as a nod to the Arts and Crafts Movement, and our cottage on the hill incorporated many of the elements of both trends.

The exterior, horizontal shiplap boards above the fieldstone foundation gave the impression of the building rising from the earth rather than previous motifs featuring vertical boards mirroring the ramrod straight trees reaching for the sky. The upper facade of the exterior consisted of brick-red shingles with cedar shingles covering the roof. The wood frame is painted forest green. A front facing gable roof sported deep eaves. The interior mirrored the color scheme with red pine panels and green wainscoting accents.

A large Adirondack style porch acted as a buffer between the outdoors and the interior leading into a large two-story room with a table for eating, puzzle-solving, playing cards and games or simply visiting. The chandelier fashioned from anchors shed light from lantern lamps hanging from the iron. A fireplace dominated the alcove off the dining area which also offered additional seating. Two wide doors could be closed to shut out inclement weather or kept wide open to invite glorious days inside. It was a basic wood-frame seasonal home that would not be out of place in the northern Minnesota lake country despite being minutes from downtown Minneapolis.

■ ■ ■

When I was about seven, I was intrigued by the still-operable, old-style wringer washing machine that consisted of a large bucket with a contraption consisting of two rollers to squeeze excess water from the newly washed textiles. The cousins were warned of a gruesome death if we ventured too close to the old warrior that lurked around the back porch. A grisly tale followed of a man whose tie was grabbed by the wringers and swallowed up to his neck. Great story, but we knew neckties were a rarity on Crown Point.

A few trees were left standing between the cottage and the hill's precipice without blocking the panoramic vista. I like to think this was an intentional salute to the Big Water's close relationship with the earth, water and the Big Woods.

Sometimes the simplest of touches provide the most joy. The lookout that juts out over the stone walkway is such a spot. A small wooden lookout was in place when my family arrived in the late 1920s. It included two short benches and provided decades of pleasure with its magnificent view of mercurial Lake Minnetonka.

One could observe the progression of a Crown Point season on our perch, from a hopeful May morning, an intense July thunderstorm percolating in the distance, the salad days of summer, a clear August night offering the chance of meteor showers and the Northern Lights, to the blustery warnings of October.

A standing-room-only crowd on the Fourth of July could watch multiple spectacular fireworks displays from the lookout. One year I counted six simultaneous pyrotechnic shows from six communities ringing the Big Water and its environs.

■ ■ ■

After seventy-plus years of use, the original lookout was replaced. Much wider, sturdier and deeper with more seating, the new version also offered a safer railing rendered in an aesthetically pleasing manner. Generations of Fruen children not old enough to appreciate the scenery retired to the girls' playhouse or the boys' bunkhouse. The girls' domicile was built for Aunt Louise and the Scriver twins, Sue and Sally. The playhouse, located in a secluded "neighborhood" at the end of Outbuilding Street, was better constructed and appointed with furniture, teacups, saucers and a teapot.

The shabby, minimalist bunkhouse had seen better days by the time I discovered it precariously jutting over the precipitous drop-off many yards west of the lookout. Assembled with dark brown stained boards, it was a musty, spartan domicile containing a bunk bed on each side covered with wafer-thin, saggy mattresses that had not seen the light of day for decades. The roof consisted of flimsy black shingles warped at the ends, barely able to keep out the elements. I tried to spend the night there once but was driven out by mosquitoes whose incessant whine was as annoying as the sting.

The row of outbuildings out back was a gloomy, quiet, dark world unto itself. Seemingly in danger of being swallowed by the forest, the compact community offered space for a variety of purposes. A twenty-foot-wide and ten-foot-deep slanting-slab-of-concrete pig pen was the first construction encountered from the west. The feeding trough was located at the top, and a wood fence on the sides of the slab's low end extended fifteen feet to give the pigs waddling room.

Walking east, the pig pen gave way to a two-story "condo" consisting of the workshop and Joe's Cabin at ground level with the icehouse and chicken coop built of cement blocks beneath them, respectively. The workshop not only housed a large selection of tools and an impressive bench but also provided space for storage.

The icehouse below had a layer of sawdust on the dirt floor and ice blocks, cut from the bay just north of Point Comfort in winter, were stacked inside after being hauled by truck up the hill. A large cube was extracted as needed with pick and tong and brought to the cottage in a wheelbarrow. The workman's cabin shared a wall with the workshop and was just big enough to accommodate a bed, table and chairs and a small kitchen. I never had much reason to spend time out back unless I was harvesting worms. It was a vestige of the World War II years. Nature was in the process of reclaiming the ghost town.

■ ■ ■

As the family grew, my grandparents expanded their footprint on Crown Point. They purchased the white house next door to the west that became available during a contentious divorce between a doctor and a university professor. It was razed in 1940 and replaced by the Fruen Brick House, which was more a conventional home than a cabin.

It was small but serviceable with two bedrooms and a bathroom upstairs and a bunkroom below. A seldom-used furnace was placed in the small basement. An upstairs air-conditioning window unit would have been a nice-to-have to battle the mid to late summer heat and humidity that almost took one's breath away and led to restless, fitful sleep, but nobody would have dared suggest buying such a modern contrivance.

Pragmatic Grandpa would have deemed such a luxury to be antithetical to island living.

The kitchen featured a breakfast table. Additional seating was available in the cedar-paneled living room as well as a card table, bookcase and TV stand. A fireplace was adorned with a wide, oversized panoramic image of Glacier National Park.

The screened porch offered a peek through the trees at the lake towards Tonka Bay and was in proximity to the bird feeders. It was located at the edge of the clearing as it gave way to the Big Woods with a path down the hill to Streater's Cove. The back door was steps away from the thick forest just past the brick barbeque grill. I never saw anyone flipping burgers there, but it was an opportunity for a pre-teen boy to practice some pyromania. I always volunteered to take all burnable refuse out back, start a mini-inferno and ensure the blaze did not reach the woods.

The front steps of the house led to the front yard and the stairway to the waterfront. The back steps gave way to a sidewalk to the cottage next door. The various slabs were composed of different materials ranging from cement to terra cotta. Imbedded pieces of stained glass decorated a few, and others had various designs, such as leaves, chiseled into the surface. As children, we traced the images by rubbing a crayon over a piece of construction paper. Aunt Margaret periodically swept the hard-packed dirt path behind the houses leading to the Scrivers.

The initial Brick House, built in 1940 and 1941, was in use for only one season before it was struck by lightning and reduced to ashes and a chimney. Arthur and Reba waited until the end of World War II before rebuilding an almost exact replica, using the same layout and materials with lightning rods on the roof. My grandparents purchased a third dwelling known as the Decker Cabin next door to the Fruens. It was nestled in the swale towards Point Comfort.

■ ■ ■

The small, white cottage was bought from two Chicago sisters for the O'Connor family, but Uncle Charles was opposed to living anywhere near water, much less on an island. He would have been happy to never cross the Mississippi and leave St. Paul. The cabin was later sold to the Granrud branch of the Scriver family.

The first improvement to the waterfront was a two-level chalet added to provide access to Crown Point in the winter without having to climb the snow-bound hill. The upper floor housed the dock sections during the off season and served as a changing room in the summer. The fieldstone foundation mirrored the cottage on the hill and vertical brown boards reached the shingled roof on each side.

A wood fence-like railing with pine tree cut-outs flanked by field stone pillars prevented an inadvertent tumble onto the rocks and water below. The cement ledge and walkway featured small stones imbedded in the surface, likely acting as "speed bumps" to provide wet feet with some traction as they certainly were not artistically interesting. For many decades the pine-paneled lower level was largely open and decorated in a spartan-like manner with a well-worn couch and some rudimentary seating including a rocker fashioned from small tree branches and an old straight-back chair.

A row of windows with shutters sporting geometric cut-outs opened in the front, feet away from the lake. The name "Fruens," spelled with twisted pieces of driftwood, initially adorned the front-facing as it reached its peak. Later, electric lanterns with red globes were added, and my father's generation flicked them on and off to signal the coast was clear to their friends waiting in their boats off the point for the party to start.

More recently the Chalet received a face-lift with some red and green accentuating the original more subdued brown. The front face and fence are now green and the window shutters red. The old shingle roof was replaced with a hunter-green metal one. Existing waterline structures are grandfathered, but no new construction is allowed without a significant setback from the shore.

Grandpa's most ambitious Big Island project was a titanic task. Ninety stone steps and a huge retaining wall, largely hidden by trees, were erected from the lake level, up the cliff to the houses. The operation took four arduous seasons to complete. Five flights of stairs and four switchbacks were designed to use the space allotted and mitigate the steepness of the climb. Cedar trees were planted on the terraces created under the switchbacks.

The railing and posts were fashioned from logs and stained brown. Midway up the second-to-last flight from the top was a niche in the wall to provide a spot to sit and rest before tackling the rest of the climb.

The brick house, Crown Point, 1941
Fruen family photo

A wooden bench was situated on the final landing but is now gone. The top of the stairway opened to a lawn large enough to accommodate the drying sails of a C-boat. *"The main workers were Charlie Carlson, a stonemason and the main craftsman, with my father and I mixing concrete and hauling boulders for Charlie to cut and lay. We did the prep work in summer, and trucks hauled fieldstone, sand, gravel and cement across the ice in winter. As the wall rose, the truck drove over to the east shore of the point and up the gently sloping back hill to dump the goods in the front yard."* (Douglas Fruen, as told to Karen Melvin and Bette Hammel, *Legendary Homes of Lake Minnetonka*)

■ ■ ■

Charlie Carlson was an artisan who could hold a stone, study and caress its surface then deftly crack it in two with his hand sledge exactly where he intended. He spent the summers on Crown Point living in the Chalet at the water's edge. Uncle Doug did the yeoman's share of the menial work as his older brothers were married, starting families and joining the Navy as the U.S. prepared for its inevitable entry into World War II. At the start, the building materials were dumped on the shoreline in winter. When the project reached the half-way point the trucks, after traveling to the island over the ice, dropped the loads on top of the hill and the construction was tackled from above. Pails of mixed cement were lowered to Charlie and the boulders lugged by hand. It was a dirty, exhausting job.

When I was spent from running up and down the 90 steps preparing for soccer season and ready to quit for the day, I thought of Grandpa, Uncle Doug and Charlie Carlson. They motivated me for one last repetition. An enduring visual is the wooden pot filled with brilliant red geraniums sitting on the sliver of wall closest to the water. In those days they were the only splash of color to interrupt the organic monument to wood and stone. A large, long stone planted next to the flowers still leans to the west. The light brownish hue is similar to the catlinite, more commonly known as "pipestone," quarried by many Dakota bands in the southwest corner of Minnesota.

The final major project was the boathouse, which matched the Chalet's style and served as the other bookend to Crown Point's waterfront. The front facade consisted of two oversized dark brown doors flanked by flagstone. Faux windows graced each end of the pine-tree-accented balconet. The green and red scheme matched the Chalet albeit to a more muted degree. With the boathouse in place, a sidewalk was laid connecting the boathouse to the main stairway and the lower-level Chalet steps.

Next to the boathouse a "Hillovator," also known as a funicular, was installed. The box-like wooden car rose to the top of the cliff and was pulled by a heavy cable that coiled around an electrically powered spindle. Its purpose was to haul luggage, groceries, spring water and the elderly to the houses above. Children were strictly forbidden from playing with the Hillovator, but that did not deter us from inspecting and earning the occasional ride to help with the cargo after it climbed Crown Point.

In keeping with his engineering concentration in waterpower development, Arthur installed a water tank, hidden in the woods, which delivered lake water to six or seven cabins. A gas-powered pump located downhill near the shore pulled water up the cliff before electricity was available. My wrench-wielding father and screwdriver-toting Uncle Dick or Uncle Doug seemed to spend an inordinate amount of time sweet-talking the motor back into action.

Charlie Carlson, stone mason extraordinaire, 1930s
Fruen family photo

■ ■ ■

By the time I made my inaugural visit to Big Island at the age of two months, the lion's share of the major projects was complete, and the family could enjoy Crown Point at a more relaxing pace. The grandchildren learned to make their own fun, and we had the run of the island up above but venturing down to the waterfront without an adult was cause for swift correction.

At night, we often gathered in the Brick House to watch the black-and-white television. The only approved programs were sporting events, most often boxing and baseball. Grandpa controlled the selection process. Predictably, he fashioned his own remote control from an extension cord split and wired to the back of the television and a push-button affixed to the other end.

A.B. called it a "Blab-Off" and used it to perfection, muting all commercials. When the inevitable ad for beer or cigarettes came on the screen, he would mute the sound and declare that "true" athletes would never smoke and drink. Grandma often played cards on the table closest to the porch. She taught me elementary card tricks but did not enjoy the game of cribbage. Mocking the counting, she imitated the sounds in a sing-song manner: *"Fifteen-two, fifteen four...."*

It was intriguing for us to explore the area near the cement-and-stone water tank. We doubted the rotting wood ladder leaning on the tank could withstand another winter, but it always did.

The Haunted House stood just off the path. I do not recall it ever being occupied. The deserted wood house appeared to be owned by a hoarder with pile after pile of magazines and other items. Perhaps the spookiest aspect of the Haunted House was a working telephone that never rang. Someone must have paid the bill. Month after month. Year after year. I don't know what we would have done had it rung.

The forest loomed over the Haunted House, adding to the atmosphere. The hot summers and cold winters of Minnesota's southern third made for an endless cycle of decay and regeneration.

To a child the atmosphere on top of Crown Point was almost biblical. Darkness vs. Light, Good vs. Evil. The dense Big Woods to the immediate north was foreboding while the Brick House and Cottage, as well as the lawn and lookout, basked in the sun. I was on guard in the dark, somber forest and emboldened in the daylight. *"It is good to know that out there, in a forest in the world, there is a cabin where something is possible, something fairly close to sheer happiness of being alive."* (Sylain Tesson, *The Consolations of the Forest*)

The Fruen family was now part of the Upper Midwest cabin culture, an essential strand in the fabric of Minnesota life. The proximity of Lake Minnetonka to our Twin City homes offered flexibility for visits ranging from a few hours, a long weekend, or more lengthy stays. Plans could change on a moment's notice, depending on the weather, to avoid a wasted weekend. With water sports out of the equation, we could enjoy the inclement weather just as much in the city while avoiding a potentially dangerous boat ride.

The short commute allowed the option of working in town and spending a quiet evening on Crown Point. I was able to play an afternoon baseball game in Minneapolis and return to Big Island for dinner.

Stone wall and stairway to the hill top. Ninety steps, 1930s.
Fruen family photo

We were fortunate to avoid the hours of windshield time experienced by the state's northern cabin dwellers: their refreshing weekend at "the lake" all but erased by frustrating southbound traffic.

■ ■ ■

Despite local assumptions to the contrary, cabin life did not originate in the Upper Midwest of the United States. Scandinavians, the Scots-Irish and Russians and others imported their styles of log cabins when they arrived in the New World. These shacks were designed solely for shelter, not leisure.

Immigrants like my great-great-grandfather Bergquist initially lived in three-sided makeshift shanties with the opening in front where the fire was located. The intermediate step in pioneer upward mobility before a multi-room log house was a one-room cabin version with a fireplace in the corner. If wall height and pitch of the roof permitted; a sleeping loft could provide more space. Wood pegs were used as steps. If it were a one-man project, the walls could only reach six or seven feet in height.

A cabin was raised quickly with just a broadax, although an additional adze and a knife made more efficient and better-quality construction. Rounded logs with the bark still attached were stacked using cut notches rather than expensive nails to fasten the wood together. When time was not of the essence, Finns preferred to prepare rough-hewn logs. Glass was an imported luxury in those early days, so window openings were covered with sliding boards or grease paper to ward off bad weather.

The Scotch-Irish immigrants and other ethnic groups borrowed the Scandinavian style of cabin architecture and brought it with them as they crossed the Appalachians in route to the Ohio and Mississippi river valleys. Little did they realize that a simple, modest design born from limited financial resources would become an enduring American symbol of simplicity, honesty and a healthy life-style.

That transformation was a long time coming in the New World. *"The log cabin was originally disdained here in America... Benjamin Franklin wrote that there are only two sorts of people, 'those who are well dress'd and live comfortably in good houses, [and those who] are poor, and dirty, and ragged and ignorant, and vicious and live in miserable cabins or garrets."* Dr. Benjamin Rush, a Declaration of Independence signatory, said the cabin dweller was *"generally a man who has out-lived his credit or fortune in the cultivated parts."* (Andrew Belonsky, "How the Log Cabin Became an American Symbol," *Mental Floss*)

So much for equality. American popular culture came to the rescue and elevated the log cabin to its eventual lofty perch. Authors, artists, musicians and politicians contributed to the simple dwelling's rise in status.

The railroads actively promoted tourism to national parks and other places of interest, stoking interest in the shrinking, unspoiled open spaces of America. Arcadian hotels and lodges sprung up to accommodate the visitors. Resorts dotted the Adirondacks, the mountains of New England, the Great Lakes and the forests of the Northwest.

A sense of the impending loss of unspoiled hinterlands and the impulse to escape the complexity – and the raw power of advancing technology – fueled the attraction for more natural surroundings. The old cabins and cottages on Minnetonka are living on borrowed time. Many elements conspire.

The suburban gentry's desire to live on "the lake" drove property taxes on upgraded shacks from the 1860s to exorbitant yearly assessments. Larger year-round homes can incur taxes of tens of thousands of dollars. Old cabin dwellers whose families owned the few yards of shoreline since the mid-19th century hope the new owners maintain part of the old site's character, but the reality is almost always a tear-down and a rebuild with a super-sized footprint.

McMansions swallow up the lots, leaving virtually no lawn or trees to soften the jarring appearance of the new domiciles blocking the views of the other homes in the neighborhood. Jon Monson of the Excelsior-based Landschute Group maintains the old homesteads *"are all in jeopardy because of the value of the property. It's civic vandalism... We want to apply deliberate, rational appraisal for determining when to save and when to start from scratch. This is a free country, but I'd rather respect the past as we go to the future."* ("Are Lake Minnetonka cottages now an 'endangered species'?" *Star Tribune*)

■ ■ ■

The demand for access to the Big Water has turned it into what is essentially a private lake. Cabins on islands escape this scenario. With no bridge connecting them to the mainland, demand and value are diminished. Since the lake is ice-bound for four months of the year, the appeal is not as strong as properties on the shore. Island cabins pose some logistical obstacles, and the pull of the Fruens' city lives sometimes intruded, but we loved our getaway that played a significant role in our childhoods.

The grandchildren were only constrained by the depth and breadth of our very vivid imaginations. Games were invented like Pinecone in the Chimney. Contestants stood on the lookout and lobbed pinecones toward the Chalet roof. While many attempts fell onto the slate shingles, points were awarded for hitting the chimney and the highly coveted bulls-eye right through the flue as the cone rattled around in the lower-level fireplace.

As a child I was intrigued to learn we had a cabin in our city neighborhood. A few blocks south of our house on Clinton Avenue was a remodeled version of a hunting lodge overlooking Diamond Lake. The marshy body of water was a favorite spot for migrating waterfowl to stop and feed on aquatic delicacies. When it was first built, the lodge was situated in the country well outside Minneapolis proper. The city grew around it, and its subsequent owners retained the original look while making improvements. I had difficulty dealing with the cabin-culture dissonance.

Craig Fruen remembered, *"I loved boating home* [to Big Island] *from Tonka Bay or Excelsior at midnight. The lake was like black glass in front and white froth in our wake, lit up by the stern light. And off in the distance, slowly growing brighter, were our red lanterns guiding us in."*

Roger and Leslie Fruen sailing on the Lower Lake
Fruen family photo

The Fruen Fleet: Boating on the Big Water

"The correspondent wondered ingenuously how in the name of all that was sane could there be people who thought it amusing to row a boat. It was not an amusement; it was diabolical punishment, and even a genius of mental aberrations could never conclude that it was anything but a horror to the muscles and a crime against the back."

Stephen Crane,
THE OPEN BOAT

ONE SUMMER DURING THE late 1950s my sister Martha and our cousin Anne, not much more than toddlers, rewrote the chorus of the Dean Martin lyric, *"standing on the corner watching all the girls go by,"* singing *"boats"* instead of *"girls"* at high decibels. The adults smirked, but the rewrite sounded plausible to the rest of us. Boats were part of the Fruen family fabric.

■ ■ ■

In the Upper Midwest, the canoe opened the vast waterways of lakes and rivers providing access to the hunting, fishing and wild-ricing areas previously impenetrable in the deep, dense forests. The dugout was a primitive, heavy vessel made from tree trunks of softer wood, usually maple, basswood or cottonwood.

The Dakota used this cumbersome style, which was unstable and difficult to maneuver in tight, fast spaces. The Ojibwe had a distinct advantage with their sleeker, lighter, watertight birch-bark canoes made from strips of birch bark sewn to cedar framing with strips peeled from

1,000-year-old dugout canoe pulled from the mud of Lake Minnetonka, 1934
Photo courtesy of Minnesota Historical Society

the roots of a spruce tree. The Ojibwe prowess on the water was a contributing factor in the eventual eviction of Dakota from the woodlands of Wisconsin and into the territory transitioning to prairie.

The 1930s brought severe drought across the country and, in 1934, the waterline on Lake Minnetonka was down seven feet from normal. Docks were extended many yards to reach the receding shoreline. Brothers Arthur and Helmer Gunnarson were working on their dock in the North Arm area of the Upper Lake when the post they were driving into the exposed soil hit what they thought was a rock. Upon further inspection, they discovered a dugout canoe – 11 feet long and 18 inches wide – that was then radiocarbon dated to 1025-1165 A.D., the oldest ever found in Minnesota.

■ ■ ■

In the early 1900s, boats were important vehicles for young love in the Gopher State. The Big Island Amusement Park rented rowboats to couples hoping to escape the watchful eyes of chaperones. When the park closed in 1911, canoe use on the Minneapolis chain of lakes exploded. In 1910 only 200 boat licenses were issued by the Minneapolis Park Board. In 1912, the number was 2,000. Applications for vessels with suggestive names like Win-kat-us, Kumonin Kid, Ilgetu, the Helusa, Kismekwik, Skizmytyt and Aw-kom-in were declined.

The Minneapolis Park Police began to patrol the city lakes in boats with spotlights to ferret out immoral behavior. A Minneapolis paper bemoaned activity so *"grave and flagrant that it threatens to throw a shadow upon the lakes as recreation resorts and to bring shame upon the city."*

Drownings were a common occurrence for many decades on Lake Minnetonka after its rediscovery in 1852 as most Minnesotans did not know how to swim. Lifejackets would not come into popular use until the 20th century when the Red Cross made a concerted effort to promote swimming lessons and water safety. William Lithgow is thought to be the first white man to drown in the Big Water when he lost a battle with a thunderstorm.

When nature was not wreaking havoc on Minnetonka, shoddy technology was. Steamboat excursions on the lake became popular later in the 1870s but, sadly, demand exceeded engineering and safety, and explosions made pleasure cruises risky. On July 1, 1880, the *New York Times* reported, dateline St. Paul, *"The steamer MARY exploded her boiler today while lying at the Hotel St. Louis dock, on Lake Minnetonka... The boat was completely wrecked, and sank in five feet of water. It has been discovered that the owner GEORGE B. HALSTEAD, of Excelsior, knew his boiler was sprung, but as there is no official inspection on Lake Minnetonka, permitted her to be run until she exploded. There is great indignation here at the carelessness with which these boats are managed."*

The *Mary* had pulled into the dock of the Hotel St. Louis and, almost immediately, the boiler exploded killing three, wounding eight and knocking many guests to the ground. The common denominator for the accidents were the defective, temperamental Ames Iron Works Company high-pressure boilers they used even when the owners had been warned by their competitor, Captain Charles May.

The *Minneapolis Tribune*, and most of the citizenry, was outraged and referred to the explosion of the *Mary* as the *"third chapter in the ample volume of Minnetonka horrors"* and *"a case of murder."* The *St. Paul Globe* report of July was more sensational, quoting the manager of the hotel, John Hinde, regarding the dead and injured: *"Mr. Plattenburg [guest]…was blown ashore and terribly injured. He lingered about an hour in great agony and expired. My head waiter, Gaines, was blown out in the lake, and his body was found an hour or two afterwards at the bottom of the lake. The engineer, Chadwick, had the top of his head blown off and looks horrible. He never knew what hurt him. The pilot John Steward was also badly injured and cannot live."*

Owner George Halstead was convicted of criminal negligence by a coroner's jury but, when the proceedings progressed to Municipal Court, Judge Grove Cooney deemed the charges improperly filed. The case was dropped.

The lives of steamboat pilots were perilous not only on the water but also on land, particularly ones who beat their wives as Edward Creelman did in 1905. At night, emboldened by righteous indignation, a group of over fifty women proceeded to the Excelsior jail to exact some lakeshore justice. When they were stopped from entering the building, they formed a block-long bucket line to a pump and passed pails of water that were dumped into the jail. When the mob finally dispersed, Creelman was found in his cell, quaking with fear.

■ ■ ■

By the mid-1880s, the Big Water had transitioned from a pioneer outlier to a resort destination for Southerners wishing to escape their suffocating hot and humid summers. Primitive cabins were dwarfed by grand hotels. Dangerous steamers were replaced by large, magnificent steamboats. Railroad baron James J. Hill commissioned the largest boat to ever cruise Minnetonka.

The 300-foot-long *Belle of Minnetonka* had a capacity of 2,500 passengers. The side-wheeler *City of St. Louis* was built in Wayzata and was the first to sport electric lighting. It measured 160 feet in length and could comfortably accommodate 1,000. The two Goliaths sometimes raced to the landing in Wayzata or Excelsior.

The advent of the Big Island Amusement Park brought thousands to Minnetonka. During the peak seasons during the first decade of the

20th century, the Park saw as many as 12,000 landlubbers visit the 65-acre park in a day. The Twin City Rapid Transit built it, in large part, to increase ridership on its new route from Minneapolis to Excelsior.

Visitors chose from three different types of steamboats. Seventy-foot-long express boats, nicknamed *"yellow jackets,"* resembled water-worthy streetcars and made multiple daily trips to Big Island as did the 142-foot-long ferry boats that could shuttle as many as 1,000 riders at a time. Excursion steamboats were hired for three-hour tours of the Big Water.

Between 1907 and 1921, Donaldson's Department Store in downtown Minneapolis offered a delivery service to homes and hotels on Lake Minnetonka via their boat, the *Isabelle,* named after the owner's wife. The range reached a quarter of a mile into the lake for island delivery. Cascade Steam Laundry offered same-day service, and for a short time the *St. Paul Daily Globe* and the *Minneapolis Tribune* were delivered by boat.

■ ■ ■

"Take the 18' Queen Merrie. This gracious lady of the big waters just likes it rough. Her clean, tapered bow was designed to quarter waves, her deep triple-keeled bottom rides a crest like a lifeboat, her long, wide deck, full-length spray rails and 38 inches of depth keep you snug and dry where other folks are bailing." (Alumacraft Corporation ad copy)

The Big Island Fruens of my youth, and for decades prior, were utilitarian by nature and valued function, dependability and durability over form. If a bateau could transport you back and forth from mainland to the island, pull you water skiing and chug along at trolling speed for fishing, then damn the cosmetics.

During the 1920s, the 1930s and the World War II years, there were few boats on Lake Minnetonka. In those early Crown Point summers, the Fruen fleet included the *Tin Boat,* a ten-foot metal boat, powered by a 3-1/2-HP motor. It featured a prow board that the family dog, a setter-shepherd mix named Skeets II, rode on proudly with ears peeled back, warding off evil spirits like the figurehead of a Viking ship.

A 13-footer with a 12-HP motor was also used to ferry people, luggage, food, drinking water and supplies. It was known as the *Speedboat,* an indication of how far recreational boating has advanced over

Street car boats used to ferry patrons to the Big Island Amusement Park.
Old Postcard

the years. It must have looked like an Upper Midwest version of *The Grapes of Wrath* when the two boats covered the short distance from Deephaven to Crown Point hauling what resembled all the Fruens' total earthly possessions.

Knowing my grandparents, I am sure they were totally organized and outfitted for a season on Big Island. My father, in his early teens, commandeered the 12-horse engine and attached it to his small, flat-bottom skiff. He skimmed the lake's surface like a bat out of hell. I recall an old Mercury Kiekhaeffer outboard motor on one of the watercrafts from my earliest Crown Point memories.

The most unusual watercraft to ply the Lower Lake waters from a Crown Point launch belonged to Joe. He was a workman hired by Grandfather during World War II when my father and his two older brothers were in the Navy. Joe helped with the grounds and a myriad of other projects. He lived in a workman's quarters out back that was logically named "Joe's Cabin." One day he was stranded on the island without a boat and wanted to go to Excelsior. A resourceful man, Joe added a log on each side of a plywood sheet he scavenged, grabbed an oar, and headed south on the lake. A friend of Grandpa saw what he thought was a mirage on the lake about a half-mile from his vantage point on the east shore. He said, *"For a moment I thought it was Jesus walking on the water."*

■ ■ ■

For a few decades, after his financial fortunes rebounded, Frank Griswold had the fastest boat on Minnetonka. It was a 30-foot, custom-made triple-cockpit runabout constructed with red-brown Honduran mahogany and a red leather-buttoned tugged interior. Chrome hardware accents such as oval step plates were used and the name *Gerry-Lo*, a combination of Frank's daughters' names, was spelled in chrome on each side.

The speedboat was powered by a V-12 Curtiss Wright airplane engine and could go up to 70 miles-an-hour at full throttle. When the engine started, a throaty roar echoed up and down the Lower Lake. My father and his siblings were thrilled when Mr. Griswold took them for rides.

The *Gerry-Lo* had three rows of bench seats that held four or five passengers each. The boat was handmade to Frank's specifications by the Dingle Boat Works Company of St. Paul at a cost of $25,000, which was five times the previous price of a top-end vessel. Griswold loved to race and, in the 1930s, he bested an aquatic airplane in a Wayzata Bay contest. *"The airplane really didn't stand much of a chance because it had to start from out of the water. But in that race, like in all of his big races, he never pulled too far ahead. He kept it close enough for the crowds to stay excited."* (Lois Griswold Shaw as told to John Mugford, *Legendary Boat to Remain on Lake*)

The three oldest Fruen boys, Dick, Roger and Bruce, had reason to visit Mr. Griswold in the 1930s when they came to get water from his spring on the Lower Lake. Grandpa Arthur did not need to undertake a time-and-motion study; it was much more efficient and prudent to take the short boat ride. By eliminating the car ride from the Glenwood spring, not to mention the wear and tear on the automobile, the process was made easier by reducing the number of transfers of heavy and unwieldy large glass jugs. The chore was made more appealing by the chance to check out the *Gerry-Lo* again.

The august Minnetonka Yacht Club was founded in 1882, and its clubhouse still sits on tiny Lighthouse Island, a stone's throw from Crown Point. Over the years the club has produced many world-class sailors. The Fruens are not among them. In the 1930s, Aunt Louise and Uncle Doug sailed a C Class scow and usually came in last during the

Frank Griswold's *Gerry Lo*. The fastest boat on Lake Minnehaha.
Photo courtesy of Woody Boater

Club's weekend races. In defense of the family's nautical reputation, Louise maintains that there was a neighboring neophyte who, on occasion, finished behind the Fruens.

In 1893, the upstart Minnetonka club shocked the sailing world by beating the best of the East when the MYC scow *Onawa* defeated the pride of New England, the *Alpha*. The provincial Bostonians said the 24-foot *Onawa* was more of a canoe than a sailboat, but the Minnetonka entry piloted by seventeen-year-old Ward Burton won by more than fifteen minutes. The winning sailboat was lighter and ballast-free, which allowed the scow to skim the surface rather than plow through it. The *Boston Herald* related the race on August 30, 1893:

The *Alpha* Beaten!

It hardly seemed possible, but later reports from Lake Minnetonka confirm the first report. How was it done? [The] Onawa has a less displacement and a smaller sail plan...Our western lakes used to be our best markets for Boston and New York back-numbers, but now! The Minnetonka yachtsmen may claim they have the fastest jib and main sailboat in this country, and for that matter, in the whole world....

■ ■ ■

When I passed one of Dad's swimming tests, I could tool around in what we affectionately called *The 18*. It was a glorified rowboat with an 18-HP Evinrude motor that sprang to life with a hard tug or two on the rope-pull starter. Responsibility came with privilege, and I learned how to tie knots and fill the metal cans with a mix of oil and gasoline. Leaving the tank in the boat empty was a cardinal sin and easily avoided with a trip the boathouse where the 500-gallon red metal gas receptacle resided. It was wise to fill the boat tanks at night to avoid smelling like fuel at work the next day.

I never actually saw a boat stored in the boathouse during the summer months. It was primarily a storage facility for water skis, ski boards, inner tubes, life jackets, a Sailfish and unidentified relics of indeterminate age or utility. Usually, a few inches of water covering the cement floor provided frogs safe harbor from hungry bass. Strands of seaweed made walking in the boathouse treacherous: A trip for gas could end with a hard, wet fall.

In the early 1960s, before the advent of the environmental movement, it was common to dump unwanted items, big and small, into the deep waters off Big Island. Divers continue to find objects on the lake bottom including intentionally scuttled steamboats and even a 1955 Mercury Monterrey four-door sedan that broke through the ice one spring, perhaps purposely abandoned. There is a secluded channel on the Upper Lake that is the burial ground for numerous jettisoned appliances that are placed on the ice until a thaw sends them to Davey Jones' locker.

In 2018, two underwater archaeologists found ten previously undiscovered wrecks. The most noteworthy find was a 21-1/2-foot wood gasoline-powered launch named *Theta,* thought to have been built in 1900 and sunk about 1920. In addition to their nautical sightings, they saw three snowmobiles, two large boulders and two entire trees, roots and all.

■ ■ ■

Our family has been extremely fortunate over the 85-plus years at Big Island to have avoided serious mishaps. There have been some close calls, but none as frightening as an incident that started innocently. Grandfather, always the engineer, had used cement tubs to stabilize the dock against the onslaught of waves. The experiment failed and he asked my uncles, Dick and Doug, to take one of the hundred-pound tubs and dispose of it in the deep water two hundred yards off Crown Point. Dick's sons, Jimmy and Ricky, were also on board the crowded craft. When they reached their destination, they wrestled the tub over the stern, but the attached rope snagged a bolt near the water line. The boat quickly sank to the bottom of Minnetonka like a heat-seeking missile. As everyone gathered their wits, treading water after their surprise ejection, Jimmy followed the family mantra: STAY WITH THE BOAT. Ninety-nine percent of the time, this is sound advice. Jimmy went down with the ship. After running out of breath and realizing the age-old advice was not pertinent in this instance, he let go of the gunwale and popped to the surface.

The now boatless Fruens yelled and gestured but to no avail. Then serendipitously, Grandpa and cousin Tommy emerged from the Chalet. A.B. was deaf, but the gesturing caught his eye. He answered with a friendly wave while turning in the opposite direction. Tommy stopped him and said, "I think they're in trouble, Grandpa. There's no boat!"

Grandpa and Tommy hurriedly came to the rescue of the rapidly tiring foursome and helped them aboard their boat. But the story does not end there.

Arthur hired a scuba diver, but he failed to locate the sunken boat. The next day a Fruen family search party, armed with an anchor and one hundred feet of rope, ventured to the approximate point of descent in an admittedly low-percentage effort to locate the boat. After dragging the bottom a few times with an old mattress spring, astoundingly, *The 18* was hooked. It breached the surface, motor and all, like an orca whale. One of the oars was standing straight up toward the sky, and a few bullheads swam inside the aluminum vessel. The boat had air tanks under each seat for buoyancy and, while one burst from the water pressure, the others did their job.

■ ■ ■

At the dawn of my Big Island memories is my grandparents' boat, an all-metal model, cabin and all. It looked like a smaller, sleeker descendent of a Civil War ironclad, Grandpa's version of the *Monitor* and *Merrimack*. To me it resembled a floating lightning rod. Dad bought an

Alumacraft *Queen Merrie* in the early 1960s. It was a tank with a tubular frame for the canvas top that could be raised during heavy rain. The roof had flexible, clear side windows that offered a bit of filtered visibility.

It was a wise, virtually indestructible purchase and withstood years of use and abuse. Its 50-HP Johnson outboard endured countless hours of water skiing and innumerable round trips to Tonka Bay, Excelsior and Orono for pick-ups and drop-offs. Dad knew his sons would be hard on the *Queen Merrie* and waited until we were older before he bought a nicer fiberglass craft for himself. We were not confined to Lake Minnetonka as Roger trailered the boat on occasion for day trips on the Mississippi, Minnesota and St. Croix rivers. Once or twice a year we would haul it to one of the myriad lakes in northern Minnesota.

When my Dad was not using it my brothers were, and our father would chastise them for various transgressions. Mike liked to perch on the seat top and work the throttle with his foot, which eventually led to a sagging seatback. When he slalom skied, he leaned way back and let the boat pull him into position. The Johnson would strain, and Dad would yell, "*Get your butt out of the water.*"

If my father had a personality flaw it would have been his impatience. He taught me to drive a speedboat, but often his instructions were frantic and indecipherable. While I was attempting to land the craft, gauging the wind and the waves, Dad would be on dry land gesturing wildly and shouting vague directions as I tried to get within jumping proximity to the dock.

Soon I had the run of the Big Water. I knew the Lower Lake like the back of my hand but was less confident, particularly at night, if I ventured into the Upper Lake. We had a cutting board used for barbeques and picnics decorated with an embossed map of Minnetonka. I stashed it in the boat and consulted it with a flashlight when needed.

I had many adventures and misadventures driving our Lady of the Lake. One day the steering wheel came off when I was cruising at full throttle. The cotter pin holding it in place had snapped. I shifted into neutral and managed to stick the wheel, still unattached, back in place and nursed the *Queen Merrie* back to our dock.

When I was 16 and dumb, I took an ill-advised shortcut between Spirit Island and Lookout Point at the entrance of Wayzata Bay and clipped the land bridge lurking a foot or two below the surface with the lower transom of the motor. I nursed the limping craft over to the closest

Queen Merrie, an 18' Alumacraft Runabout
Fruen family photo

marina, and a helpful worker sympathized with my plight. (Maybe he had an irascible father, too.) He made a quick repair and sent me on my way, seemingly good as new. The next morning Dad asked if anything happened to the Johnson. I confessed and was once again amazed by his unsettling omniscience.

One benefit of having older cousins and brothers is the truism that sooner or later they will do something foolish and shift the focus from my foibles. The Big Island duo of brother Mike and cousin Ricky headed up to visit Brown's Bay cousin Colt Bagley in the 14-foot Alumacraft with a 7-1/2 horsepower Mercury motor. They took the outboard from its usual perch and attached it to Uncle Ralph's new hunting skiff. After a pull on the starter cord, the motor revved to life. The putt-putt Mercury proved to be too big for the new hybrid experimental vessel. The stern reared back, took on water, and immediately sank to the bottom of my uncle's lagoon.

The hardest part of boating for me was threading the needle in tight quarters while backing the boat trailer into the water. There was usually a large audience at the landing waiting their turn and adding to the pressure factor. When the trailer was attached to the station wagon it seemed that turning the wheel was a counterintuitive action, as the trailer turned in the opposite direction of what I expected. If not careful, I turned the car, trailer and boat into a pretzel. It was best to maneuver the vehicle and trailer into a straight-shot scenario.

My Northeast Lower Lake cousins on my mother's side of our family, George and Colt, had a one-boat Armada in their formative years. They prowled Brown's, Wayzata, Gray's and other bays and engaged in naval battles with other combatants. The skirmishes usually ended with the frenemies sharing milk and cookies at one of their houses. George and Colt are a few years older than I and tormented me on occasion, but I appreciated their attention, and seeing them was a nice change of pace from my Big Island cousins.

It was rare when Dad messed up, but it was secretly gratifying to me. Early one perfect summer evening, we planned a picnic on Goose Island – a small, uninhabited one-acre spit of land in the Upper Lake. We proceeded at a slow speed and, per his custom, Roger started the coals in the grill to coordinate with our arrival.

He spotted the wave from a large boat, but it was too late. The grill tipped, the contents spilled, and all hell broke out on the *Queen Merrie*. As the dogs lunged for the raw hamburger meat, my father scooped the glowing briquettes into the water with his bare hands as the Astroturf on the floor began to melt in spots. Rarely given to profanity in front of the family, Dad uttered some words he had learned in the Navy.

■ ■ ■

Despite his occasional bouts of churlishness, my father was our personal Neptune whether he was picking up visitors on the mainland or taking his children, nieces, nephews and grandchildren water skiing. Sometimes he took a breather on the dock, handing the driving duties over to Uncle Dick or one of the older boys. Roger would soon be greeted with a wall of water as the skier would tilt a ski, giving Dad a thorough drenching. Everyone knew it was coming and scrambled to safety, but Roger played along, sputtering with mock outrage as the young ones shrieked and the dogs barked.

When he was not behind the wheel or getting an impromptu shower, my father tinkered with various projects, often fixing nylon ski-tow ropes or the ones attached to the boats. He spliced the rope, meticulously fashioned loops and melted the frayed ends with his lighter to make a seamless connection. His medium was nylon rope and he was a master. To him, these activities were as therapeutic as yoga or a massage.

■ ■ ■

I was not as accomplished a skier as my brother Mike or cousin Ricky, but I had a few tricks. My best was a complicated maneuver executed with a two-ski start. After a spin around the cove to the west, I lifted my left ski and moved it behind my back where, holding the tow rope with one hand, I removed the ski with the other and balanced it on my shoulder, now skiing on one. When passing the dock, I floated the loose ski toward the dock and continued in slalom mode.

When my childhood friend, Chris Briscoe, made his annual visit from California, we performed some tandem stunts. Both of us skied well outside the wake, then converged to the middle as one of us lifted his tow rope high while the other crouched and sped underneath the rope to the far side. Mike outshone us, though. He started from the

Chris Briscoe and the author prepare for synchronized water-skiing tricks.
Fruen family photo

shoreline end of the dock, hopping on his bare left foot while holding his right ski just off the metal surface. He timed his jump into the water perfectly, and the slack in the rope disappeared as his slalom ski slapped the surface.

■ ■ ■

At summer's end when there was a hint of autumn in the air, Dad took his annual spin around the south side of Big Island on a pair of water skis. Everyone looked forward to this event, and the older boys jockeyed for the right to drive the boat and hopefully dump Roger into the lake. His outfit was always the same: his trademark red cap, sunglasses, white t-shirt and Scotch plaid swim trunks. So confident was he as the sun glinted off his gold watch band! He often had a drink in a plastic cup, showing defiance to those who would dunk him and bravado that he would survive the outing unscathed.

The action was almost choreographed. When Dad ventured beyond the confines of the wake, the boat driver immediately turned in the same direction, creating slack and causing the rope to sag and my father to sink to thigh level while he feverishly gathered the tow rope to keep it taut. He timed his exit perfectly, let go of the handle, coasted the last few feet and gently sat on the dock.

My father did not tolerate this kind of showboating from us, but he gave himself a pass regarding the dangers of a human body colliding with metal. Although the annual event was eagerly anticipated, it was bittersweet as our Big Island summer was on the wane. Roger took on the role of Crown Point's benevolent dictator after Grandpa died. This is the place where Dad was happiest. He had been around the world, but Big Island was his province.

Minnehaha Falls early 1900s
Photo by Harry Emerson

Minnehaha Creek

"'Hark' she said; 'I hear a roaring and a rushing.
Hear the Falls of Minnehaha calling to me from a distance."

Minnehaha in the throes of death, Henry Longfellow,
SONG OF HIAWATHA

MY NEIGHBORHOOD GANG OF elementary school marauders didn't know the twenty-two-mile streamlet running by our southwest Minneapolis homes linked Lake Minnetonka's Gray's Bay to the Mississippi River. We did not know its historical and cultural importance, nor did we care about the creek's past as a transportation corridor and food source as it alternately meandered and rushed to its destination. We paid no attention to the beautiful homes bordering Minnehaha Creek, many of which resemble larger footprints of English stucco cottages.

Our world was wedged between the creek on the north, Diamond Lake on the south, Lake Nokomis to the east and Lake Harriet to the west. Our home on Clinton Avenue, less than a block away from Minnehaha, was a smaller, ivy-covered version built in the 1920s as the city of Minneapolis spread south.

We called it "the Crick" in deference to colloquial dialects we probably learned from *Tom Sawyer* or the *Adventures of Huckleberry Finn*. We did not embrace the Queen's English when we were out of earshot from our parents and teachers. Our attempts at being worldly resulted in what we felt was eloquent profanity, even if we did not understand the meanings of many of the words.

The creek was our crew's dominion in the summer. Our miniature, heavily wooded Amazon River jungle. We swam and used a knotted rope swing to hover over and drop into a deep spot. We caught crayfish and, upon learning they were not much fun, threw them back. The gang built wobbly forts on the shore with fallen branches, soggy cardboard, and other materials we could scrounge.

The police would kindly run us off, and sometimes a group of "big kids" chased us away albeit more roughly. Billy, Andy, Steve and I – and other part-time co-conspirators – returned undeterred to resume our activities.

Like most boys, we were budding arsonists. After we built Aurora or Revell plastic ship models, sniffed a bit of the Testors' glue and admired our handiwork, we took the boats down to the creek. After pilfering one of our parents' lighter-fluid cans and some matches, we doused the models, strategically placed some Black Cat firecrackers on board, lit the fuses and launched the ships on their way to an inevitable, disastrous fate. As the vessels floated downstream, the scene looked and sounded like Pearl Harbor in miniature.

■ ■ ■

When it was swelteringly hot and humid in July and August, we rode our bikes along the creek paths we used as our expressway to the bowling alley on 48th Street and Chicago Avenue to roll a few games and enjoy the air-conditioning. Whole-house air-conditioners were not common in Minnesota then. My parents bought a window unit, but it was located in their bedroom. They did not share.

The bowling alley, Parkway Lanes, sold soda ("pop" to us in those days) and candy – an ideal venue for us. Once twelve-year-old Billy flirted with a perfect game, falling painfully short in the final frame. On a rainy day, we had the option to catch a movie at the Parkway Theater next door. It was a cheap outing: twenty-five-cent admission plus a drink and some candy. Movie theaters had not yet discovered the outrageous price points and margins they could extract from their captive audiences.

Saturday matinees brought droves of raucous kids shouting, "*We want the show!*" as they dropped their open boxes of Atomic Jawbreakers on the slanted cement floor, adding to the din and drawing hoots of derision. The red velvet seats took a beating as the restless crowd bounced up and down. After a cartoon or two, the feature began. We preferred movies like the *Seven Voyages of Sinbad, Swiss Family Robinson or Journey to the Center of the Earth.* The scary *13 Ghosts* offered special effects enhanced by 3D glasses handed out at the door.

■ ■ ■

Throughout its history and still today, Minnehaha Creek passes by numerous points of interest. Sites include wetlands, meadows, wildlife habitat, a Target store, a boardwalk, parks, an elementary school, a civic center, locations of six old flour mills, ghosts of Native American villages, manicured backyards, neighborhoods and Hiawatha and Meadowbrook public golf courses.

Minnehaha runs under many old, architecturally interesting bridges and adjacent to the beautiful Minnehaha Parkway. It flows into and out of Lake Hiawatha, passing unobtrusive bronze statues close to the tourist attraction, Minnehaha Falls, which continues to attract visitors from the world over since being immortalized in Henry Wadsworth Longfellow's 1855 epic poem, Song of Hiawatha:

> *Where the Falls of Minnehaha*
> *Flash and gleam among the oak-trees,*
> *Laugh and leap into the valley.*
> *Gleaming, glancing through the branches*
> *As one hears the laughing water*
> *From behind its screen of branches.*

■ ■ ■

Norwegian immigrant Jacob Fjelde settled in Minneapolis in 1887. The sculptor is most famous for his statue honoring the valiant First Minnesota Infantry at the Battle of Gettysburg. The regiment sustained heavy losses in prior battles: First Bull Run (20 percent) and Antietam (28 percent).

The unit, 262 strong and outnumbered five to one, suffered 82 percent casualties staving off the Confederates as they attacked a key vantage point, Cemetery Ridge. The Minnesotans repulsed three Rebel advances in keeping their position on the hill on July 2, 1861.

The next day, bolstered by reinforcements, the unit helped repel the Pickett-Pettigrew Charge, losing seventeen more men. Many years later, during a May 30, 1928, Gettysburg Battlefield address, President Calvin

Statue of Minnehaha and Hiawatha. Located on the bank
of the creek just before it tumbles over the falls.
Photo courtesy of Minnesota Historical Society

Coolidge proclaimed, *"Colonel* [William] *Colvill and those eight companies of the First Minnesota are entitled to rank as the saviors of their country."*

Fjelde joined the ranks of admirers of Longfellow's poem and was commissioned to create a plaster sculpture of Minnehaha held by Hiawatha to stand in front of the Minnesota Building at the 1893 World's Columbian Exposition in Chicago. The public clamored for a bronze version of Hiawatha and Minnehaha to be cast, and the project was funded largely from pocket change donated by the school children of Minnesota.

Controversy ensued when critics cited the decidedly Anglo-and-romanticized features of the Dakota maiden and the Ojibwe warrior as inauthentic. The sculptor said he relied on photographs for detail as he was unable to find any Indians to model. In 1912, the statue was cast in bronze and, after a ceremony, placed on the bank of the creek before it tumbles over the Falls.

■ ■ ■

Minnehaha Creek links two important Dakota religious sites: Lake Minnetonka and a location between the Falls and the Mississippi River. Eddie Benton Benais, a full-blooded Ojibwe from northern Wisconsin and Grand Chief of the Mdewiwin Society, explained its significance while testifying in a 1999 court case. *"Between the Falls and that point* [confluence of the creek and the great river] *there were sacred grounds that were mutually held to be a sacred place. And that the spring* [Coldwater Spring] *from which the sacred water should be drawn was not very far... There's a spring, near the Lodge, that all nations used to draw the sacred water for the ceremony."*

Benais' grandfather told him many tales of his trips to the location that he had made as a boy traveling on foot, horse or canoe. The various tribes – Dakota, Ojibwe, Sauk, Potawatomie and Meswaki – shared the spring, believing *"that it is forever a neutral place and forever a sacred place."* In 1820, the Dakota sent a birch-bark scroll invitation to the Ojibwe to meet at Coldwater to forge a peace agreement. The on-and-off enemies accepted. Many generations of Ojibwe-Dakota intermarriages helped ease the enmity between the two tribes.

"In the years that followed the events of 1820, Coldwater Spring was

the habitual camping place of the Ojibwe who came to Fort Snelling, the Indian Agency [Lower Sioux] *and the nearby Dakota communities. Ojibwe and Dakota traded, danced, and participated in ceremonies there for many years."* (Bruce White, *MinnesotaHistory.net*)

The Dakota had been frequenting the area for centuries and called the area at the junction of the Mississippi and Minnesota River's *Bdote* (Where Two Waters Come Together) Many sacred sites are in the vicinity. In addition to *Mini Owe Sni* (Coldwater Spring) close locations include *Oheyawahi* (Pilot Knob) and *Taku Wakan Tipi* (Carver's Cave).

Missionary Stephen Riggs devoted forty years of his life working with the Dakota and observed, *"The Mdewakandtonwan think that the mouth of the Minnesota River is precisely over the center of the earth and that they occupy the gate that opens into the western world."*

■ ■ ■

"Early in the Spring [1820] *Col. Leavenworth discovered the fountain of water where the troops now are, & to which they moved as soon as the ice would permit. It is a healthy situation, about 200 feet above the river, and the water gushing out of a lime stone rock is excellent. It is called 'Camp Cold Water.'"* (James Duane Doty, Camp Cold Water, July 31, 1820)

The soldiers building Fort Snelling moved from the bluffs to Coldwater* in 1820, making it the first U.S. settlement in Minnesota. It became a bustling, crowded place with stables, a blacksmith shop, a trading post, a steamboat landing and even a hotel.

It took three summers to complete the fort, and the men moved into the completed outpost designed to defend U.S. interests as the country moved west and the encroachment onto Native American lands caused predictable conflict. Officers at the fort tried to negotiate peace between the Ojibwe and the Dakota to facilitate the steady stream of furs and tax revenues for the U.S. government. Finally, the bastion acted as a deterrent to British expansion in the Northwest. The fort, first named Fort St. Anthony, was called the *"citadel in the wilderness"* by author Evan Jones.

■ ■ ■

---

*In 2010 the Cold Water Spring location was put under the auspices of the Mississippi National River and Recreation area with the hope of reestablishing the original oak savannah and prairie landform.

Our pre-teen interest in the tourist spot was not motivated by intellectual curiosity, but the fifty-three-foot Falls was magical nonetheless, particularly when the creek was running high. Our squad lost its pioneering spirit before we reached the Mississippi, two miles from the Falls. From above the Falls and below, we viewed where it landed in a pool of water before flowing into the Mississippi. We walked downstream through the glen, possibly passing Coldwater Spring.

In the early 1900s the variety of fish drew people to the creek, and Coates P. Bull remarked, "*Sucker and redhorse each spring swam from Lake Harriet through the outlet into Minnehaha... Settlers, even from Eden Prairie and miles to the west, brought their spears to harvest bushels of these fish to eat and feed to pigs... Farmers could and did go down with pitch forks and pitch the fish out onto the banks for their fish fry.*"

Bull also observed a bounty of wildlife along the little stream near the present site of Edina including muskrats, mink, otters, and osprey and additional fish species such as pike and sunfish. Even today a rogue northern pike or muskie will spill over Gray's Bay Dam to prowl the pond created by the dam at Minnehaha Mills.

My mother remembered another aspect of the creek, Longfellow Zoological Gardens. Robert "Fish" Jones had been driven from his home and zoo at the outskirts of downtown Minneapolis due to a growing number of complaints concerning the sounds and smells of his menagerie. He found a more remote location, so he and moved to a location along the creek and expanded his operation. Jones diverted Minnehaha to form ponds for his aquatic animals. Almost immediately after the grand opening in 1907, the favorite crowd attraction, three seals, escaped. While two were easily recaptured, the third took off down the creek, went over the Falls and took a right when it reached the Mississippi River. The seal was finally located almost fifty miles downstream at Red Wing. Apparently, the sea lions decided not to swim to freedom and stayed in their rookery.

Mom loved the performances at the Zoo House, which showcased the antics of bears, monkeys, lions and leopards. There was also a camel and an anteater. The little train that circumnavigated the grounds was a popular attraction, and all the cars were named after characters from the "Song of Hiawatha." When the Big Island Amusement Park closed in 1911, Jones transferred the exotic birds he had earlier sourced.

■ ■ ■

In July 2019, two Edina boys – 12-year-old Mac Hoekstra and 14-year-old Owen Sanderson – had the best Minnehaha Creek fish story to tell. The boys were floating downstream on inner tubes when they spotted what turned out to be a seventy-year-old sturgeon right below them. They borrowed a slip-knotted rope from Owen's father, somehow looped it around its tail and pulled it from the creek to measure the six-foot monster. The neighborhood's "telegraph" network kicked into high gear, and soon a mob of excited children were hopping up and down, screaming with excitement.

The fish tail scratched Mac on the chest as the estimated 100-pound leviathan was wrestled to the ground, measured, photographed and pushed back into the water. Initially the Minnesota DNR officials were skeptical but, when they came to investigate, they located it under the 56th Street Bridge.

Their first efforts to capture the primitive sturgeon and relocate it to the Mississippi were unsuccessful. It is believed that the fish entered the Minnehaha from Minnetonka's Gray's Bay during the rainy spring when the lake and creek levels were both extremely high. DNR spokesman Harlan Hiemstra was perplexed by the situation: "*There have been these legends of a large fish that could be a sturgeon, or it could be a muskie, in Lake Minnetonka. They have not been officially confirmed by a fisheries biologist. You can have again one of these remnants of a prehistoric era show up swimming through Minneapolis or Edina … That is cool.*"

The boys had broken the law by "noodling," or fishing with one's hands, but Hiemstra did not seem worried. "*I don't think anybody's too concerned about that. It's not what we should do with fish, but hey, boys will be boys in that regard.*"

I do not believe the experts ever located the sturgeon again, but I need to get in touch with our old gang and propose honorary membership for Mac and Owen. They have the right stuff.

■ ■ ■

My grandmother, Reba Watson Fruen, was born along the creek at Edina Mills in 1890, a few years before the operation wound down and ceased operations. Little did she know then that grain milling held a prominent place in her future. Four partners built the Waterville Mill in 1857 on Minnehaha Creek where a small fall created an opportunity for a dam. The dam harnessed the waterpower and a millrace to direct the current over the waterwheel. Oats, barley and wheat that the farmers hauled in by horse-drawn wagons were then milled.

The peak of the enterprise came during the Civil War years when it operated twenty-four hours a day to meet the needs of the troops at Fort Snelling. Scotsman Andrew Craik purchased the mill in 1869 and renamed it "Edina" after his hometown, Edinburgh. He made improvements by building a huller and a drying kiln to specialize in oatmeal and pearl barley.

Craik expanded into retail packaged goods by selling his flour to a downtown Minneapolis department store. A full-fledged community sprung up near the operation including a school, church, post office, blacksmith shop, store and a carriage builder. The Watsons moved to 2917 Bloomington Avenue in Minneapolis when Great-grandfather John was appointed superintendent of Hennepin County Schools.

In the 1930s, the Depression and the drought put tremendous pressure on the food supply chain and the pocketbooks of Minnesotans, and many took to hunting for sustenance. "*On a few occasions during the Depression years, Dad took his shotgun over to the cornfields on farms south* [of the creek at] *York Avenue and shot a pheasant for supper. Rabbits, squirrels, ducks and deer were also the meat for supper on rare occasion.*" (Jane King Hallberg, *Minnehaha Creek: Living Waters*)

Our pre-teen bodies grew, and our private creek haven looked smaller and smaller. Summer Camp, organized sports and a newfound preoccupation with girls distracted us from the old stomping grounds. At sixteen the access to cars expanded our horizons but, every now and then, we were drawn back to the creek when our attention was piqued.

Flooding was a nuisance for homeowners with wet basements, but it was a source of excitement for us when we went to see large, ugly carp flopping on the ground or when an armored vehicle was used to smash the ice jam under the Humboldt Avenue Bridge. The Creek had been our oyster, but we were starting to emerge from our shells.

■ ■ ■

Grinding stone from Edina Mills
Photo courtesy of City of Edina

The only time I remember my father Roger expressing any interest in the creek was in June 1964 when the Minneapolis visit of President Lyndon Johnson drove him to distraction. It was an arid summer when LBJ came to town to attend Svenskarkarnas Dag, a Swedish Summer Fest attended by almost as many politicians as Swedes. The creek was barely a memory, making the Falls noticeably less impressive.

Dad complained when the Minneapolis Park Board spent over $500 pumping water into the creek by opening fire hydrants so the Democratic president, vice-president and governor could have a photo opportunity. Roger was really on a roll, sputtering *"Johnson… Humphrey… Rolvaag."* As a thirteen-year-old wise guy, I was tempted to ask, *"Where is Mayor Hofstede?"* but knew better.

■ ■ ■

In the late 1960s my nephew and niece, David Jr. and Tracy, had a spur-of-the-moment adventure on the creek. Like Uncle Ross they had their gang and, one day, they decided to travel down Minnehaha in large inner tubes. Eight of them, all pre-teens, shoved off at Edina Mills, coincidentally where Grandmother Fruen was born seventy-five years prior. These were different times, and their parents were blissfully ignorant of their whereabouts.

There was no preparation or planning, but the children had boundless energy. Passing through neighborhoods on their tubes, they were scolded by some adults and greeted by many more. Parched and hungry, a kind woman brought them sandwiches. They cupped their hands and drank creek water. Upon reaching stretches of slowing current, they jumped from the creek onto terra firma and, toting their tubes, sprinted ahead to hasten their progress.

At one point the retinue encountered a man and his son fishing. The boy had hooked a carp while hoping to latch onto something more appealing. The fish had tucked itself in a muddy hole against the bank to avoid capture. Tracy was the youngest, so she was nominated to "*noodle*" the carp. She succeeded and after bare-handing the fish and tossing it on the ground, the journey recommenced minus three co-conspirators who called it quits. The afternoon was waning, and Junior and Tracy knew they were close to their grandparents' house.

They also knew Grandma Leslie baked the best chocolate chip cookies. Tubes in hand, the remaining five set out to find 5232 Clinton. Tracy was taught to memorize her grandmothers' addresses, and they walked a few blocks to find no one there. My father eventually appeared and deposited them back at their home. No cookies.

■ ■ ■

A tragedy that occurred in the neighborhood the year before I was born and four years before we moved there haunted my dreams for years. On the night of March 7, 1950, Northwest Airlines Flight 307 attempted a landing at the Minneapolis-St. Paul Airport in a blinding snowstorm. Visibility was poor, resulting in a low approach to the runway, and the left wing of the Martin 202 twin prop nicked a seventy-eight-foot flagpole in the Fort Snelling National Cemetery.

The crippled plane continued in a northwest direction to circle and essay an emergency landing but, shortly after passing over our future home, the wing fell from the fuselage over the Washburn Water Tower, often used as a beacon by pilots when nearing the airport. The plane

Roger and Leslie Fruen's home on 5232 Clinton Avenue South
Fruen family photo

then plowed into a home on Minnehaha Parkway. It was just under four miles from its planned destination. *"It's among the most beautiful parkways in the Twin Cities. Thousands of people walk, run and bike the trails that follow the meandering Minnehaha Creek through south Minneapolis. But on March 7, 1950, the scenic neighborhood is where then 15-year Dianne Doughty's family was ripped apart. 'Everything just exploded, and I have no idea. Your first reaction is self- preservation and I just jumped up and dove out the window."* (Bill Hudson, WCCO-TV)

Dianne was downstairs at watching television with her parents who also used the same escape route after impact. Her younger siblings, Janet (10) and Tommy (8), had no chance. They were already asleep upstairs, and the plane's fuel fed the conflagration. In addition to the Doughty children, ten passengers and three crew members perished.

A simple rock with a plaque now rests on the parkway bank across from the rebuilt Doughty home to honor the victims. I was fascinated by the story when I heard it. Being too young to process the horror and proximity of the crash and the fragility of life through reason, Flight 307 regularly seeped into my subconscious and my sleep cycle for a few years. And, on the rare occasion, still does.

■ ■ ■

At one point the area the around the Falls was more notorious than natural. Of course, where there are soldiers there are women. And the area of the falls in the late 1800s was more of a bacchanalia than the touristy area now where children play and eat ice cream cones.

Dance halls and pavilions appeared and drew streetcar loads of young women, many underage, who arrived to drink, meet men and participate in the debauchery. The lascivious behavior was met with outrage from the more "upstanding" citizens.

The noise, tumult, fights, coarse language, drunkenness and clandestine liaisons met with strong resistance from the nascent neighborhood and predictably, the conflict ended up in court.

Eventually the Minnehaha Falls environs gave way to the more family friendly scene of today, but not before Oscar F. G. Day wrote a satirical version of "Song of Hiawatha" published in the June 28, 1899, *Minneapolis Tribune.*

> *"All around was wild carousel—beer was*
> *foaming, men were swearing—*
> *Maidens in their teens were dancing with*
> *the veriest abandon—*
> *Lingerie was elevated, shrieks were there*
> *of drunken orgy—*
> *Men were pasted, others battered and the*
> *free fights she saw there*
> *Broke the heart of Minnehaha."*

When I return to Minneapolis, I often take a drive on the Parkway. It is not a sepia-toned nostalgia tour, just a beautiful trek past the old neighborhood. If a memory interrupts my reverie, so be it.

The Bryn Mawr gang in 1927. Roger Fruen is in the center holding the plane.
Fruen family photo

Summer in the City

"Winter and summer, then, were two hostile lives, and bred two separate natures. Winter was always the effort to live; summer was tropical license. Whether the children rolled in the grass, or waded in the brook, or fished for smelts in the creek, or took to the pine-woods, or chased muskrats and hunted snapping turtles in the swamps, or mushrooms or nuts on the autumn hills, summer and country were always sensual living, while winter was always compulsory learning. Summer was the multiplicity of nature; winter was school."

Henry Adams,
THE EDUCATION OF HENRY ADAMS

MY 1950s AND 1960s childhood benefitted from the freedom and amusement afforded by an urban neighborhood that was safe but adventurous for a boy with an imagination. My summers were not programmed except for a week at YMCA Camp Iduhapi when I was younger and a week at Hockey School when I reached my teens.

I played first base for the Pearl Park baseball team and, the year we won the Minneapolis city championship, everyone on my team received a blue ribbon from the sponsor, Northland Dairy, which I still have somewhere. The simple token was more meaningful than the participation trophies that are prevalent now. There were no uniforms. We played in blue jeans and Minnesota Twins caps. While our families and friends cheered, nobody was overly concerned about our self-esteem. It was just a game, after all, and if we lost one there was another chance to rebound in a few days.

Our coach was a no-nonsense woman, Marge Frederickson, whose day job was the supervisor of officials, umpires and referees for all the

Minneapolis Park Board sports leagues. She drilled us on the funda-
mentals, always wearing her Gilligan-style bucket hat. We were razzed
before the games for having a female coach, but most of the time our
opponents were chastened when the games ended.

When I turned 15, I became an usher for sporting events and
worked at most of the 81 Minnesota Twins home games except for the
infrequent weekday afternoon games during the school year. It was a
great job for a kid, getting paid to watch major league baseball. I became
a favorite of Bob Sims, who owned the ushering service. He gave me
some plum assignments like opening the bullpen gate for the Mustang
convertible that delivered the relief pitchers. As the years went by, this
custom faded as it was determined a professional athlete should be able
to jog a few yards to the pitcher's mound.

The arrival of the Twins was the most exciting thing to happen in
my small world. At the age of ten I lived and died with my heroes, and
my parents often hid the Sports section of the *Minneapolis Tribune* from
me the morning after a night game if the news was bad.

It is an inexorable wait for spring to arrive in the Upper Midwest,
and it would be a shock to people from warmer climates to see the kind
of conditions Minnesotans tolerate to participate in outdoor activities.
Twins' April home openers are sometimes "snowed out." Kids slosh
through mud and slush to play baseball in their parkas. Men wearing
water-slicked windbreakers huddle together as they pull their golf carts
down fairways, dodging snow flurries and sleet.

There are eventual signs of hope. The crab apple tree in our backyard
always seemed to bloom in a riot of small, pinkish flowers on Mother's
Day. The small crab apples were the perfect size to use in backyard and
alley combat but wreaked havoc when chewed and spewed by the lawn
mower. By the end of the school year, a large lilac bush along my walk
home from the bus stop erupted in a purple, fragrant portent of warmer
days and nights.

■ ■ ■

One knew spring had finally arrived when the glass storm windows
were removed and replaced with the screened versions. Our Southwest
Minneapolis house, a few minutes from the airport, was right in line
with one of the primary runways. In early spring, late fall and winter the

storm windows would rattle from the planes' vibrations. Other times of the year, phone conversations were interrupted until the aircraft cleared our neighborhood.

Lying in their bed at night, my parents could see the descending plane's lights so clearly that their first instinct was to duck. Dad seemed more carefree when the snow melted, which made us all look forward to summertime at "The Island." Cabin Fever is a real phenomenon in the Upper Midwest.

Roger always drove Pontiacs that were leased through the company every two years. The first one I remember was an impossibly long, very pink, mid-50s Bonneville sedan with a white hardtop. In the 1960s he got into the station wagon habit. No matter how hard we tried to convince him to lease something sportier, he would never diverge.

Since my mother didn't drive, we had one car until I reached the age of 16. Dad tried to teach her to drive soon after they were married, but it was an experience fraught with danger. Mom was not a "linear thinker" and had no grasp of or interest in mundane matters such as turn signals, gears, lanes, signs, brakes or gas pedals. We had a one-car detached garage, and a narrow one at that, which was entered via the alley behind our house.

The garage had a small brick fireplace and chimney in the front left corner that used coal in the winter back in the days before Sears Die Hard batteries. The alley side of the gray stucco garage took a beating as I stood in the Fairbanks' driveway and threw my rubber-coated baseball against the wall thousands of times and fielded ground balls as they rebounded back to me. One can still see the vestiges of the now-patched hole I burrowed with my pitches.

I think my Dad felt somewhat trapped by his sense of duty to his father, his heritage and his obligations as a breadwinner. While there is certainly comfort in family and routine, it can also be an overload, particularly when you often spend the weekends together, too. Roger Fruen was a born salesman: affable and outgoing but, given the chance to reinvent himself, he may have chosen another career. The routine wore on him. Dad would have liked a bit more adventure. Perhaps take a risk.

None of that seemed to matter as much in the summer, when we were freed from the constraints of a Minnesota winter and able to spend time on Big Island where my father grilled burgers and hot dogs and worked on a myriad of projects involving dirt, grease, sawdust, paint and the vast array of hand tools in the shed out back.

Mother could often be found kneeling by her backyard garden with spade in hand as her skirt billowed around her in a perfect circle. A certain sign of warmer weather came when she removed the Styrofoam cones protecting her roses from the Minnesota winter. There were other flowers too, thriving in the weedless environment. She planted mint next to the house, and I often was asked to pick some to garnish my parents' summer drinks. A Gin Fizz or Tom Collins were warm-weather favorites.

■ ■ ■

Days we were not at the island were spent on the loose with my friends. We had the run of the neighborhood, checking in at home at lunch time and returning for dinner. Our bicycles increased our range into more of South Minneapolis. We could pedal to Lebow's Drug on Nicollet Avenue and buy some gum, a candy bar, baseball cards or slurp a cherry phosphate at the soda counter.

I never bought comic books as I could read about Superman and Archie across the street at Milt's Barber Shop. One time Milt leaned over and conspiratorially whispered to the rookie barber giving me a crew-cut, "*Be careful with this one, his mother is fussy.*" I didn't worry much about tonsorial matters until girls appeared on my radar and I was trying to develop my Beach Boys "surfer swoop" under the watchful eyes of my parents and the hair police at school.

In the early 1960s, a swath of houses was cleared through South Minneapolis to make way for Interstate 35. Nine hundred homes were displaced, and fifty residential blocks were cleared. The bulldozers gutted the heart of a wonderful neighborhood and left it vacant for years until the construction crews reached that stretch of the freeway. It was another playground and we fashioned underground "forts" using the stray bits of rubble as our building materials. The real fun was in the construction of the pit "houses." It turns out that sitting in the dirt and the dark with a flashlight is not all it is cracked up to be.

We shifted gears and made a baseball diamond with a backstop, but no matter how many times we dragged the infield with a discarded door, rock-induced bad hops were a significant hazard. We reverted to playing at Pearl Park. The Park transitioned from the shallow, swampy Pearl Lake beginning in 1936 when *"...about 15,000 yards of fill were dumped and graded in the south end of the 'swamp' to improve the skating area. Later, with the help of federal work-relief crews, the park board stripped a foot of peat off the bed of Pearl Lake and raised it two feet by using 60,000 yards of fill acquired from the airport, where federal crews were grading for new runways."* ("Pearl Park," Minneapolis Park and Recreation Board)

Pearl often flooded in the spring and, in the autumn, the sod on the north end was often spongy and our football spikes tore the turf when cleat met sod. The reconfigured wetland did not go quietly.

Charles Loring is considered the "Father of Minneapolis Parks" and, subsequently, Theodore Wirth led the sculpting frenzy of the city's parks, parkways and waterways. It was the landscape architecture's version of the "Whack a Mole" game. It seems every action had a counter reaction that needed to be addressed. In 1911, a celebration to showcase and promote the City of Minneapolis was highlighted by the "Wedding of Waters."

The dredge-happy Park Board had created a canal to join Lake of the Isles and Lake Calhoun (so named at the time), and its unveiling was to be a highlight of the week-long event. A canal does not have the broad appeal of Minnehaha Falls, and a lack of rainfall throughout the spring and early summer reduced the city's main attraction to dribbles.

■ ■ ■

A solution was floated. Divert Minnehaha Creek to Lake Amelia (now Nokomis). Empty Rice Lake (now Hiawatha). Dam the Creek's exit point from Amelia to fashion a holding pond to supply the Falls with a steady supply of water. After the canal project was complete, there was no time to institute this circuitous strategy, and the celebration proceeded. *"...a fifty-foot waterfall written about by a Harvard poet, which attracted visitors from around the world was a bit more impressive to most people than a short canal under a busy road and railroad tracks. The Minneapolis PR machine could call the city the 'Venice of North America' all it wanted with its new canal, but visitors' imaginations were still probably fueled more by the images of the famous poet's noble heathen, beautiful maiden, and 'laughing waters.'"* (David A. Smith, "The Worst

Homes demolished or moved to make way for I-35W. Downtown Minneapolis
is in the distance. *Photo courtesy of Hennepin County History Museum*

Idea Ever #8: Power Boat Canal from Minnetonka to Harriet," *Minneapolis Park History*)

Perhaps inspired by the water-scaping frenzy, but more likely attracted by the potential of self-aggrandizement, engineer Albert Graber
proposed expansion of Minnehaha Creek into a 30-foot-wide, nine-
mile-long channel from its Lake Harriet outlet to Lake Minnetonka's
Gray's Bay. It was to be an express lane for city dwellers' power boats to
significantly cut the travel time to their summer cottages. Graber was
involved in a commercial project at Lake Mille Lacs and was eager to
cash in on another.

His enthusiasm was evident when quoted in a newspaper article
claiming to have the support of "*members of the board of county com-
missioners, capitalists, attorneys and real estate dealers. The plan, say the
promoters, would enable residents of summer houses on the big lake to
have their launches waiting at the town lake.*" (*Saturday Evening Tribune*,
May 28, 1911)

This attempt to cash in on the City of Lakes' efforts to develop recreational amenities even had a blueprint for contingencies. The dam at Gray's Bay would need to be removed. If this caused the level of Minnetonka to fall, water could be siphoned from the Minnesota River watershed and thus limit the chronic seasonal flooding. In theory.

By the time the dredging ended in the early 1930s and after twenty-three years of moving earth, over six million cubic yards of earth and flora had been removed. Smith said, "*That's enough muck and gravel to fill five football fields to the height of the IDS Center in downtown Minneapolis.*" The city was and continues to be an excellent steward of its natural gifts, and perennially places in the top five, if not first, in the rankings of U.S. city park systems.

The Park Board was imaginative, prescient and bold in its approach. It provided access to the lakes while leaving room for walking paths, bike paths, horse paths and eventually automobiles. Acquiring land and digging dirt were not the end of the process. Thousands of trees were to be planted while parks, skating rinks and parkways all need to be maintained and, in many instances, staffed.

There were cutbacks during economic downturns when acquisitions and new projects were delayed. Minneapolis was still passionate about its parks system. It was a priority. Somehow the money was always there for essential maintenance.

■ ■ ■

Civic boosters proposed a summer festival to celebrate and market the watery wonders of Minneapolis and provide a civic counter-punch to the St. Paul Winter Carnival. The Mill City was eager to pridefully extoll its progressive and modern virtues in contrast to the not-so-clean image from the thirties when labor unrest was rampant and the presence of gangsters gave Minneapolis the nickname "Mobapolis." The Aquatennial was conceived to repair the city's tarnished image. Along the way it evolved into a unique urban celebration of lakes, rivers and waterfalls.

A wildly successful tradition launched in 1940: The Minneapolis Aquatennial. The promoters, the Civic and Commerce Association, went all out. Marketed as The Best Days of Summer, there were 70 different events ranging from parades, fireworks, a rodeo, synchronized swimming and acrobatic diving exhibitions.

Minneapolis punches south. Pearl Park and Diamond Lake await development. 1930s photo.
Photo courtesy of David C. Smith

Aquatennial "Water Follies" with synchronized swimming featuring Olympic and professional performers, 1952.
Photo courtesy of Hennepin County Museum

A 450-mile canoe race began in Bemidji and ended in Minneapolis. At night, 400 fountains in Bde Maka Ska, the largest lake in Minneapolis, erupted. When darkness fell on the city, 800 shimmering lights performed an aquatic minuet. Gene Autry, and his horse Champion were the Aquatennial's first special guests, and Bob Hope was the initial Grand Marshall. Boxing champ Joe Louis attended.

A Queen of the Lakes was crowned as well as a Commodore who reigned over the celebrations and appeared at the formal ball. The Aqua Follies offered sophisticated Busby Berkely Hollywood extravaganzas with water ballets, skits, and humor performed by swimmers imported from Tinsel Town. The featured divers were Olympians.

We attended the special 1956 Aquatennial to celebrate the centennial of the founding of Minneapolis. The 40-block-long Torchlight Parade along Nicollet Avenue passed under our perch behind the large windows in a dentist's office that was a few stories off street level in the Medical Arts Building. Unfortunately, my only memory involves my sudden urge to use the rest room.

The bathroom in the hallway was locked for the evening. I was five years old, and certainly toilet trained, but when my father suggested I use the sink in the office I was wary. Was this a test? The grand homage to the watery wonders of Minneapolis sent me not so subliminal messages. Soon I had no choice but to comply, and there were no repercussions.

■ ■ ■

Living in the City of Lakes meant we shared the neighborhood with all sorts of little creatures, and it was not uncommon to see a mallard hen and her ducklings waddling down the street on the way to the Creek or Diamond Lake. Antediluvian-appearing salamanders lurked in window wells, and every now and then a fugitive, primitive looking snapping turtle would show up. We entertained ourselves by offering it sticks to split in two.

One day I found a medium-sized painted turtle in our yard. Considering myself a budding St. Francis of Assisi, I gingerly placed the reptile in the front basket of my hand-me-down black Schwinn and pedaled the short distance to Diamond Lake. As I lowered it to the sandy shore, it bit me and lumbered off as I understood the adage: no good deed goes unpunished.

As a pre-schooler I often went downtown with my mother Leslie to visit Grandmother Harrison and meet other friends and family members for lunch. We often went by taxi, and I regaled the driver with my car knowledge. I knew the make of almost all automobiles and when I did not, I asked Mom to read the chrome script nameplate. Once a cabbie kept exclaiming, *"I'll be God damned"* every time I shouted out the make of a passing car.

Grandmother Harrison lived at the Hampshire Arms at 9th Street and 4th Avenue. The 400-room residential hotel, built in 1892, had seen better days and even at my young age I noticed the now-shabby glory of the place with washed-out wallpaper and the threadbare carpet in the hallways. She was usually found sitting at a table in the corner of her living room. She wore her robe and always had a piece of tissue at the ready, stuck in a sleeve in case of a sneezing or coughing fit.

Grammie played solitaire next to a cache of cigarettes and an ashtray. She proudly introduced me to the other women on her floor. Never have I been so popular with the ladies. In the summer we went to the roof that was full of geriatric sunbathers. It was a kaleidoscope of senses. The sun reflected off the black asphalt roof, creating a *"tar beach"* accented by essence of creosote. The sounds of traffic and honking horns rose from the street five stories below.

■ ■ ■

By sixth grade I rode the city bus by myself, which was the 12-year-old equivalent to getting the keys to the family car. I now was able to navigate the downtown Minneapolis streets without my mother in tow. I walked to Nicollet Avenue and took the 18A bus. I had doctor and dentist appointments in the Medical Arts Building, which was the nexus of Minneapolis medical and dental care. Suburbia still deferred to the city in many ways.

During the school year we were rewarded with a "skip day" if we made the honor roll. Some of my fellow academicians, usually Steve Mitchell, Mike Melander, Rob Pearson and I met downtown and availed ourselves of all the attractions. In the summer we were on our own recognizance and free to head downtown on a whim, hinging on our ability to convince our mothers that we at least had a plan. We effortlessly cruised the canyons of downtown Minneapolis. We easily could have done it blindfolded. Our main drag was Hennepin Avenue, and our downtown world only deviated a block or two to the east. In the 1600s, what is now Hennepin was a footpath used by the Dakota that connected from the Mississippi River, where they met Ojibwe or European traders, to Bde Maka Ska and their semi-permanent lakeside villages.

After Minneapolis was settled by the Yankees, Germans and Scandinavians, the avenue became a magnet, offering low-priced meals and lodging for seasonal migrant workers who were brought in to move timber for the logging industry and harvest grain for the mills. Eventually, Hennepin became the city's theater district, with over 30 theaters lining the avenue.

In the 1950s, urban renewal came to much of the downtown area, pushing what were considered undesirable elements like flophouses, seedy bars, prostitution, adult bookstores and the people who frequented them, to Hennepin Avenue.

As a teen, Minnesota comedian Lizz Winstead was fascinated by the variety of life on Hennepin and the differences between the strip and the rest of Minneapolis, which she called "*Lutheran-occupied territory*" in her memoir, *Lizz Free or Die*. Her mother referred to Hennepin as "*a morality free zone.*" The bar Moby Dick's was a constant source of irritation for police, and Winstead detailed its clientele as a mix of "*bikers, pimps, hookers, and a lot of other folks with lesser ambitious career aspirations... Moby's had a big clear jar on one end of the bar filled with AA chips, because at Moby's if you came in and dropped your AA chip in the jar, you drank all day for free.*"

Bars like Mousey's, the Gay 90s and Augies were a constant source of irritation for the police, who were called to break up the inevitable brawls or drag a patron to the drunk tank. A paddy wagon was always at the ready. In ninth grade my friend Holly walked me through Mousey's doors like she owned the place. She did not, of course, but her father, Al "Mousey" Ostrowsky, did. After much pleading by his daughter, Al showed me the baseball bat and handgun he kept under the bar. I was impressed.

While we weren't old enough to belly up to the bars, we had lunch at our favorite restaurants as a prelude to our other downtown rituals. Herman's Lunch was a classic, no-frills, one-story building sandwiched between the YMCA and another building. We sat at the counter

Hennepin Avenue, Minneapolis, Minnesota

Old postcard

A 1955 photo of Herman's Lunch. Home of the 25¢ burger.
It was located on 19 S. 9th Street in Minneapolis.
Photo courtesy of Minnesota Historical Society

on spinning stools and ordered cheeseburgers, fries and cokes. One-cent "Ask Swami" vending machines were perched on the long Formica countertop and asked that you pose *"any question that can be answered 'yes' or 'no'"*. It also offered "fortunes and predictions."

When we were in the mood for Italian we ate at Luigi's on Hennepin. The restaurant served generous portions of pasta with a sweet red sauce at a reasonable price. We always played the jukebox, and one day Mike Melander and I repeatedly shoved coins into the slot and spun the Rolling Stones' first Jagger-Richards written single, "The Last Time," over and over. The title was prophetic, as eventually the manager told us to knock it off.

Many summer afternoons we would catch a movie at one of the remaining grand old theaters such as the Gopher, State and Orpheum. Many of buildings were built in the 1920s in styles ranging from Italian Renaissance to Beaux Arts to Neo-Classical.

As the popularity of vaudeville waned, the Orpheum evolved into a major movie house. In 1940, "Gone with the Wind" was a 2,579-seat sellout for every showing for three straight weeks. I was there front and center in 1965 when "Thunderball" smashed all attendance records. Some of the decorative highlights of the Orpheum include six Pompeian friezes in the lobby and the magnificent 15-foot, one-ton chandelier in the theater.

As we matured, our favorite genre of movies was international intrigue featuring heroes like James Bond and Matt Helm. Sean Connery and Dean Martin seemed to be the essence of cool, and there was a whiff of sex that was titillating to our pubescent libidos and more gratifying than leering at our fathers' Herb Alpert "Whipped Cream and Other Delights" album covers.

Our crew also loved the femme fatales in movies like "How to Murder Your Wife" (Verna Lisi), "A Shot in the Dark" (Elke Sommer), and "Cat Ballou" (Jane Fonda). We admired these beautiful and voluptuous women from the safety of our theater seats. However, had we met a woman like that face to face, we would have run home to our mommies.

We may have talked a good game but, in reality, we felt more comfortable with winsome, wholesome Minnesota girls our own age. The gang also enjoyed other types of movies such as "The Great Escape," "A Hard Day's Night" and "PT 109." We went with our families to see movies like "Dr. Zhivago," "How the West Was Won," "Music Man" and

"The Sound of Music." It was okay to be seen with your parents and little sister at the neighborhood theater when going to see blockbusters.

■ ■ ■

The squad often visited the Downtown Bowl. We felt as if we were entering a black-and-white film noir set descending the stairs and emerging at the bottom into the bowling alley. The place was enveloped in a blue haze of cigarette and cigar smoke and inhabited by the residents of the nearby hotel. Just like the rest of our Hennepin Avenue destinations, the Downtown Bowl was safe enough, if not spiritually uplifting.

The posse minds its own business and was polite to everyone, kindly rebuffing the random panhandling drunk whose faulty radar mistook us for men of means. Half the fun, though, was surreptitiously imitating the characters we encountered and adding new words and phrases to our lexicon. The more scatological and ribald the better.

Finally, no downtown excursion was complete without a stop at A & B Sporting Goods, Shinders and Rifle Sport. A & B had the widest assortments of sporting goods in the Twin Cities. We cruised the aisles and admired the baseball gloves and bats and all the hockey equipment.

Shinders, may it rest in peace, was a newsstand but so much more in the depth and breadth of its offerings. They sold every newspaper imaginable – domestic and international. They had rows of paperback novels and magazines ranging from *Archie* comic books to the tawdry *Humping Housewives*. Baseball cards, candy and gum were located by the cash registers. We tiptoed into the adults-only back room and perused the large collection of lascivious literature. We gawked until we were booted out. The whole atmosphere gave us a glimpse of what we thought New York City must be like.

Rifle Sport was the favorite stop of our downtown routine. It was located on Hennepin, sandwiched in between the fleabag Rand Hotel and a slew of bars. The alluring marquee lights featured pulsating bulls' eyes on each end and were nearly impossible to resist as we walked by. A wall-mounted fortune-telling machine greeted us inside the door.

There was a large assortment of arcade games including two styles of bowling: one featured a swiveling cast-iron bowler controlled with a knob. The other used a metal puck that slid across the wood surface toward the pins that retracted into the machine, depending on your aim.

We had to watch where we rested our hands as the automatic puck return could smash our fingers.

There were race car games and a hockey game with two spinning metal men, one at each end. A large machine-gun-mounted, World War I-style aircraft was used to pelt battleships and planes in our favorite shooting machine. The baseball game had background noises and lighted base runners circled around the bases on the playing field. A basketball game had two players with badly chipped paint-mottled bodies. Your player was on offense and the defender kept thrusting his arms upward in an effort to stuff your shot.

In the middle of the main room were a change booth and office, a photo bay and a small chamber where anyone could create their own record. The recording was played back at high volume before the machine spit it out. No swearing was allowed during a rendition of "Louie, Louie" lest some skinny guy with a sleeveless, dirty white t-shirt and a surgically attached cigarette would confiscate it.

The old-school wood pinball machines were in the back and could not be used by minors as they were considered gambling contrivances. The vintage machines were the classic two-flipper type, not the multiple-flipper styles found today. Since Rifle Sport was always our final destination, we had to make certain we saved enough change for bus fare home.

It took some time for our eyes to adjust to the bright summer sun beating down on the sidewalk when we emerged from the arcade. We split up and walked to our various bus stops as the refracted heat and light shimmered off the surface of Hennepin's blacktop.

Arthur Fruen's car broke through the ice on Minnetonka's Upper Lake on New Year's day 1930. The incident was featured on the *Minneapolis Tribune*'s front page on January 5.
Photo courtesy of Minneapolis Tribune

Winter on the Big Water

FRUEN'S AUTO BREAKS THROUGH ICE
AT MINNETONKA: SIX RESCUED

Alderman Fruen's party took a short cut across the ice to save time. It was a short cut that ended in catastrophe when 200 feet from shore the ice broke and the car, stuck in a crevice, began to sink. Only Mr. Fruen's quick thinking saved the day. He put the children on the roof of the slowly sinking car. Rescuers arrived just in time, and the party walked a plank to safety after their icy bath.

Front Page, *Minneapolis Tribune*, January 5, 1930

MY GRANDFATHER, MY FATHER and his two brothers, Dick and Bruce, spent New Year's Day at Big Island and were making an intermediate stop on the Upper Lake before heading home to 56 Russell. Following a "road" in the snow, the car hit a depression in the ice and partially sank. After his heroics, Arthur had frostbitten legs; the children were said to suffer from "nervous shock." When another vehicle tried to pull the car out, the chain snapped and the half- submerged auto fell to the lake bottom approximately twenty feet below the surface.

By mid-winter there are ruts in the snow resembling roads to various points. Whenever we drove across the ice from Excelsior to Crown Point, my father insisted we keep our hands on the handles, holding the door slightly ajar. One day I asked him why. He explained that if the doors are closed, water pressure prevents one from opening them if the car is submerged. This was sufficient to satisfy my curiosity until I learned of the icy ordeal he survived at the age of ten.

Driving on frozen lakes obviously involves some inherent risks. Minnetonka's lakescape is a collection of twenty-nine "kettle lakes,"

177

or bays, many connected by channels. Underwater currents can cause variances in ice thickness. Shifting winds and compressed ice ridges can create open water, and every winter there are deaths from cars plunging into the icy depths. If drowning is not the cause, hypothermia is.

A uniform ice thickness of twelve inches is considered safe for driving on Lake Minnetonka. The speed limit for cars and trucks is 50-miles-per-hour during daylight hours and 30-miles-per-hour at night. Close to shore and ice houses, the maximum speed allowed is 25. There have been DUI arrests made on the frozen waters of the Upper Midwest. A man was arrested on Wisconsin's Lake Winnebago while sitting in his car. The vehicle was stopped 300 yards from the shore with a blown tire. The driver registered .365 on the Breathalyzer, more than four-and-one-half times the legal limit.

■ ■ ■

"Ice fishing is no longer cold. Stay at a nice resort, eat a delicious breakfast, take heated ice transportation to your fish house. When you arrive, the fish house is on fish, the thermostat is set at 70 degrees, and the holes are drilled and cleaned. You're ready to fish." (Joe Henry, *Lake of the Woods Tourism*)

Had I known one could enjoy upscale amenities on the ice, I may have been more interested in the sport. Today the serious, ice anglers can enjoy luxurious accommodations bigger and nicer than our family room at home. The most tricked-out feature sleeping quarters, a kitchen, bathroom, big-screen television, high-end sound system and perhaps a ping pong table.

My experiences are less elaborate. When I was six or seven my father drove me across frozen Pelican Lake to a low-tech ice shanty where a friend was fishing with the simple jigstick he shook up and down to attract crappies, sunfish or the occasional walleye. He may have been using a minnow or a Swedish Pimple lure. I was losing interest when a turn of events turned into one of my young life's most vivid memories.

A large fish slowly entered the field of vision. Dad's friend dropped his jigstick and grabbed the spear resting in the corner of the shack. He expertly thrust it downward and pulled it back with the attached rope. Impaled was a large rough fish, perhaps a Buffalo Fish. He removed it from the tines and tossed it outside.

Fascinated by dead things, I watched in awe as the fish was frozen stiff before it hit the snow in double-digit, sub-zero temperatures. I inspected the unappealing creature and the spear holes in its body. On the way back to terra firma I rode a battered gun-metal-grey snow saucer tied to our car bumper. Like water skiing, with a little body English I could venture outside the vehicle's "wake" into fresh snow. *"First off, there's a certain thrill to a sport where you hang a couple of ice picks attached to a rope around your neck so that if you fall through the ice you can claw your way out. Tennis just doesn't have that kind of adrenaline rush... There's all manner of electronics, tackle, heated vests, heated socks and if the ice picks don't give you a sense of security, there's a $199 'float coat'—an insulated jacket that doubles as a flotation device if you go through the ice."* (Tim Krohn, "Grumpy Old Men on the Ice," *Free Press*)

The sport, foreign to many, is so entrenched in Minnesota's winter culture that I thought nothing of heading to a friend's icehouse to fish in his "four-holer" while watching a hockey game on television. His directions were simple. *"It's the pink stucco house halfway between the Tonka Bay point and Gale's Island. You can't miss it."* One learns to layer their clothing when ice fishing, and it's not the fashionable type of layering. The labels are not haute couture: a pair of Gopher Glove chopper mitts and Mukluks – moccasins on steroids favored by Eskimos and the Inuit to trudge through snow, water and slush. A variety of rumpled t-shirts and sweatshirts from the corner of the closet, some long underwear, jeans, a parka and a beer company giveaway stocking cap complete the ensemble. This type of preparation, however, is way too fussy for me. I am more of a heated icehouse aficionado, not the sit-outside-on-an-upside-down-bucket-and-shiver type.

■ ■ ■

The first improvement my grandparents made at their newly acquired Crown Point property was a stone building of Swiss design on the waterfront to use as a base of operations in winter. The two-story "Chalet" was erected in the early 1930s with some furniture and a large fireplace on the lower level. The upper level was utilized mostly for storage. Our family would venture there once or twice every winter, but the most memorable visit came on New Year's Day 1967.

Our plans included a "picnic" and a viewing of the Cowboys and

The cottage in winter
Fruen family photo

Packers championship football game. That day became the coldest in Green Bay history. The temperature was -13 at kick-off, and conditions deteriorated as the contest wore on with the wind making it feel like -50 by game's end as the rays of the sun dipped behind Lambeau Field and shadows blanketed the stadium. The University of Wisconsin-Eau Claire marching band gamely tried to perform but had to stop after the woodwind instruments froze, metal mouthpieces stuck to lips and seven members were taken to the hospital and treated for hypothermia. An elderly spectator died from exposure.

After referee Norm Schacter tore the skin from his lips after removing the whistle from his mouth, it was decided the officials would use hand signals instead. CBS commentator Frank Gifford quipped, *"I'm going to take a bite of my coffee."* Ed Gruver, in his book *The Ice Bowl*, wrote, *"The players had become gray, ghost-like figures moving at a slow, painful pace."* The Packers won in the final sixteen seconds.

The temperature was similar in Minneapolis without the brutal winds. This didn't stop us. After all, we were hardy Minnesotans! Mom, Dad and sister Martha decided we would make the jaunt to Crown

Point *al fresco* rather than by car. Brother Mike and wife Sandy joined the four of us. Some cross-country skied while others trudged behind, pulling Flexible Flyer sleds carrying the food, beverages and a small, old black-and-white television to watch the game.

Surprisingly, it was not an uncomfortable crossing. We were properly swaddled in winter gear with long underwear girding our loins, scarves wrapped around our faces and wool knit stocking caps pulled down well below our ears, leaving a slit for vision. The exertion from the two-mile trek kept us warm.

Upon reaching the Chalet a fire was started for warmth and cooking. The doors to the upstairs were closed to trap the heat. Dad chopped a hole in the ice for water to boil the bratwursts. Mike, Sandy and my parents were all great cooks and entertainers, and we had a summertime-style picnic. Potato salad, beans, cole slaw, chips and all the condiments made a great bratwurst meal. Most important to me was a healthy dollop of sauerkraut for my sandwich.

Hot chocolate and coffee were the only departures from the warmer-months' fare. More exotic culinary offerings were served but, at the age of fifteen, I was not a fan. I did enjoy pulling a prank, though. With no better rationale than this is the type of dumb thing brothers do, I moved the sled placed over the hole in the ice that prevented an unpleasant frigid bath, packed the opening with snow and smoothed it.

Like a moth to a flame, my sister stepped in the booby trap and executed an unplanned and painful version of the splits with her right leg plunging into the lake and her left leg stretching parallel to the lake's frozen surface. When she was rescued and pulled from the hole, Martha's right pant leg immediately froze stiff. I was told to give her my jeans, and I spent most of the afternoon in my long underwear while waiting for her Levi's – draped over the fire screen – to thaw and dry. While anxious to get my pants back, I was not the most popular family member that day.

■ ■ ■

Every few years the ice conditions (early cold with little to no snow) are perfect for a variety of sports on Minnetonka. A more or less smooth surface is perfect for skating or hockey, although an errant pass can result in a long chase, particularly against a stiff wind, as the puck skitters

Crown Point waterfront in winter
Fruen family photo

into the distance. In very cold temperatures skate blades squeak due to the greater difficulty of creating friction and the resulting thin line of water that allows the skater to glide.

Skate sailing is exhilarating and a little daunting. The skater holds a large kite-shaped sail propelled by the wind and controls the direction and speed by shifting the angle. Some sails have a vinyl window that allows a view of what otherwise would be the blindside. I loved the out-of-control feeling but knew I could toss the sail at any time to coast to a more manageable speed.

Ice boating, known as *"hard-water sailing,"* is another winter sport not for the weak of heart. The boat frame is supported by three long, sharply honed runners and steered with a shorter one. Speeds of over 100-miles-per-hour have been reached by the Skeeter class of ice boats. Regattas and races used to be held on the Big Water with discarded Christmas trees serving as markers for the slalom course. Minnetonka hosted a memorable contest in 1890 between a team from Lake Pepin (a widening of the Mississippi south of St. Paul) and the home entry.

The Lake Pepin team used a heavy vessel named *Cyclone* and a lighter style with silk sails, the *Phoebe*. Minnetonka countered with a *"jack rabbit"* boat, the *What-not,* piloted by George Bassett with his teenage sister Nancy acting as his crew. During the deciding race, George slipped on the ice at the start, and the *What-not* left without him. Nancy navigated the blustery winds alone and finished first.

Once in a blue moon, conditions conspire to create "black ice." A slow freeze, no wind or snow, no nearby springs or currents and perfect timing combine to set the stage for nature's gift. Ice crystals form in a vertical, uniform and parallel manner, allowing light to penetrate. It takes days to complete the process, and the trickiest part of enjoying the beauty of black ice is being in the right place at the right time. The unblemished surface is fleeting.

The clarity and smoothness is remarkable as fish swim below you, and the smallest of rocks are visible on the lake bottom. Moving further from shore, the surface turns jet black as the water depth prevents the light from penetrating. Minnetonka becomes a sculptor's studio as blades carve the ice into geometric patterns. Behind the skater the ice is marred, but ahead lies a mile or two of unblemished perfection. The sensation is other worldly, giving the impression of skating on a black cloud.

Organized sports tournaments are held on the ice and snow. Softball is popular, and orange balls are used for obvious reasons. The Wayzata Chilly Open *"takes all that's stuffy about golf and inverts it for a come one, come all engagement. No golf experience or clubs required— anything from hockey sticks to canoe paddles will suffice, so long as it can drive a tennis ball down an icy fairway. Argyle knickers? Nah. Chilly Open etiquette is to dress as foolishly as possible while taking to the tundra."* (Jerard Fagerberg, *Minnesota Monthly*)

Other activities include a Chili cook-off between ten or so restaurants and "Snowga" classes on the frozen lake. Yoga in the snow.

The North American Pond Hockey Championship is held in January in Excelsior Bay with the proceeds from tickets, raffles and concerts donated to charity. There are twelve small-scaled rinks with over 70 teams and 700 players participating. The men's age groups range from Mites to an over-45 bracket with many ex-college players, ex pros, some women's teams and old timers lacing up the blades.

For those who embrace winter rather than fight it, there is a sled dog race called the Klondike Dog Derby that circumnavigates much of the southern Lower Lake shoreline. It begins in downtown Excelsior and ends with a circle around Gale's Island before heading back to the starting point.

St. Paul celebrates what may be Minnesota's top winter outdoor event. The city took umbrage at an 1885 New York newspaper report calling the Capital City "*another Siberia, unfit for human habitation.*" The Carnival was born in 1886 and celebrated its 135th anniversary in 2021. "*She was alone with this presence that came out of the North, the dreary loneliness that rose from ice-bound whalers in the Arctic seas, from smokeless, trackless wastes where were strewn the whitened bones of adventure. It was an icy breath of death; it was rolling down low across the land to clutch at her.*" (F. Scott Fitzgerald, *The Ice Palace*)

The prominent attraction is the Ice Palace that first appeared in 1886 after it was fashioned by 27,000 blocks of ice with a tower reaching 106 feet. The edifice inspired F. Scott Fitzgerald's short story that was based on his wife Zelda's unpleasant, frigid visit to St. Paul from Alabama. Her character, Sally Harper, ventures north to meet her fiancée's family and suffers from culture shock as she becomes lost in the maze of the Palace.

The early Winter Carnivals featured horse races and sledding contests on frozen St. Paul lakes. Bands of Dakota rode into town, pitched their tents and participated in the events. Activities have expanded over the decades to include outdoor concerts, parades, fireworks and ice-sculpture contests. During the National Hockey League All Star Game in 2004, the Bare Naked Ladies performed on an ice stage outside the Palace. They didn't play nude, and I spotted gloves on the hands of some of the Ontario lads.

King Boreas and Aurora, Queen of the Snows and their court are elected to preside over the festivities. St. Paul has set a high bar as an example of the possibilities of embracing winter rather than fighting it. City people sometimes are under the impression that they control nature when the opposite is true.

Winter on Minnetonka is not always just about recreation, particularly on an island. It is the most opportune time to bring building supplies across the lake by truck. Countless loads of rock, river stone, cement, wood and sand were dumped on top of Crown Point's hill and at the waterline during the 1920s, '30s and '40s to construct the various buildings taking shape in Grandpa's vision of our family retreat.

A different kind of icehouse was crucial to summer cabin life until electricity, refrigerators and freezers debuted on Crown Point and the rest of the island in 1940. While there was a limit to the lake's bounty of food and timber, there was an inexhaustible supply of ice to be harvested with little chance of crop failure.

The ice industry was important enough to merit its own magazine, *Cold Storage and Ice Trade Journal.* Eighteen-inch blocks of ice were cut, drilled, lifted by tongs and hauled by horse and wagon over the more gradual slope around the corner from Point Comfort to the ice shed shared with neighbors and shaded by the stand of Big Woods at the rear of the property. During the sweltering months of July and August, Big Island children sought refuge there and welcomed the whisper of winter cooling the perishables and the possibility of uncovering a ripe watermelon among the sawdust, hay and ice.

Earliest Glenwood-Inglewood delivery wagon.
One horse until tandem teams were introduced.
Old postcard

Crown Point Critters

*"I am fond of pigs. Dogs look up to us. Cats look
down on us. Pigs treat us as equals."*

W.C. Fields

AT FIRST GLANCE, BIG Island has a pedestrian variety of animals. Over the decades, deer antlers have been found but never the bucks that sported them. The winter ice provides an escape route and apparently the closely spaced trees of the Big Woods outlier are not to their liking. There are squirrels, raccoons and a variety of birds. Cardinals, black-capped chickadees, woodpeckers and finches visit feeders and hummingbirds hover to drink sugar water from red platters. Baltimore orioles flock to an orange half sitting on a railing. Great-horned owls can be heard if not seen.

Exotic birds lived in the large aviary at the Big Island Amusement Park when it opened in 1906 courtesy of Robert "Fish" Jones. He was given the nickname he loathed after operating a fish market for ten years at Hennepin Avenue and 16th Street in Minneapolis. He was one of the city's great characters, wearing a silk top hat and sporting a Van Dyke beard while walking in elevator boots to mitigate his short stature.

Jones promenaded around the downtown area in a Prince Albert suit accompanied by massive white Russian wolfhounds. He was a devoted amateur ornithologist with an extensive knowledge of birds and was hired to travel to Europe and acquire a selection of fascinating winged creatures for the park.

Ring-necked pheasants, native to China, were introduced in Minnesota when a game farm was established on Big Island for breeding purposes in 1915. The Minneapolis Street Railway Company donated the abandoned park land and old wood to construct the pens for hatching and rearing. The old buildings were renovated for management.

Robert "Fish" Jones, amateur zoologist and proprietor
of the Longfellow Zoological Garden. *Old postcard*

Big Island in Lake Minnetonka to Be Used as a Game Preserve

All that portion of Big Island, Lake Minnetonka, owned by the Street Railway company, will be used next spring and summer for a preserve for game bird breeding.

Frank D. Blair, field secretary of the Minnesota Game and Fish Protective league, obtained the necessary permission from C. G. Goodrich yesterday.

Ducks, pheasants and many other game birds are to be raised in pens on the island.

Big Island game farm announced. *Photo courtesy of of Minneapolis Tribune*

Ruffed grouse and bobwhite quail were also raised, but breeding ring-necks was the top priority.

The project was extremely successful with adults released into the wild and eggs distributed to farmers and hunters to raise and release. Eventually the farm was bulging at the seams and the birds were taken from the island and moved to a 200-acre site on the Upper Lake in Mound, Minnesota. In thirteen years, the farm released 25,000 pheasants into the wild.

Minnesota's inaugural pheasant-hunting season was in 1924, for Hennepin, Scott and Carver counties only, and the sport has grown exponentially from the small experiment starting with forty hens and ten roosters on Big Island. If an Ancestry.com existed for pheasants, the birds of Minnesota and the Dakotas could trace their genealogy back to Lake Minnetonka.

■ ■ ■

I was a budding zoologist as a child and collected frogs, toads, garter snakes and maybe a grasshopper or two, placing them in a cardboard box after creating what I perceived to be an appealing environment. The deal forged with my parents was predicated on the release of my captives by sunset, and a no-critters-in-the-house codicil although, on occasion, a frog was found in the dog's water dish in the morning.

One spring, when I was not much more than a baby, a thunderstorm separated a raccoon kit from its mother and was adopted by our family. Grandfather named it "Kefauver" after the Tennessee senator who first gained fame for his investigations into juvenile delinquency and organized crime.[*]

■ ■ ■

Our pet had the full run of Crown Point and would scramble up the legs of my high chair to battle me for my breakfast. He would also scrap with my mother's Pekingese, DeeDee, for her food. One might wonder

---

[*] During a primary battle in 1948, Kefauver's opponent, E.H. Crump (the head of Minnesota's Democratic Party) accused Estes Kefauver of being in league with "pinkos and communists" while acting like a sneaky raccoon. The Yale Law School graduate donned a coonskin hat and countered, "*I may be a pet coon, but I'm not Boss Crump's coon.*"

Keyfauver, our orphaned pet raccoon
Fruen family photo

why my mother and father were so *laissez faire*. They were the opposite of helicopter parents and let their children take their lumps. The Fruens espoused the theory of "no blood no foul." My older cousins tricked Kefauver by giving him a sugar cube, then following him to the waterfront to wash it, only to see the treat disappear.

We had our share of pesky Minnesota summer insects, but I was fascinated by the beautiful dragonflies often perched on my fishing line. There are about 140 species of the iridescently colored creatures in the state, and fossilized ancestors dating back 325 million years have been discovered. The four-winged dragonfly can fly up to 30-miles-per-hour and hovers, glides, moves forward and backward and up and down like a helicopter.

The insect's presence is indicative of good water quality. Its large compound eyes provide an almost 360-degree field of vision, which aids its voracious appetite. They consume large quantities of mosquitoes, a skill that should make the dragonfly revered in the Upper Midwest. Once I was amused to see two of them flying in tandem, linked together, until my older, wiser cousin Tommy explained what they were doing.

■ ■ ■

Farm animals were a common site on Crown Point during the 1920s, '30s and '40s. Every spring our island neighbor, Albert Scriver, would begin a two-day hike from Minneapolis with the family cow and dog to Huntington Point in Tonka Bay where the mainland is closest to Big Island's Recreation Point. They were met by a rowboat, and Albert would hold the rope while the cow swam the short distance.

They continued their journey through swampy terrain, thick woods, over hills and across the channel until they reached their destination. The cow was then allowed to roam with a bell around its neck until it was milking time. The cow is long gone, but the Scrivers still have the bell and use it to signal mealtime.

In the spring, Grandfather purchased 100 chicks that he kept in a straw-lined corner of the garage in the city under an electric heating cover and contained by a six-inch-tall fence. There was often a line of neighbor children eager to look at the chicks. Grandpa did not discourage them as he felt it was good for the birds to get acclimated to humans. When spring temperatures rose, the chicks were given access to the backyard at 56 Russell, which was more bucolic than the garage.

At the close of the school year, the surviving 85 or 90 chicks were transported to Crown Point by boat and lived in the cement-floor chicken coop – known as the Chicken House – below the Workman's Cabin. The birds stayed in a fenced yard for the first few weeks, adjusting to the change in venue. They were then allowed to roam until night when they retreated into the Chicken House to be safe from raccoons and the occasional weasel. One day Great-grandmother Emerson heard scratching at the back screen-door of the cottage and opened it to find a hen. The chicken walked right in, went to a corner of the back porch and laid an egg. This routine was repeated throughout the summer.

During the World War II years, Grandpa brought four or five piglets to the island and slaughtered them every fall. This augmented the family's meat rations, and he enjoyed another animal-husbandry experience. The process was gruesome. In the autumn, the pigs were stunned with a bolt pistol, then hung on a hook to drain the blood after cutting the carotid artery. The head was removed, the carcass cut in half, washed and the butchering begun. Most of the meat was transferred to the large walk-in freezer in Bryn Mawr.

The experience was unpleasant for everyone, particularly the pigs, but Uncle Doug tried to benefit by making a football from a discarded bladder. His mother told him that is why they call them "pigskins." What Grandma did not tell him is that the bladder needed to be emptied first. Doug doused himself with urine. At least the chickens were pleased by the whole process as a bit of pigs' blood was added to their feed and drove them into a frenzy.

One year a ham dinner was interrupted when one of the adults, in a sterling example of too much information, told the children they were eating "green ham." The expression, now all but vanished from the vernacular, did not refer to the color but the difference between a fresh ham and a cured one. Aunt Louise recalls her initial revulsion but was mollified by the fact that a fresh (or green) ham is generally the entire hind leg of a pig and is very tender. Satisfied by the explanation, she continued her meal.

The goats were a hazard. The kids head-butted in play, but the adults meant business when their territory was breached. Getting between them and their food was another bad idea. The younger Fruens stayed on high alert while outside.

■ ■ ■

Both my parents grew up in households with a menagerie of dogs and cats, and a few stand out in the annals of Crown Point. The first Fruen dog to roam the island was Bugsy, a Boston terrier named for his bulging eyes and mobster Bugsy Siegel. He did not live long, succumbing to Canine Epilepsy.

Next came Skeets I, a shepherd-setter mix, followed by Skeets II, a Llewelyn Setter. Skeets II was really Uncle Doug's dog. My uncle played hide-and-seek with Skeets II by heading into the dense woods and climbing a tree after giving Skeets a firm "STAY" command. After a half-hour or so, Grandma would release the dog and encourage him to, "Go find Douglas!" He made a beeline for his master deep in the Big Woods. When Skeets II became old and feeble, Grandma and Grandpa waited for my uncle to return from Naval Officer's Training in San Diego so he could say goodbye to his pet before it was euthanized.

DeeDee, a Chinese Pekingese, was the first pet of my immediate family that I recall. My only Big Island memories of her come from photographs, usually involving a tussle with Kefauver the raccoon. There is a picture of the Pekingese nestled in the cockpit of the family sailboat, which gave her credibility as a Crown Point dog. The pedigree was developed as a companion to the ancient Chinese royal family. DeeDee was a nickname coined by my father, referring to Damn Dog. She did have the imperious manner of her breed after serving the elite for centuries but was pugnacious to a level way above her weight class.

After DeeDee our family acquired Suzie, a chocolate-colored miniature poodle whose scrappy personality belied the reputation of the breed. She loved chasing balls of any kind, a habit that almost ended her life one summer day on Big Island. We were playing baseball in the hollow and, after my friend tossed the ball in the air to hit it, Suzie jumped to catch it and was hit squarely in the head by the bat. She dropped to the ground unconscious.

Dad brought her out back behind the old pig pen, certain she was mortally injured. He pushed on her chest and resuscitated the poodle. She was wobbly at first but slowly regained her coordination.

Two days later we were returning to the island from Excelsior when Suzie, snapping at the water spray, leaned too far over the right stern gunwale and fell into the lake. Dad was running the *Queen Merrie* at full throttle and, when we noticed her absence, she was far behind. The dog swam in three tight circles to orient herself and headed for Crown Point. We turned back and plucked her from the lake. Suzie was no worse for wear.

Suzie was not a water dog but was active and often on the move. One day I noticed her running around the waterfront with my fishing rod and reel in tow. She had chomped on the piece of breakfast bacon I had pierced through the hook. Greatly alarmed, I tried to remove the hook from her gum but had no luck.

Skeets II patrols the Crown Point waterfront
Fruen family photo

Great-grandmother Emerson guiding her one horse open sleigh
Fruen family photo

As a last resort I asked Dad to intervene. Any concern I had of his displeasure was alleviated by his enthusiasm for the project. He was a frustrated veterinarian or ER surgeon and reveled in tweezing bee stingers, ingrown toenails and splinters from his children, nephews, nieces and grandchildren. My father took a pair of pliers from the tackle box and snipped the barbed end from the hook, easily pulling the rest from Suzie's mouth. I was impressed not only by his skill but also his passion.

A few years later for reasons unknown to me, we picked up an Old English Sheep Dog that was registered as Princess Mink-A-Rug. She had spent the first six months of her life in the lobby of the downtown Minneapolis Radisson Hotel and was an undisciplined, whirling dervish of white-and-gray dog hair.

Her crazy personality was enhanced by her mismatched eyes: one dark brown and the other light blue. Princess loved the water, jumping in and dog paddling to us only to leave red welts on our backs from her frantic scratching. She barked at virtually everything. She was an annoying dog that was not Big Island material in my book.

We had to monitor the dogs as we battened down the hatches of the *Queen Merrie* before our car ride home from Minnetonka. Suzie and Princess had a knack for locating and rolling over dead fish. This made for an unpleasant but – thankfully – short trip back to the city.

■ ■ ■

I tried to construct a small pond under the lip of the chalet balcony to hold my catches of panfish but, no matter how tightly and high I piled the stones, the fish always escaped. One summer we acquired ten mallard ducklings and kept them in a covered pen built in my old panfish-holding area. They shared it with the blue-black mud wasps that built nests underneath the Chalet ledge overhang.

They were sheltered from predators like owls and raccoons and ate insects, water plants and feed pellets specially concocted at the Fruen Mill. The ducks were great entertainers. Every day we released them and took them for a swim as they dutifully followed us in formation behind the rowboat. A loud, smelly outboard motor would have been a deal-breaker.

Fall arrived, and we had a picnic at our next-door neighbors in Minneapolis. When I looked at my meal, I was horrified to find the grilled remains of one of my summer friends. In my first act of civil disobedience, I pushed the plate away.

As a child I was an obsessive little fisherman. At the start I went old-school with gear consisting of a small red wooden "dropline" spool around which the black string was wound. My first bobbers were the balsa wood "slip" style until I graduated to a classic Eagle Claw round, red-and-white plastic design. Ross was moving up in the fishing world, if only on Big Island.

When Dad was convinced that I was serious about the hobby, he bought me a Zebco starter spinning rod and reel with nylon line. I was very pleased but also understood my father had an ulterior motive. The metal casing over the reel made it almost impossible to turn the line into a tangled mess.

My preferred bait was a succulent earthworm, and I knew just where to find them. Right between where the last slab of pig-pen concrete ended and the Big Woods began, the soil was extremely black and fertile, covered by a layer of last autumn's rotting leaves. That was where the worms lurked.

As a boy I used a red Hills Brothers coffee can to house my bait and kept it right next to the bar of soap Grandfather used for his daily bath in the lake. At the end of the season I liberated the surviving worms and put the can in its winter location, a shelf just inside the door of the upper level of the Chalet.

Minnetonka remains a first-class fishery for large and smallmouth bass, panfish, northern pike and muskie, the *"freshwater barracuda,"* that can reach 50 inches in length and over 50 pounds. When landed it is a large angry boatmate. Seventy percent of a muskie's diet consists of fish but muskrats, mice, frogs and even ducklings are often consumed. In alternate years, walleye and muskie are stocked in Minnetonka.

■ ■ ■

Carp were introduced in the 1880s and have been a target for extermination ever since. Once, some of the older Fruen boys caught a carp and affixed an empty Glenwood-Inglewood plastic gallon spring-water jug to the body of the fish. As it swam away, the carp was visible for a long time with its personal buoy keeping it close to the surface. Besides being butt ugly, the common carp wreak havoc in lakes with game fish.

They also uproot vegetation, which destroys habitat by stirring sediment. This hurts water clarity and releases nutrients that promote the spread of green algae.

In 2018, the Minnesota Department of Natural Resources began a ten-year program, named *Carpicide,* to remove carp from Lake Minnetonka by using specialized nets that were baited with cracked corn to attract the fish. Barriers have been installed to block access to spawning grounds. Some carp have been taken to the Wildlife Science Center in Stacy, Minnesota, to feed the wolves.

In the beginning, I just fished off the dock that provided excellent cover for panfish and the occasional largemouth bass (the basic hog-jawed, bucketmouth variety). The sunfish I could handle, but a bass on the line required assistance. They did not go quietly.

Dad coached me and made sure I learned how to set a hook and not let the fish swallow it. Eventually I learned the concept of catch-and-release. Dad taught me how to scale, clean and debone a fish. Anything I caught was to be cleaned and eaten or put back in the water. I learned sportsmanship and conservation, even if the lessons were a bit self-directed. Who wants to spend an afternoon with a Rapala filet knife and smelly fish when the sun is shining and the water is a perfect summer temperature?

■ ■ ■

Uncle Dick, Aunt Margaret and their four children spent most of the summer on Big Island when I was growing up. Aunt Margaret was the most avid, patient and proficient angler in our family. She fished whenever the boat traffic was minimal, usually in the morning or at dusk. She always wore shorts and some sort of light jacket with a cigarette dangling from her lower lip as her only accessory.

She could speak perfectly well as she multi-tasked - casting, smoking and talking – and many boats stopped by our dock if Aunt Margaret was flipping a lure. They wanted advice, tips, hotspots and maybe some island gossip. She was the Oracle of Crown Point.

To this day, Lake Minnetonka ranks as one of the top bass-fishing destinations in the country. In May 2020, *Bass Angler Magazine* ranked the Big Water #8 in its annual "Top Ten Bass Fishing Spots in the U.S." Minnetonka hosts big-time professional bass-fishing tournaments.

Grandpa Arthur displays his catch
Fruen family photo

One of my most cherished fishing memories is an early morning summer outing with my older cousin Ricky. We awoke at dawn and, after a quick breakfast, we took one of the smaller boats to the Big Island channel, turned right into the small lagoon and beached the small craft on the sand. I snapped a classic top-water lure, the Jitterbug, to my leader.

A double-cupped metal lip made the bait shift from side to side on the retrieve, creating a motion that bass find very appealing. That early morning, the lure was irresistible. I aimed the first cast at the closest edge of some lily pads. I felt this was a good strategy as the largemouth bass and many other species use cover to launch attacks on smaller victims.

I overshot my target, and the Jitterbug landed on the far side of the vegetation. However, a large Bucketmouth, looking for a frog breakfast, hit the lure like a ton of bricks. My Jitterbug didn't even have a chance to jitter. As I reeled in the line, I had to drag the fish back *through the garden*" and had a sinking feeling as the bass offered no resistance. The lure was covered with green seaweed, leaves and water lilies, but underneath the flora was a four-pound bass. It had managed to be snagged by both sets of treble hooks and was rendered helpless.

I was prepared for disappointment but was surprised and pleased to discover the fish was still attached to my lure under all the aquatic vegetation. I landed that bass.

Ricky and I moved to the south side of the channel. I hooked another nice-sized largemouth, but fumbled it and, after a single bounce on the sand, the fish escaped back into the water. As we headed back to Crown Point, my cousin complimented me on my prized catch. Excitedly I replied, *"Yes, and I almost caught the other one!"*

Rick responded, *"We don't talk about the ones that get away."*

The 1991 Halloween Blizzard dropped 28.4" of snow in Minneapolis.
Photo courtesy of Star Tribune

Minneapolis: City of Frozen Lakes

"Good morning, good morning!
Sunbeams will soon shine through
Good morning, good morning to you!"

Nacio Herb Brown and Arthur Freed,
GOOD MORNING

I WOKE TO THIS loathsome, insipid, insidiously cheerful song blaring from my parents' clock radio every school morning for twelve years. I think the dial was glued to 830 WCCO on the AM band. The station was a nationally recognized force. At any time during the morning, half of the listening public in the market tuned into the station. At night the clear channel signal was so strong that I was able to listen to North Stars hockey games from my fifth-floor dorm room atop a Vermont hill. Pilots flying over Minneapolis and St. Paul saw most of the lights in the homes below shut off in unison after WCCO's thirty-year on-air veteran, Cedric Adams, wrapped up his 10:00 PM news report.

WCCO was the go-to source for weather information, corny humor and school-closing reports that was the only part of the programming that piqued my interest. I was always disappointed when my school was not mentioned. Minneapolis knew how to move snow and no attention was paid to the dangerous, double-digit negative temperatures often experienced in January and February. The end result was fewer snow days off than one might expect.

The "Good Morning" song was preceded by Maynard Speece's Farm Report, which Dad followed religiously as it pertained directly to his livelihood. Maynard gave listeners pork belly futures pricing, and every other imaginable commodity, from South St. Paul and Chicago. Speece was so dedicated to his job that he gave his report one Monday morning in April 1968 from his Redwood Falls hospital bed. The day before he had visited Bob Starr's Cedar Rock Ranch, and a horse kicked him in the ankle, an injury requiring 22 stitches.

During elementary school I rode a bus resembling an orange shoe box to Breck School on the west bank of the Mississippi River. Before I began first grade, my mother and I made a trial run to my bus stop, which was located 2-1/2 blocks from home on a blind curve and across the perilously busy Diamond Lake Road. After that I was on my own. In winter the wait seemed interminable and the ride was fraught with danger as I had to avoid the big kids who skulked in the back. The older boys offered details on the intricacies of sex. All of it was wrong. By the time I exited the bus, I was already tired and often very confused.

■ ■ ■

The heat was cranked up in the classrooms, and I often struggled to pay attention while fighting off an involuntary nap. My classmates and I looked forward to music and winter sports like hockey, wrestling and basketball. I played hockey and in the days of outdoor rinks spent hours of time shoveling snow to give the varsity team a clean sheet for their practice.

Our headmaster, F. Douglas Henderson, was a canon in the Episcopal Church and a Canadian by birth. He told a group of hockey parents, anxious for some indoor hockey facilities, that they needed to build him a chapel before a hockey arena would become a priority. He kept his word and, by my sophomore year, we dropped the shovels and grabbed

Early hockey on Lake *Bde Maka Ska*
Courtesy of Vintage Minnesota Hockey

our sticks, but not before we had had our daily all-school get-together in the simple beauty of the stone, wood and glass Chapel of the Holy Spirit.

Lunch was a respite for most although not for the underclassmen rotating in and out of the job of "biddy," which was a euphemism for "waiter." Delivering the food and taking the carnage away was the least of a biddy's worries. I breathed a sigh of relief if I were assigned to a table with a pleasant senior at the helm who didn't make me eat my vegetables. There was pressure to be at the front of the biddy line and there was a bit of hand-to-hand combat and shoving and pushing involved. The students were hungry and restless; waiting for food did not play well. The bland menu was rotated but not totally predictable except for Friday's fare of fish sticks.

Study hall was an oasis later in the day. We could choose to read a book, play chess or study. As a seventh grader, the essence of *savoir-faire* was to go to the open period armed with a dog-eared James Bond paperback in one blazer pocket and a magnetic chess board in the other. Studying was the least popular option. And, yes, we were the antithesis of cool.

The general consensus deemed *The Spy Who Loved Me* the raciest tome in Ian Fleming's Bond body of work. Despite the standards and watchful eyes of the faculty and administration, there were still plenty of chances for mischief. We were not angels.

■ ■ ■

Between classes when we went to exchange books, professional wrestling bouts were reenacted with the victims flung into the locker doors serving as metal "ropes" in our make-believe ring. Bodies bounced, and the sound reverberated down the hall. Tie knots were cinched up so tightly by marauders that the victims sheepishly headed to the bookstore where the beleaguered Mrs. Kellogg cut the ruined cravat with her pinking shears.

One learned who to avoid as the younger Upper School students tiptoed to the relative safety of the next classroom. Someone always had a broken leg or ankle, so the unwitting spent the school day sporting the dusty imprint of a rubber crutch tip on the back of their black blazer. Fart jokes helped relieve the boredom of studying Chaucer, Dante and Donne.

Armpit and hand-powered impersonations were *de rigueur*. In elementary school we took the 3:30 bus home, which was more enjoyable than the morning trip. The older boys involved in sports took the 5:00 bus, which gave the younger riders a respite.

My Breck School years were a dichotomy of strict behavioral and academic standards coupled with progressive, intellectual freedom. At the start of classes every year, we looked around to see who didn't pass muster and was not invited to return. Morning chapel was a mixture of hymns, a sermon, announcements and often guest speakers including U.S. congressmen and other notables.

■ ■ ■

The person who most embodied the spirit of Breck during my era was Major John Hudson, an Englishman with an impressive mustache decorating his stiff upper lip. He was part of the British Expeditionary Force at the Battle of Dunkirk and bore the wounds he suffered on his arm.

I am not certain of his title, but Upper School Head Disciplinarian would be a good description. Major Hudson commanded respect and didn't pull his punches when a miscreant drew his attention. He had a good sense of humor, though, and left you with just enough encouragement, and an implied wink, to think there might be hope for you yet. The more serious indiscretions were handled by our indecipherable headmaster. Canon Henderson was a man who used silence as a tool, leaving his subject to sing like a bird in abject defeat.

The Major achieved his goal of becoming an ordained deacon in the Episcopal Church and served as a vessel of the bishop with an emphasis on social service. He also contracted incurable cancer. When he informed the student body of his illness, he reassured us that he was not afraid and "was no stranger to death," referring to the action he saw in World War II.

The entire Upper School attended his memorial service at the striking neo-Gothic St. Mark's Cathedral overlooking Loring Park at the fringe of downtown Minneapolis. The funeral was replete with the usual pomp and circumstance of a High Episcopal service with uplifting hymns like "Jesus Christ Has Risen Today" and "All Things Bright and Beautiful." The service was an unforgettable outpouring of love, sorrow, honor and gratitude.

■ ■ ■

Autumn in Minneapolis was a truncated prelude to winter. The football season started with crisp fall nights and often ended in snow flurries or something more substantial. I was a member of the Pearl Park Hawks in 5th and 6th grades. We played in the Minneapolis Park Board league against teams from other neighborhood parks. Some opponents were familiar, like the boys we met at YMCA Camp in the summer or those we played in other sports.

The Hawks practiced at the north end of Pearl Park on what was just a patch of grass rather than a lined football field. We were coached by a man named Sparky and his overqualified assistants. They knew their football, and our leader was perhaps the best motivator I have ever encountered. We would have climbed Mount Everest in our football cleats if asked.

Sparky was a vitamin salesman with a trunk-load of samples and a supply of small plaster "*dog bones*," painted gold that had "Our Hero" etched in the middle. They were handed out after games to the top performers. I wanted one badly and was eventually rewarded. I still have one in a box somewhere.

Night games were especially exciting. We had to "make weight" so injuries were minimized and, after the weigh-in, we proceeded to the field to warm up under the lights. Dad procured our white jerseys with red accents through a "deal." Maybe they were a bargain, because the jerseys were hockey-style, not football. I played offensive and defensive guard and was serviceable, making up for a lack of natural talent with effort and a high football IQ. I hung on the coaches' every word.

While I remember bits and pieces of some of the games, there was one that stands out in my memory. We played the Nicollet Park (now Martin Luther King Jr.) squad on their home field under the lights. They were an all-black team, and Sparky sensed some trepidation among his players. We certainly had met blacks before but not many children. The Nicollet team was well-drilled and even added some twists to their routine.

On the opening kick-off, they executed some call and response. When the kicker shouted, "*What do we eat?*" the other ten players responded, "*Raw meat!*" The place kicker replied, "*Let's go get some!*" and pounded the ball downfield. Before the game, Sparky had us huddle for the pep talk and, leaning in conspiratorially, said, "*These Negro kids are just like you with one difference. They hate to be tackled right below the knees.*" This, of course, was spurious by omission since tackling low was effective no matter the skin color.

Emboldened by this inside information, we took the field and won 14-2. And yes, we learned the Nicollet Park team was just like us. We had a great season and finished with a 5-3 record. I earned a gold "Our Hero" dog bone or two.

■ ■ ■

When the snow came, we returned to Minnehaha Creek, stood high on the south-side bluff and lobbed snowballs at cars heading east on the parkway. Once we pelted a police car and ran like the wind in different directions. The gang played tackle football on a 45-degree angle on the hill, plodding through deep snow, bouncing off the wooden slat-and-chicken-wire fence designed to prevent a mini avalanche from covering the road. Boot-hockey games were held at Steve's backyard rink with periodic timeouts to let his little sister Amy skate for a while.

There was a tree in the middle of the ice surface which we learned to use as a "pick" to frustrate our opponents. A league was formed with two-man teams sporting homemade jerseys. I was a Montreal Canadien. We ran up and down the ice chasing a ball fashioned from white hockey tape.

Minnesota is a hockey-crazy state and the sport helped our family tolerate the winter months. Growing up, I had skate issues. Dad must have been pinching pennies when he bought my first pairs. The source was the used skate department at Nicollet Hardware. I recall one pair that was so floppy that the boot offered the support of a thin leather wallet. This leads to the myth of "*weak ankles.*"

I am no physiologist, but the real problem is ill-fitting or poor-quality skates. Once I proved I was serious about the sport, my father opened his pocketbook and bought me new ones. At least I wasn't shamed into wearing hand-me-down figure skates or worse, white Bunny Hugs with little pom-poms. That was the expressway to derision.

Pearl Park featured a large open skating surface, two hockey rinks framed with rickety old boards and a warming house. The wide expanse of ice was perfect for races and games. Pom Pom Pull Away was popular as was the forbidden Crack the Whip, a more dangerous version of what you might have seen at an Ice Follies show.

Skaters were added one at a time to form "the whip" which was circling the center of the ice going faster and faster with each addition. Towards the end it became more difficult to catch up to the last link. It was thrilling, with an element of danger, as the immutable law of centrifugal force launched the final participant towards the heavily traveled Portland Avenue. The rink attendant eventually shut the game down, but it restarted when he skated off to deal with other rule breakers.

One of the hockey rinks was dedicated to the older, more skilled boys. Rink rats like me were relegated to the other surface. We practiced our shooting against the boards with the objective to make as loud a noise as possible when puck met wood. Lifting the disk off the ice was also a priority with backhand shots offering the best opportunity for success. When the objective was to impress a girl leaning over the boards, I set the puck on its edge which guaranteed lift-off.

Hockey games at Pearl Park were often held under severe conditions. Our "bench" was a snow bank and, if wind was a factor, we changed ends at the mid-point of the third period to ensure fairness. Skating "uphill" was difficult. Games were postponed if the temperature plunged below -20 degrees Fahrenheit. I don't remember much about my Pearl Park hockey career, probably because I rarely got a chance to touch the puck. My skating was not good enough. In sixth grade I switched positions from forward to goalie. It was a good career move.

Approaching the warming house, the wooden stairs, deeply rutted by decades of skate-blade abuse, suggested an impending visit to yesteryear. The interior was dark and hot – cave-like with an ancient cast-iron stove fueled with coal and broken hockey sticks. A brass rail encircled it, always draped with wet socks, chopper-mitt liners and the odd scarf hissing from the steam and stench rising off the wool.

Younger kids often bore the stigma of *"idiot mittens"* fastened to their outerwear sleeves by metal clips to prevent losing a pair. Children whose mothers made them wear snow pants suffered the ultimate indignity. Skate guards were strewn under the benches, and it was a challenge to find a matching pair when it was time to leave. Digging through the warming house lost-and-found carton was almost always fruitless.

Pearl Park hockey rink
Photo courtesy of Minneapolis Park Board

The decibel level was high as the young crowd boasted and counter-bragged about their exploits on the ice. There was usually some crying due to frost-bitten toes or the pain from an inadvertent step on a sockless foot. At a younger age our skates were dull as butter knives, so the damage was minimized. It was a short walk home, but I tarried in the warmth and the tumult.

■ ■ ■

Two Minneapolis parks produced world-caliber winter athletes. In January 1934, some 50,000 fans attended the U.S. Outdoor Speedskating Championship held at the Powderhorn Park oval. In 1947, Olympic team tryouts were held there. The final nine-man team included four members of the Powderhorn Skating Club, most notably Ken Bartholomew, who won the Silver Medal in St. Moritz, Switzerland. Minneapolis was considered one of the world's speedskating capitals, which makes sense as Scandinavians brought the sport across the Atlantic.

Chicago Olympic medalist Leo Friesinger praised the carefully groomed ice surface at Powderhorn, *"It is a pleasure for me to return to Minneapolis and skate on the best ice in the United States."* Speedskating is a grueling sport demanding strength, stamina and grace. The United States has won 67 Olympic speedskating medals, the most of any the country has garnered in the winter games.

"This form of amusement is as distinctly Scandinavian as lutefisk, groet, kringles and shingle bread. With skis on his feet a man can skim

swiftly over the soft snow in level places, and when a slope is convenient the sport resembles coasting in an exhilarating and exciting form... One or two of the contestants were skillful enough to retain their equilibrium on reaching terra firma again, and ski on to the end of the course, arousing the wildest enthusiasm." (*Minneapolis Tribune*, 1891)

Glenwood Park (now Theodore Wirth) is adjacent to the Glenwood-Inglewood and Fruen Milling Company site and, when it expanded in 1909, the acquisition of land offered many opportunities to provide more amenities to its frequenters. Norwegian immigrants introduced Nordic-style skiing: cross-country and jumping, known then as ski running and ski jumping. The topography of the Kenwood and Bryn Mawr neighborhoods was tailor-made for the sports.

"Tomorrow will witness the greatest ski contest that ever took place in this country. For several years our Norwegian cultivators of the ski-sport have worked assiduously to introduce their favorite sport in this country, but their efforts although crowned with success, did not experience a real boom until the Tribune interested itself in the matter and gave the boys a lift." (*Minneapolis Tribune*, January 29, 1888)

The sport reached the U.S. in 1883, and the first formal tournament was held in 1887 in Red Wing, Minnesota – a Mississippi River town south of St. Paul. The initial Minneapolis event took place on Kenwood Hill in 1888 with the Norwegian Turn Club, the Vikings Club and Der Norse Twin Forening members participating in front of an estimated 3,000 onlookers. Younger, spryer spectators perched in trees or on idle freight-train cars along the course for a bird's-eye view.

The 1924 Olympic ski jumper trials took place in Glenwood Park on January 6, 1924, and three Twin City entrants were selected for the squad: Hans Hansen, Anders Haugen and Sigurd Overby. The park board was so enthusiastic that it predicted in the 1924 annual report that the Mill City would host the Winter Olympics in 1928 or 1932. This did not transpire, and the jumping facilities at Glenwood eventually faded into obscurity. Minneapolis did not produce a national champ until John Balfanz won in 1964.

Dad's boyhood wintertime activities were like mine. His Bryn Mawr gang skated, had snowball fights and sledded down "Fruen Hill." My father and his two friends won the Holsum Bread Snow Sculpture Contest, sculpting an elephant with icicles for tusks. One difference from the late 1920s to my 1950s childhood was fashion. I wore an *"ear*

Norwegian Ski Club, Minneapolis. Fueled by Scandinavians who immigrated to
Minnesota, the area soon became the epicenter of cross country skiing.
Photo courtesy of Minneapolis Tribune

T.C. Bear shoveling snow,
early April home game postponed.
Photo courtesy of MLB

Holsum Bread Ice Sculpture
Contest winners.
Icicles turned into tusks.
Roger Fruen (center) and
the other sculptors.
Fruen family photo

brassiere," which was a wool band that covered one's ears and not much else. The Bryn Mawr boys of Dad's era sported leather aviator pilot hats. My generation's go-to spring, summer and fall headwear was the Davey Crockett inspired, faux raccoon hat with a tail.

T.S. Eliot described April as *"the cruelest month,"* which was no surprise to Minnesota eight-year-olds. Glorious spring days were sandwiched between spirit-crushing meteorological events to remind us that we were still in the grips of a defiant winter. We battled back by playing catch – yearning for the start of baseball season – in our boots and parkas, plucking errant throws from mud or an ice-encrusted pile of dirty snow.

The Fruen's haven between the city and the wilderness. Despite the farm animals, it was not the "pastoral ideal," but close enough for the Fruens.
Fruen family photo

The Pastoral

"I will arise and go there, and go to Innisfree,
And a small cabin build there, of clay and wattles made,
Nine bean-rows will I have there, a hive for the honey-bee,
And live alone in the bee-loud glade,
I will arise and go now, for always night and day,
I hear lake water lapping with low sounds by the shore;
While I stand on the roadway, or on the pavement grey,
I hear it in the deep heart's core."

William Butler Yeats,
THE LAKE ISLE OF INNISFREE

I RECALL IN MY earliest Big Island memories the small version of an English Rock Garden tumbling from the front of the Brick House. The stones could be used as steps but rarely were. The garden seemed to command an arm's length invitation, much as one would study a painting in a gallery. Daisies, lilies of the valley and various grasses shared the space with bees and monarch and tiger swallowtail butterflies. It was an oasis of simple beauty and quietude on the often cacophonous Crown Point.

The Pastoral Ideal has been a pervasive theme in literature dating back centuries with imagery that includes gardens, farms, ponds, babbling brooks, meadows and shepherds. D.H Lawrence called it the *"spirit of place."* In Virginia, the colonists wanted the Garden Eden as a refuge, but not at the expense of progress, success and wealth made available by the market for tobacco in England and the use of slave labor. Their New England counterparts had little leisure time during their efforts to battle the elements and soon, the native Pequots.

■ ■ ■

"Then the little locomotive shrieked and began to move: a rapid chugging of exhaust... Soon it ran once more at its maximum clattering speed between the twin walls of amazed wilderness as of old. It had been harmless once... But it was different now. It was the same train, engine, cars, caboose, yet this time it was as though the train...had brought with it into the doomed wilderness...the shadow and portent...and he knew now... that after this time he himself...would return no more."

William Faulkner,

THE BEAR

By the 1820s, in the words of author Leo Marx, *"the machine was in the garden."* The Industrial Revolution brought rapid change. The land, harbors, lakes and rivers were transformed into more effective modes of transportation. Canals and roads were chiseled through the waterways and the forest, and the invention of the steam engine revolutionized the movements of people and goods.

Tracks were laid for the first major railroad, the Baltimore and Ohio. For the most part, there was little objection to the technological advancements that were greeted as progress and, after all, America was still a cornucopia with frontier to spare.

"Americans have long tended to see city and country as separate places, more isolated from each other than connected. We carefully partition our landscape into urban places, rural places and wilderness. Although we often cross the symbolic boundaries between them – seeking escape or excitement, recreation or renewal – we rarely reflect on how tightly bound together they really are."

William Cronon,

NATURE'S METROPOLIS: CHICAGO AND THE GREAT WEST

The ideal is a sublime buffer zone between the complexities of the city and the hardships and dangers of the wilderness.

Lake Minnetonka escaped the Industrial Revolution due to its hidden location largely unknown to European settlers until the early 1850s. Farm run-off and lumber-milling detritus were the first polluting agents in the Big Water. Invasive species began to intrude. Carp in the 1880s and by the turn of the century, curly leaf pondweed. Soon the Hotel Lafayette began dumping raw sewage into the bay. As transportation improved

with the advent of automobiles and streetcars, throngs of Minneapolitans descended on the lake. When the railroad reached Wayzata, tourists
from all over the world arrived.

■ ■ ■

The Iron Horse was a double-edged sword. There is no denying the benefits of the expansion of the "*Iron Road,*" but the push westward also
brought destructive consequences. An unholy relationship was formed
between the U.S. government, the Dakota, Lakota and other plains
tribes, the railroad and the bison. After the Civil War, General William
Tecumseh Sherman and his troops protected the construction of the
Transcontinental Railroad from the attacks of Lakota and Cheyenne
fighting not only for their way of life but their very existence.

The tens of millions of bison provided the Native Americans with
more than just food. The hides were used to fashion clothing, blankets,
robes and shelter. Stomachs became pots or water flasks. Bones were
re-imagined into tools as well as spears and arrowheads after the marrow was extracted. Even dried bison excrement was utilized as fuel for
fires.

Sherman espoused the simple military strategies of cutting off the
enemy's food supply and breaking their spirit. The beasts were not only
killed to feed railroad workers but also in sport. "Wild Bill" Cody, General George Custer and other lesser-knowns cut off the bisons' tongues
and humps that were considered delicacies. The rest of the bodies were
left to rot.

Hunting expeditions by train were coordinated by "sportsmen" who
had military escorts. The engineer adjusted his speed to match the gal-
loping bison herd. Rifles were fired through open windows and platforms at the helpless thundering herd. Hills of skulls were piled beside
the tracks. It was not long before the bison population had dwindled
from an estimated 30 to 70 million to merely 200,000 animals.

Indigenous Americans, despite their image of an idyllic coexistence
with nature, contributed to the carnage and waste in addition to alter-
ing the landscape to fit their needs. Chutes were made and underbrush
burned to channel moose, deer, bear, elk and others to watering holes
where they were easily dispatched.

About 6,000 years ago, the method of *"buffalo jumping"* was introduced to kill the huge beasts in greater numbers. The strategy was known as *pishkin*, roughly translated to "deep blood kettle." Rock walls two to three feet tall were piled along a stretch of prairie as much as a few miles long. Men waving hides and shouting from behind frightened the bison into stampeding.

Bison have a strong herd instinct that was almost impossible to stop once the first few plunged to the canyon floor. Hunters were stationed at the bottom with stone mauls and spears to finish off any animals injured but still alive. Women worked until dusk to harvest hides, meat and other prized parts.

Meat not harvested, dried and smoked by morning was inedible. The process was cruel. Crippled, mangled bison writhed in pain for hours until they were killed by hunters. Many were suffocated when crushed by others cascading down, leading to excess and waste when it was not possible to process the dead at the bottom of the pile. The decimation of the Great Sioux Nation's life source drove them to the negotiating table where they signed treaties, soon broken, relegating them to reservations and forcing them to rely on the whites for sustenance.

■ ■ ■

Arthur and Reba Fruen had no misconceptions regarding the Pastoral Ideal when they acquired the Crown Point property. The geographical proximity to home and office precluded an extended period of relaxation and rumination. Barking dogs and rowdy children jumping, splashing and shrieking had little resemblance to Walden Pond.

The family parcel on Big Island has always been a casual place for family and friends. It was a place to entertain and celebrate at the unique enclave so close to the city. The Rock Garden notwithstanding, it was my grandparents' Ideal.

Prior to European contact, the Dakota inspired fear in other bands due to their tall stature, imposing strength and proud bearing. Not yet ravaged by disease, starvation, desperation and the firearms of the French and their native allies, the Iroquois, the Dakota commanded respect and helped reinforce the myth.

White incursion and disruption of countless years of their culture made it impossible for the Dakota to live up to the ideal. They chafed at the government's attempts – in keeping with Thomas Jefferson's agrarian vision – to turn them into farmers and the strategy to Anglicize their children. Ripped from their home and culture, the young natives dressed in the Anglo style and were taught English at Indian Schools to ensure assimilation. In a short period, the *"Original People"* changed from the Noble Savage to the Wretched Indian. Perhaps the conflict between the two cultures may be attributed to religious and spiritual differences. The natives viewed themselves as a part of nature, an equal to the animals, plants, rocks and other objects they believed possessed spirits. The European immigrants, in the Judeo-Christian tradition, believed they were *"The Chosen Ones,"* separate from nature and deserving of all the riches the land offered. Native Americans prudently used the fauna and flora, mindful of future needs, while the New England colonists and their descendants did not plan. They were focused on survival in the here and now.

This was the harsh environment Great-great-grandfather Andrew Bergquist encountered in 1853 in Minnesota as did William Fruen seventeen years later.

■ ■ ■

The Scrivers arrival on Big Island pre-dated the Fruens. By the time Arthur, Reba and their children landed on Crown Point advancements were in place, but it was not gracious lake living. Creature comforts were few: no indoor plumbing, no electricity, no potable water nor a Hillovator to carry people, food, glass jugs of Glenwood Inglewood spring water and supplies up the steep hill.

Hiram Scriver rowed a boat to Excelsior where he drove his car to the St. Anthony Falls Bank and reversed the process when the workday ended. Grandpa Fruen was ferried to a garage that he and a few neighbors rented on Gluek's Point in Lynwood where they kept their cars. Uncle Doug recalls dropping his father off at the tender age of seven or eight and returning to Big Island, so the boat with a motor was available during the day.

When guests arrived at the parking lot on Gluek's Point, there was a sign detailing the Morse Code-like system to contact the islanders for a ride. Our family's code was long-short-long, which was communicated by horn honks or, at night, the flashing of cars' headlights.

By the time I reached the age of reason, the Scriver clan had expanded to include other branches: the Baileys, Granruds and Burchs among them, but they were collectively known as the "Scrivers." I heard tales of cutting grass by hand, first slashed with a scythe down to a manageable height and then trimmed with a sickle.

Grandfather Fruen had a wide labor pool of strong grandsons at his bidding. I was at the tail end of the first wave of grandchildren and inherited the more menial chores. I was everyone's apprentice: Dad, brothers, uncles and older cousins had no issues delegating chores to the youngest.

I mowed the large front lawn with a push mower over hill and dale while being plagued by mosquitoes, bees, gnats, chiggers and streams of sweat down my face. My white Jack Purcell tennis shoes (every sneaker was a "tennis shoe" then) turned green with wet grass. I did not complain, because no one appreciated city-boy whining.

Eventually we acquired a Toro power lawnmower that certainly made the task easier but still required attention with the speedier process. Once I rolled my ankle on a garter snake, and toads were dodged to prevent a grisly outcome.

One summer at the age of fourteen or fifteen I was given the job of digging a hole for the new septic tank. This was a chore for the lowliest of grunts. Me. There was little direction given beside the circular outline of the hole and the guidance to *keep digging.* Grandpa was approaching 80 and was slowing down, but he checked my progress every hour or so. I often thought I was finished, but Arthur's standards were more stringent than mine.

My unenviable status continued during my least favorite Crown Point activities: setting up and taking out the metal dock. At least in May one could look forward to the coming Big Island season. The sections and framing structure of the dock were hauled down the flight of steps from the upper chalet level to the water. The grease-smeared nuts and bolts were taken from winter coffee-can confinement.

The weather was brisk early in the spring and the wet, cold fingers often resulted in a fumble. I was the designated fetcher. If the offending fastener fell close to the shore, I could lie on my stomach and reach it with my hand. If a little deeper, I sat on the finished portion of the dock and grabbed the nut or bolt with my toes. As we progressed outward, I was forced into total immersion. The reverse process in October was demoralizing as it signaled the end of the summer. The water was just as cold as May, and the wind was a harbinger of winter.

■ ■ ■

If a grandson were to spend an extended time (a week or more) on the island, he had a morning schedule. Breakfast with Arthur was always the same – cereal for the youngster and Fruen Milling Company's Cream of Rye and some prunes for Grandpa. The morning was spent working on various projects.

After lunch we were left on our own to explore and enjoy the afternoon. My Fruen cousins Ricky, Jimmy, Tommy and Sue were usually in-residence next door to the Brick House. During my grandparents' later years, Uncle Dick and Aunt Margaret were there in case of an emergency.

When Ricky told me the ending of one of his work sessions with Grandfather, I refused to believe it. He headed to the Chalet "*ice box*," which had the standard pan underneath to catch the liquid of melting ice. He took two cans of beer and handed one to Arthur, who drank it right down. I was in shock and a little jealous. Grandpa was a proponent of disciplined living but was not a stick-in-the-mud.

Jimmy was quiet but took time to show me the ropes around the Lower Lake. We went on a tour of tiny Gale's Island, which was fascinating in its use of a small footprint less than two acres in size. In addition to a unique octagonal house, there was a tennis court and a footbridge to the spit of land called Cape Cod to honor their Massachusetts origins, aiming straight at Crown Point. Harlow and Elizabeth Gale bought the island, then named Gooseberry, in 1872 for $2.45. They wanted to name the island Brightwood, but the locals made Gale's Island stick.

Jimmy also taught me how to cook a Big Island delicacy: a hot dog split down the middle and stuffed with cheese. A piece of bacon wrapped around the dog held the delicacy together with three toothpicks, and the concoction was broiled in the Brick House's old but dependable oven. I could survive now, if necessary, on a dict of RC Cola, spring water, cereal, fish and gourmet hot dogs.

■ ■ ■

Arthur and Reba Fruen's Christmas card. Eloise Butler transplanted the Lady Slippers from the banks of Bassett's Creek to her nascent wild flower garden.
Fruen family photo

Tommy is two years older than I and the creator of the magnificent tree house cradled in the branches of a massive oak tree a few feet into the Big Woods at the northern end of our property. A few boughs stretched from the trunk at right angles, providing the perfect frame for the two-story edifice. Tommy scavenged most of the materials from the island, where nothing was ever really discarded. The treehouse was well built and offered a superb view over the cabins towards Excelsior, Tonka Bay, the southeasternmost end of Big Island and Gale's Island.

Ricky Fruen was the unofficial Mayor of Big Island during his teens. On summer weekdays, he took walks from Crown Point in a counter-clockwise direction down the hill past Point Comfort all the way to the Veteran's Camp. He knew everyone along the path and stopped to visit along the way. Rick was a bit of a lady's man and had a few Big Island romances.

He walked past the cabin of a friendly old hermit and was often given a gift from the man's garden such as a bunch of carrots, which Rick politely accepted. He was going to buy a candy bar at the Veteran Camp commissary, and carrots were a low priority. He usually gave the vegetables to campers.

Ricky and my brother Mike were close in their late 70s. In an act of familial symmetry their sons – Scott and Todd respectively – also grew up on the island together and fulfilled the scenario my grandparents had envisioned forty-some years earlier. The dads were our family's best water skiers and befriended John Hiram Burch from the extended Scriver clan. I was eight years younger and considered *"Johnny Hi"* to be the island's first superstar. He was a superb skier. When he slalomed, he had such control that his body seemed almost parallel to the water, a few inches off the surface in his water ballet.

■ ■ ■

Moccasin Flowers bloomed among the ferns at Glenwood Springs. Better known today as the Lady Slippers, the flower is a species of the orchid family, the state flower of Minnesota and now rarely seen. Eloise Butler was a long-time high-school science teacher in Minneapolis who was passionately dedicated to the study and preservation of wildflowers. She was granted a thirteen-acre portion of what is now Theodore Wirth Park surrounding a tamarack bog to create a wild garden oasis.

Glenwood Falls at Theodore Wirth Park
Fruen family photo

Crown Point lookout on a quiet day
Fruen family photo

Big Island and Great-grandfather Fruen's fern-covered Glenwood Springs were two such places linked by botanical kismet. Ms. Butler boated to Big Island to find specimens like Squirrel Corn – a plant with fragrant white heart-shaped flowers that thrived in the rich soil of the deciduous Big Woods.

Lady Slippers proliferated along William's stretch of Bassett's Creek, and Eloise and her volunteers transplanted them into what became the Eloise Butler Wildflower Garden and Bird Sanctuary. Arthur Fruen was a charter supporter and was involved as an ex-officio Park Board official. Upon his death, Grandpa was honored by the association as a *"great conservationist."* The Pastoral Ideal may be a poet's pipe dream, but the 13-acre site on the western edge of Minneapolis comes close, albeit a bit frantic on the weekends.

Late on a Lake Minnetonka weekday afternoon after the boaters scatter to their docks and trailers, the wakes dissipate and – weather willing – a hush comes over the southeastern end of the Lower Lake. A Crown Point benediction.

At Belford, home of James Ford Bell and Louise Heffeleinger Bell. My mother's
cousin Billy Dalrymple is the hatless man with the majestic pose.
His wife, Evelyn "Chici" Dalrymple, sits in the upper right.
Courtesy of Minnesota Historical Society

Snobbery is Relative

"Of all the snobs the Reverse Snob is possibly the most snobbish; he is so sure of himself that he intentionally puts other people in a position where they have to play his game or feel like snobs themselves. The false simplicity of the Reverse Snobbery stands in glaring contrast to the genuine simplicity of the genuinely modest man."

Russell Lynes,

SNOBS

GUILTY AS CHARGED. A strain of anti-snobbery runs through the Fruen family. Admittedly I suffer from my own version of this malady. Two early childhood visits to Lake Minnetonka's Gold Coast are vivid in my recall.

As a preschooler I accompanied my mother by boat to the annual St.-Martin's-by-the-Lake Episcopal Church Country Fair on the grounds of the Sweatt family's 75-acre "farm" straddling the borders of Wayzata and Minnetonka on the northeast Lower Lake. I knew something was afoot when I was dressed in my humiliating Sunday-school outfit: a blazer, short pants, dress shirt, knee-high socks and a bow tie. Mom probably made me wear saddle shoes, too. This clashed with the unofficial Crown Point dress code.

Even at the tender age of four the Sweatt estate was impressive. The grounds were meticulously groomed with breathtaking gardens. I crossed the little bridge that spanned a moat multiple times. The Sweatts were avid equestrians, and the stable was a large, exquisitely designed version of a medieval Norman-style brick cottage with a thatched roof, home not only to the horses but also the riding master.

The thoroughbreds had about five acres to roam and graze when they were not in the paddock preparing for their next appearance in the show ring. The Sweatts engineered a 1927 merger between their Minneapolis Heat Regulator Company and Honeywell. I had not reached the age of reason and did not equate the buildings and lakeside grounds with money, but the experience was impactful in a manner I would later understand.

■ ■ ■

My other early experience in the vicinity also occurred in the mid-1950s. My Uncle Ralph was staying in a guest house at Belford, the home of James Ford Bell Sr. and his wife Louise Heffelfinger Bell. Belford sits on a high hill with a commanding view of Lake Minnetonka. It was built in a Mediterranean style of architecture with the white stucco and a red-tiled roof prominent in the construction.

Originally, Belford was a summer home built by James Stroud Bell who moved to Minneapolis from Philadelphia to work for the Washburn-Crosby Company. His son, James Ford Bell, followed in his footsteps and learned the flour-milling business that eventually merged with three other operations to form General Mills. James and Louise converted Belford to a year-round domicile.

My memory comes in a curious reverie. I was alone at the large open-air rectangular pool across the driveway from the main residence, playing with my toy sailboat. The pool was surrounded by columns supporting the roof that created a narrow alcove for sitting and walking. The architectural style would not look out of place on a Greek island. I am certain that the pool house closet had an extensive stock of libations. Being alone seems odd for a boy in short pants. The adults must have been in the main house, perhaps on the porch that offered the best vista.

A decade or so later my friend Chris Briscoe visited from Santa Barbara with his high school classmate Peter Wingate. We had been invited to the Winslow family home (later named Tanager Hill) with 750 feet of shoreline to the south on Minnetonka's Smith Bay and to the north, 200 feet on Mud (Tanager) Lake.

The 32-acre spread was recently described as the *"most extraordinary and admired estate on Lake Minnetonka."* For once, the details were not exaggerated by the listing agent: This was no *"unique fixer-upper."*

The mansion was built in 1939 for the future chairman of the agri-business monolith General Mills, Charles Ford Bell. An iron gate opened to reveal the white brick Georgian Colonial manse of over 13,500 square feet included six bedrooms and ten bathrooms. On the grounds were a six-car garage, two caretaker homes and a guard house. The swimming pool (and pool house), tennis courts, a greenhouse and a 3,500-square-foot guest house also graced the grounds.

Before leaving for the Winslow estate, I selected my attire. Chris and Pete then rummaged through my closet to find some suitable clothing as their traveling wardrobe consisted of dusty, fragrant shorts, t-shirts and sandals.

We drove to the Winslows. Joe and Betty were gracious hosts and gave us a tour although, in my mid-teens, I was more intrigued by their daughters. One can view the interior by watching the classic, original 1972 version of "The Heartbreak Kid," starring Charles Grodin, Cybill Shepherd and Eddie Albert as her chronically disagreeable father. Towards the end, many locals appeared in brief cameos, including Betty and Joe.

We survived a short, harrowing ride to the Woodhill Club. Joe was at the wheel, Betty rode shotgun and the rest us were squeezed in the back. Joe was convivial but terrifying as he spent most of the trip turned almost 130 degrees to engage in conversation with his passengers.

The Winslow property was eventually purchased by Irwin and Alexandra Jacobs (only the third owners) and was on the market for $22 million at one point. After the Jacobs' deaths the price tumbled to $12 million, and the inevitable plan to chop up the now 20-acre site into six developments received approval from the city of Orono. Smaller lots gobbling up views, shoreline and the probable demolition of the storied estate will result. Attorneys for concerned neighbors have expressed alarm at the violation of setback ordinances and increased traffic with the addition of a honeycomb of neighborhood streets and turn lanes on the existing lakeside roads.

■ ■ ■

With these early encounters, and others, I consider myself a snobbery cognoscenti. I have witnessed haughtiness from all angles and observed many of the subspecies. I have been the victim of snobbery from those

Pool party at Belford. The roaring twenties.
Fruen family photo

looking down and those looking up. People will judge you in myriad ways: wealth, education, geography, clothes, appearance, housing, accents, cars, intellect and genealogy.

Snobbery does not stop there. Every day new forms appear: wine, food, beer, coffee, music, lettuce, dog food, cell phones, bottled water, ergonomically correct bicycles, baby strollers and many more types of objects provoke snobbery. Now cannabis has joined the fray. Strains, hybrids and edibles are now topics of exhaustive discussions and displays of one-up-man-ship.

Music snobs are quite pretentious. I enjoy many types of music and consider myself well versed in the different varieties. Classical, opera and jazz snobs can be the worst. There are purists in every genre like the bluegrass snob who gives a musician bona fides if he built his own five-string banjo.

I have two friends who clucked behind my back regarding the "*country crap*" I listened to over the years. Imagine my satisfaction when they remarried and were suddenly born-again country aficionados when their new spouses liked that kind of music. I like what I like. I don't check to see which way the wind is blowing.

Dad used to call me "*Redneck*," and he also listened to some classic country. My father stood quite low on the rungs of the snobbery ladder and had friends from all over the map including childhood buddies, friends from the Navy, the neighborhood and business. He was, however, a real-do-it yourself snob. He was very handy and scorned my skills in this area. Roger was impatient and, anytime I fumbled on a project, he snatched the tools from my hands and took over.

One time my father met with the headmaster of Breck School and suggested introducing a shop class into the curriculum. Canon Henderson said, in his usual succinct manner, "*We'll prepare Ross for college, you teach him how to use a hammer.*"

■ ■ ■

Minnesotans have perfected a peculiar type of regional snootiness that centers on a common bond of superiority and smugness from their ability to endure brutal winters. "*Nobody has it tougher*" is a common theme, and there is a competitiveness regarding the accessories to endure life on the tundra. Snow blowers have canvas cabs with windows to protect the operator from wind gusts and blowing snow.

Farmers compete in the summer with elaborate sound systems for their tractors and air conditioning to combat hot, muggy conditions. There is a strong Minnesota bond fashioned by the ability to survive the weather extremes. I contributed to it by foregoing a hat or gloves even in the dead of winter except when I was moving snow.

Fruens are Lake Minnetonka Reverse Snobs. If your family hasn't lived on the lake since the Roaring Twenties, you are *arriviste*. The McMansions dotting the shore are considered garish. Old cottages, trees and 5,000-square-foot homes are torn down to make way for 8,000-square-foot monsters that tower over their neighbors, sucking up every square inch of the property and the character from the shoreline. We consider snowmobiles and ATVs to be vulgar as are boats that are way too big for the lake and the weekend warriors who do not know how to pilot them.

People have looked down on the Minneapolis house where I grew up as being too small, but they did not understand my mother. Dad was restless and sporadically tried to get her to upgrade, but she would not have it. She favored stability after her transient childhood, and she was not moving. It taught me a lesson regarding the unimportance of "things." It was a great, tight-knit neighborhood and a wonderful place for kids. The Fruens lived on Clinton Avenue just south of Minnehaha Creek and a block west of Pearl Park for 42 years.

My father, despite his scorn for the mechanically disinclined, came close to being snobbery free. He was truly modest and walked effortlessly in many worlds and assumed people were inherently good, unless they were Democrats. If he had negative opinions of others, he usually kept them to himself, but sometimes he just could not help it. Every now and then a yard sign for a Democratic candidate would pop up near our house amid the forest of Republican ones. Dad would sniff and say, "*University Professor.*"

My mother's make-up was a bit more Byzantine. She was born into a life of privilege and spent her summers on a hill overlooking Brown's Bay and winters in a rented house or apartment in the Lake of the Isles neighborhood. Many years she was sent to boarding schools when her parents' alcohol addictions prevented a stable home environment. She enjoyed talking about the grand old days, which she romanticized, but she was perfectly happy with her life on Clinton Avenue.

Leslie was proud of her family and friends. No matter what the circumstances, she thought they all were simply great and could not believe her good fortune to have them in her life. Her family and home were tantamount and, after her disjointed childhood, she loved the security of her marriage and snug neighborhood.

After World War II, Glory Conary, my father's cousin and my mother's childhood friend, introduced them. Soon, romance took center stage. The housing market was extremely tight with demand for homes outstripping supply and infrastructure. Beyond the burgeoning first ring of suburbs were farmland, and suburbanites commuted to downtown Minneapolis much of the way on dirt roads.

After their wedding, my parents moved into a basement apartment in Minneapolis that they affectionately called "*Leslie's Lower Level.*" Not the penthouse, but it was their first home and they loved it. Status was not a consideration. They were simply happy to find a place in the city in the tight post-war real estate market. After all, if subterranean living became confining, they could escape to Big Island.

In a 1975 Dave Mona's *Mpls.* magazine tongue-in-cheek passage described "*Minnetonka Chic*" as "*living in Cottagewood, owning a Lund*

Runabout and a Ford LTD wagon, shopping at Nygren's in Excelsior, having season tickets to the Guthrie, dining out at the Spring Lake Soda Fountain, and skiing at Lutsen."*

While satirical, this rang true at the time. Opulence and conspicuous consumption were harder to find on the lake then and that suited the Reverse Snobs. After all, many of the Cottagewood residents grew up in Minneapolis and attended Washburn or West high schools.

In her later years, mother Leslie was confused by the new wave of lakesiders who made their fortunes through avenues she did not understand. Hedge fund managers, baseball players, internet savants, musicians, restauranteurs, a hair-care accessory marketer, a man known as The Liquidator, and the perpetrator of a $3 billion Ponzi scheme whose view is now obstructed by prison bars. Their homes are wedged between those of the old aristocratic grain millers.

■ ■ ■

Make no mistake, I do not begrudge anyone making money and applaud their success. But are elephantine homes incurring yearly real estate taxes approaching $100,000 necessary or just a chance to preen and display ornamental feathers like peacocks?

There is a small kettle lake connected to the western end of Brown's Bay by a short channel. It was a frequent go-to spot for us to ski. It is isolated with a smooth surface and little to no boat traffic. There was one caveat. If one fell, it was immediately clear why the small, shallow bay was originally named *Little Muddy.* The bottom is sludgy and the water quality and clarity poor. We quickly learned to keep our mouths closed if we tumbled. It is on the State of Minnesota Impaired Waters List.

As the demand for Big Water property continued, the land around *Little Muddy* became gentrified with impressive homes. A déclassé name was not acceptable anymore, and it was rechristened Tanager Lake. (This is a little too presumptuous for me – like putting lipstick on a catfish.) It remains a great spot for crappie fishing, though.

During the 1960s, a great upheaval invaded the world of traditional Snobbery. The rough line of demarcation was the JFK assassination

---

*Lutsen is a famous ski resort near the north shore of Lake Superior between Duluth, MN, and the Canadian border

and the emergence of the counterculture. Prior to November 1963, the WASPISH denizens of the Eastern seaboard from Boston to Palm Beach who attended Ivy League Universities or Seven Sisters colleges reigned supreme. They were Boston Brahmins, haunters of the Hamptons or hailed the from Philadelphia's Main Line.

The men worked at ancient, prestigious *"white buck firms"* such as law practices, banks and other financial institutions sandwiched between liquid lunches and golf. The nickname refers to the style of footwear the Anglo Saxons wore at prep school at Andover or Exeter and college in places like Cambridge or New Haven: white buckskin with red soles. They belonged to selective country clubs, drove big cars, drank cocktails and were Republican and Episcopalian or Presbyterian.

■ ■ ■

In the mid 60s, the counterculture gained traction and, as the youth attracted to the new lifestyle went to college, joined the work force, married and started families, America's values evolved. A status conversion occurred, espousing trends like smaller is better, cheap chic and environmental awareness. Cadillacs, Lincolns and sports cars gave way to Volkswagen Beetles and vans.

The Ivies and elite liberal arts colleges began to value merit over DNA, ethnic quotas were reconfigured and the doors were opened to gifted public-school graduates. The anti- establishment beatniks gave way to hippies, who morphed into Bohemians. They did not despair over success and money but curled their lips at those who used money to leverage their social standing.

The newspaper's Society page is long gone, but the game of golf is a microcosm of the hauteur of snobbery. Bryn Mawr was an incubator for the sport in Minneapolis. St. Paul's Town and Country Club beat Minneapolis by five days, opening nine holes for play just a chip shot from the eastern Mississippi River bluffs on June 9, 1898.

Bryn Mawr's Minneapolis Golf Club opened on June 14, 1898, with nine holes and a few hazards to make it more challenging. With few social amenities, it was considered a *"business man's course"*. David C. Smith, the reverent caretaker of Minneapolis Park history, detailed the origins: *"It's worth noting that the most thorough description of the new course and club appeared on May 15, 1898 in the* [Minneapolis] *Tribune's society column, not its sports pages. The list of the first 200-plus members reads like a who's who of early Minneapolis society: Pillsbury, Peavey, Heffelfinger, Jaffray, Rand, Lowry, Bell, Dunwoody, Christian, Morrison, Koon, Loring."* (David C. Smith, "The Mother of All Minneapolis Golf Courses: Bryn Mawr I," *Minneapolis Park History*)

Soon, many of the members organized a spread overlooking the west shore of Bde Maka Ska, then called "Lake Calhoun." The original nine-hole course was soon expanded to eighteen. The club, with a nod to the Lakota band, was named *Minikahda, "by the side of the water."* The impressive two-story, white clubhouse opened in 1899 featuring a large wraparound porch overlooking the lake and a portico with four Corinthian pillars facing the course.

Minikahda hosted the U.S. Open (1916), the U.S. Amateur (1927) and the Walker Cup in 1957 but is now considered too short a track for today's big, stronger flat-bellied long hitters who play with the advantage of technological advances in equipment and livelier golf balls. The course is still challenging for the best of amateur golfers demanding precision and a well-thought strategy for every hole.

Bryn Mawr was not finished being the incubator of prestigious golf clubs. *"Bryn Mawr was about to be plowed under for housing, and Minikahda was full, so the time was right to establish a new Minneapolis club. There had been newspaper speculation that the location search might go as far west as Lake Minnetonka, but the men wanted a site within twenty-five minutes of downtown Minneapolis on a streetcar line. After inspecting sites near Diamond Lake, Glen Lake, Twin Lakes, and Lake Nokomis, the group found their ideal site: three adjoining farms, totaling 146 acres, bordering on Mirror Lake in Edina."* (Rick Shefchik, *From Fields to Fairways*)

The Bryn Mawr course bounced back from the Minikahda defection and was open for the 1900 season. Soon, city housing began to encroach on the golf course to the point that *Minneapolis Journal* writer Earl C. May claimed a player might come upon *"a cellar dug where a green used to be."* In 1909, the Bryn Mawr club morphed into Interlachen Country Club that provided rolling, oak tree-lined fairways and more land to provide other amenities such as tennis, trapshooting, horses and various winter activities. It was west of the city but close enough to see downtown Minneapolis.

Interlachen has hosted many major tourneys including the U.S. Women's Open, the Ryder Cup, the Walker Cup, the U.S. Men's Senior Amateur and the Solheim Cup, but the most legendary event was the 1930 U.S. Men's Open.

Grandfather Harrison was an avid, superb amateur golfer who won the Maryland Chevy Chase Club men's championship at age 19 and usually played at the Woodhill Club, a long-iron away from Lake Minnetonka, after he married my grandmother and moved to Minneapolis. He brought my young mother to the final round and witnessed Bobby Jones' miraculous *"lily pad shot"* on the 18th hole.

Jones, the eventual champion, topped a shot while distracted by two children who ran onto the 18th fairway during his backswing. Witnesses say the ball bounced off the pond a few times before resting safely on terra firma, leaving the fortunate Bobby with a 40-foot uphill putt that he promptly drained for a birdie.

One might think the finish would be enough excitement for one day. Grandpa was thrilled when an errant Chick Evans shot glanced off my mother. I guess he was basking in reflective glory. Mom was a seven-year-old tomboy and likely shook it off but did not share the enthusiasm exhibited by Cleve Harrison.

In addition to the 100-plus-degree heat and the thrilling Bobby Jones finish, change was in the offing. A significant transition began in the stuffiest of sports. And perhaps a portent, in a larger sense, of the future a few decades down the road. The sporting press from around the country was taking notice of what was happening out there where the forest ends and the prairie begins: *"Golf has outgrown the supercilious silk stocking clique which controlled it during its gutta percha* [early crude golf balls] *infancy. The Midwest has done more than any other section to popularize the royal and ancient game. Certainly Minnesota has contributed its part in the last three years by helping to dissipate the aroma of snobbishness."* (George Trevor, *Amateur Golfer*)

The nine-hole Bryn Mawr Club was ground zero for two of the country's most venerated old golf courses. *"The cozy little club with its congenial membership was crowded out by the growth of the city and thus passed into history what was once an organization which was within the reach of the small salaried man and yet claimed as members some of the most prominent businessmen of the city."* (*Minneapolis Morning Tribune*, May 14, 1911)

■ ■ ■

While golf is certainly a big and easy target, there are a myriad of other aspects to consider. Like many other factors of the new upper class, politics have become a hybrid. Anti-war activists have discovered that success isn't so bad when there are bills to pay and children to raise have embraced an ideological middle ground.

Great-grandfather William Fruen would be intrigued by the various types and flavors of water available today. Once again, he was ahead of his time, introducing flavored spring water *"made by the pure flavor of the choicest Concord Grapes."* If the product has *"artesian"* in the description, that is a big selling point. Some suppliers slyly imply glaciers are involved. Smart Water is *de rigeur*: vapor-distilled and fortified with calcium, magnesium and electrolytes.

Quirky home décor is also celebrated. My brother Mike bought what was really a glorified cabin overlooking a pond tucked just south of Interstate 394 west of downtown Minneapolis. After a year or two, he tore down the old house and built a new, much larger modern home to his specifications. It has a substantial setback from the water with a splendid view of the abundant wildlife.

Pews from an abandoned church in northern Michigan grace his living room. A door with an etched glass window leads into his pantry. Antique knobs from God-knows-where adorn many doors. He did not intentionally go Bohemian as he enjoyed the art of the deal more than stylish affectations, but the resulting look is do-it yourself Restoration Hardware.

I have experienced snobbery, upwards and downwards, sometimes regarding the same subject. Some assumed I was haughty because I went to a private school. Then New England preppies scoffed at Breck School in fly-over land and, having never heard of it, wondered if there were indoor plumbing or a threat of Indian attacks. I let them know that, indeed, my classmate Richard was a Dakota band member.

A good example of convoluted Lake Minnetonka snobbery began innocently enough. I was at the boat landing in Tonka Bay and took on a hitch hiker who was heading to a party on Big Island just across the channel from Crown Point. As we approached, my rider was heckled as the modern *"ironclad"* called the *Queen Merrie* who did not live up to

Not to be outdone by Charles Gibson, James J. Hill built the Grand
Lafayette Hotel, which opened to great fanfare in 1882.
Photo courtesy of Minnesota Historical Society

the rarified standards of the other guests. Apparently, they were special.
They did not appreciate the ramming power of the *Queen Merrie*. They
did not embrace the Fruen philosophy of function over form, nor did
they know that dressing like a Kingston Trio cover-band was at odds
with Big Island protocol.

I smiled evilly as I sped away. I had spent many hours on that very
land and in the water rolling boulders and adding rip-rap to stabilize the
hill. My father then sold the property to the son of a former Minnesota
attorney general, who had fancy friends. Complicated and confusing.

There are certainly patrician pockets of old-school pretension remaining with green-and-pastel-pink-clad people named "Kip" and
"Bitsy" who earned their money the old-fashioned way: They inherited
it. In their defense, ones of their ilk that I know, no matter their political
stripes, are usually generous with not only their money but their time.

Today's snobbery landscape is full of many permutations and con-
tradictions. Reverse Snobs may be the Kings and Queens of the Snobs.

We perceive ourselves to be so emotionally sound and grounded that we rise above the fray and do not need to adopt affectations to boost our self-worth.

When a new Hulu series generates "buzz" around the water cooler, the Reverse Snob might say, "*I don't watch much television. Just PBS and Meet the Nation.*" This not only suggests a whirlwind schedule but also intimates a degree of erudition. In a nutshell, the Reverse Snob values what the garden-variety snob scorns and scorns what a regular snob values.

■ ■ ■

Lifestyle minutia are scrutinized to an unimaginable degree. Brutally snooty rules are endless a la "*not our kind, dear*" or the age-old "*nouveau versus old*" divide. Around Lake Minnetonka, as in most rarified social atmospheres, Reverse Snobs are counterintuitive: snobbish about snobs. I do not pretend to understand it all nor am I immune to its superficiality. In fact, I wish I never broached the subject in the first place.

OUTRAGEOUS!

A Dastardly Piece of Legal Vandalism.

Minneapolis Enumerators Arrested in the Night.

Outraged Minneapolis Says—

ARRESTED!

Minneapolis Census Enumerators Charged With Padding the Returns Come to Grief.

Scheme to Swell the Population of the Flour City Knocked in the Head.

But Here's St. Paul Slant

MASON A LIAR

Shown Up in His True Light by Ed. Stevens.

No Frauds Committed by the "Manufacturing Annex."

And Minneapolis' Side Again

Here's the way the 1890 census war between Minneapolis and St. Paul "broke" to the public. First two headlines show contrast between manner in which Minneapolis and St. Paul papers, respectively, dealt with the St. Paul-inspired raid in which Minneapolis census men were arrested. Last headline, from a Minneapolis paper, shows the indignant attacks on Mason, the detective whose affidavit concerning Minneapolis frauds started the war.

Accusations fly between Minneapolis and
St. Paul over fraudulent census controversy.
Photo courtesy of Twin Cities newspapers

My Dad Can Beat up Your Dad: The Rivalry

> *"...just the other day the Enemy Paper [Minneapolis Star Tribune] couldn't resist pointing out that lately Minneapolis 'is in the national spotlight, leaving St. Paul in its shadow.' The EP covers its city in such a way that everybody is 28, jogs, is about to enjoy a gay marriage ceremony and has enough money for gardening and kitchen renovation. St. Paul might as well be one of those towns in Northern Wisconsin where the lone brick building is an old school with '1923' engraved in the stone!"*
>
> Joe Soucheray,
> St. Paul Pioneer Press, August 3, 2013

ST. PAUL VERSUS MINNEAPOLIS. Antipathy existed in spades from the start of Anglo settlement. Sometimes downright combative. During the 1930s, *Fortune Magazine* reported that the only thing one needed to know about the two cities is that "*they hate each other.*" But make no mistake, there is a distinction. No matter the topic, whether politics, business or sports, the citizens of Minneapolis and St. Paul are ready to drop the gloves.

Minneapolis started out as St. Anthony Falls, but the New Englanders who first came to tame the fast water of the Mississippi and facilitate bringing the bounty of the northern woodlands and the western wheat fields to market toyed with the idea of naming the town Lowell in deference to their eastern roots. Minneapolis was chosen: a manufactured name combining the Dakota word for water and the Greek word for city.

St. Paul, perched on hills and the banks of the Mississippi, is often thought to be the last city in the East. The rounded apexes of the state capitol and the St. Paul Cathedral are reminders of the town's historical roots. The skyline of Minneapolis with its towers of stone, metal and glass appears as a mirage from the vast prairies to its west. The City of Lakes is considered to be the first western city. Minneapolis is said to be quirky, trendy, brash and even funky where St. Paul is known as staid, traditional and resistant to change.

■ ■ ■

When ex-wrestler, then Governor Jesse Ventura, appeared on the "David Letterman Show" in 1999, the host goaded the Guv into choosing Minneapolis as his favorite Twin City. If nothing else, Jesse was always a straight shooter but should have stopped there. However, encouraged by the pot-stirring Letterman, he insisted on elaborating and taking a shot at St. Paul: "*Whoever designed the streets must have been drunk, because in Minneapolis, you know if you're on Thirty-second Street, Thirty-sixth Street is four blocks away. In St. Paul, there's no rhyme or reason. It's not numerical. It's not alphabetical. You know, I think it's those Irish guys. You know what they like to do over there.*"

As the last sentence was uttered, Governor Ventura made a gesture with his fist and thumb in a drinking motion. Realizing his blunder he said, "*Oh, am I in trouble now.*" He had a point about the haphazard nature of the streets. They run so erratically that at one point in downtown St. Paul, 5th Street, 6th Street and 7th Street all intersect. Still, it was not a politically expedient comment and if Ventura wanted to blame someone about insobriety in the Capitol City, he could have begun with the bootlegging Pierre "Pig's Eye" Parrant.

Pig's Eye was a French fur trapper so named because one eye was marble-tinted and set off-kilter in the socket. A white band circled the pupil. He arrived in the area in 1832 and lived in a squatter's colony in the vicinity of Fort Snelling. He began distilling liquor and laid claim to a piece of land on the banks of the Mississippi just upstream from what is now downtown St. Paul. He opened a bar there called Pig Eye's Pandemonium at the entrance of Fountain Cave. His patrons were river boaters, local residents and soldiers. The location became so popular that mail started being addressed simply to Pig's Eye, and the appellation stuck.

The community may have been called that in perpetuity if it weren't for Father Lucien Galtier, a priest who was horrified by the name and Parrant's sinful ways. In 1841 Galtier built a small chapel and performed an exorcism allegedly incanting, *"Pig's Eye, converted thou shalt be, like Saul; Arise, and be, henceforth, Saint Paul!"* Minneapolis and St. Paul were linked in print for the first time as the "Dual Cities." Personally I prefer Twin Towns. More alliterative.

■ ■ ■

Egos and condescension prevailed.* Minneapolis newspapers were the more pompous: *"This city is known abroad as a moral, upright city, and its citizens are noted for their honesty, integrity and enterprise; and many a person has referred with pride to the fact that no house of 'ill fame' could flourish here. Our city has been so free from prostitution and the standard of morals so high, that there has been no need of reference to this evil."* (*Minneapolis Chronicle,* "The Social Evil," April 30, 1867)

St. Anthony and Minneapolis were settled primarily by Yankees from New England and New York. They valued education, diligence and high moral standards while turning a blind eye to the unsavory aspects of the burgeoning city and whitewashed the truth. St. Paul was a bit more self-aware and embraced its eclectic citizenry of Irish immigrants, woodsmen, soldiers, Native American agents, fur traders and frontier toughs. The rivalry and resentment between the two towns were evident as early as 1851 when the *Minnesota Express* described a brawl from a decidedly St. Paul point of view, *"It must have shocked the nerves of St. Anthony [who] has always represented their town as a perfect Pecksniff in religion and morals...often has St. Anthony said, 'See how much better, more industrious, more temperate and moral I am, than that rowdy St. Paul... A few fights and rows at the Falls, will cure our perfectionist neighbor of rolling up her eyes at the sight of a dog fight or a gin cocktail.'"*

The two settlements clashed from the beginning often over economic issues but also for pride fueled by petty jealousies. St. Paul won the

---

* Competition between three early settlements near the vital confluence of the Mississippi and Minnesota rivers was fierce from the beginning. St. Paul, Minnesota's capital, became the first of the three to be incorporated in 1854. St. Anthony was incorporated the following year. Minneapolis waited until 1867 to be incorporated. In 1872, St. Anthony was annexed into Minneapolis.

Arthur Fruen's proudest civic project: the new Minneapolis Auditorium
Old postcard

Iconic Grain Belt Beer sign. Located on Nicollet Island next to the Hennepin
Avenue Bridge. The Schmidt Brewery was a fixture on St. Paul's West 7th Street.
Photo courtesy of City of Minneapolis

first battle and acquired the mantle of territorial capital. At the time the city was larger, more influential and could flex bigger political muscles. The battle for bragging rights as the head of Mississippi River navigation simmered for decades and involved the placement of dams, locks and control of waterpower. In the end, it really did not matter as not far upstream from the Upper Lock at the Falls of St. Anthony, the river becomes too shallow for boats to carry much cargo from the north. "*After an economic crisis in 1857, everyone lost everything. The effects of that crisis were more serious in St. Paul. The city had to rebuild with a shortage of capital, creating an atmosphere and opportunity for diverse groups to participate but slowing the city's growth.*" (Allen Brown, *Minneapolis vs. St. Paul*)

Even lakes were dragged into the conversation. In a symmetrical geographical coincidence, the two cities are both bookended by lakes: St. Paul by White Bear and Minneapolis by Minnetonka. In 1880 the *Minneapolis Tribune* boasted that the Big Water's grand hotels proved it "*THE summer resort of the state*" while St. Paul's White Bear Lake "*can no longer be regarded as a rival.*" The *Chicago Times* insinuated itself into the conversation in 1883 declaring, "*Minneapolis people entertain that Minnetonka is exclusively a Minneapolis institution, and that St. Paul people who visit come only as strangers with an enemy's eye....*"

The sibling rivalry continued when Minneapolis built an immense exhibition hall at the Falls to display the city's industrial potential. It was erected largely because of the indignity suffered when the state agricultural fair was whisked away to St. Paul.

Literati, both domestic and foreign, weighed in on the tale of two cities early on. Mark Twain, in his travelogue *Life on the Mississippi*, opined the towns "*sprung up in the night.*" "*When I was born St. Paul had a population of three persons; Minneapolis had just a third as many. The then population of Minneapolis died two years ago; and when he died he had seen himself undergo an increase, in forty years, of fifty-nine thousand nine hundred and ninety-nine persons. He had a frog's fertility.*"

Visiting French writer Leon Paul Blouet, using the *nom de plume* Max O'Rell, observed the two towns "*are near enough to shake hands and kiss each other, but I am afraid they avail themselves of their proximity to scratch each other's faces.*"

■ ■ ■

The Minnesota State Fair began in 1859, and a permanent site was chosen in 1884 roughly halfway between the two cities at the location of the Ramsey County Poor Farm. The compromise calmed the waters for a few years. *"The two cities were separated only by a thin well-bridged river; their tails curling over the banks met and mingled, and at the juncture, under the jealous eye of each lay, every fall, the State Fair. Because of this advantageous position, and because of the agriculture eminence of the state, the fair was one of the most magnificent in America."* (F. Scott Fitzgerald, "A Night at the Fair")

The Census of 1890 was likely the biggest kerfuffle. Minneapolis had first surpassed the population of its neighbor in 1880. The next time around, accusations of cheating flew back and forth. A Deputy

An all-you-can-drink stand at the Minnesota State Fair.
The fairgrounds were placed in neutral territory to avoid inter-city disputes.
Photo courtesy of Minnesota Historical Society

Marshall from St. Paul arrested seven census takers and brought them back across the river with six bags of evidence for arraignment. The newspapers fanned the flames. The St. Paul paper pontificated: "*An abominable outrage of justice and dignity...a city which stands ashamed in the eyes of the nation... Villainous plot to pad the Minneapolis census by more than 100,000 names.*"

The Minneapolis newspaper headlines were equally incendiary: "*The Mask of Hypocrisy Torn from the Malignant Face of St. Paul! It Means War.*"

A total recount was undertaken, and gross inflation was discovered on both sides. St. Paul reported 225 people residing at the Union Railroad Depot. They claimed 25 were living in the barbershop of the Ryan Hotel. Minneapolis counted some citizens twice: once at work and again at home. Fictitious houses were invented by the hundreds. When the dust finally settled, it was determined that Minneapolis had inflated its totals by 11% and St. Paul by 7%.

The two communities fenced over the location of businesses, schools and other entities. The Federal government nudged the battling siblings toward consensus over the location of the Ford factory by deciding power would be supplied by the High Dam (a dam between both cities), and St. Paul prevailed after it agreed to pay half the cost of a bridge to Minneapolis. The University of Minnesota issue was solved by giving each city a large campus.

When major league sports first came to the Twin Cities the first two teams, the Vikings and the Twins, made their home at Metropolitan Stadium in Bloomington, an inner-ring suburb of Minneapolis with proximity to St. Paul. Throwing the Capital City a bone, the teams were named "Minnesota" rather than "Minneapolis" to avoid blowback from potential season ticket holders on the east side of the river.

The Mill City has bragging rights for pro sports championships as the Minneapolis Lakers captured two NBA crowns before moving to Los Angeles. Perhaps the silliest example of the rivalry occurred in the mid-1960s. The two city councils could not agree on Daylight Savings. For a few weeks, Minneapolis was behind St. Paul by one hour on the clock.

In 1997, hockey became a bone of contention when St. Paul Mayor Norm Coleman tried to convince the Hartford Whalers to relocate to St. Paul. In a clandestine move, Minneapolis made a counteroffer to lure the team to the Target Center. To this day the Xcel Center in St. Paul and the Target Center compete over major concerts and other events. It is estimated that the counteroffers end up costing the winning venue well over $50,000 each time. Sid Hartman, legendary *Minneapolis Tribune* columnist, displayed his typical lack of *bonhomie* when the NHL franchise, the Minnesota Wild, called the Capital City's beautiful Xcel Energy Center home, referring to St. Paul as "*East Berlin.*"

Both cities have excellent theaters, multiple music venues, highly rated colleges, top-notch park systems and museums. Minneapolis is home to the American Swedish Institute and St. Paul to the Minnesota History Center. In addition to the natural beauty of the metro area's lakes and rivers, both towns have charming neighborhoods.

St. Paul's Summit Avenue is considered to be America's finest existing example of Late Victorian (or Queen Anne) architecture and stretches from the Mississippi River to downtown. The avenue features a wide center island flanked with mansions accented by slate roofs, balconies, colonnades, turrets and *port cocheres* leading to the carriage houses. Summit is anchored in the east by the Beaux Arts St. Paul Cathedral and the James J. Hill House built by the railroad baron in 1891 for $930,000. Its amenities include an art gallery, a greenhouse, a two-story pipe organ and seventeen chimneys. The Governor's Mansion is located on Summit closer to The Father of Waters.

Sinclair Lewis, a left-leaning author who excoriated his hometown of Sauk Center, Minnesota, in *Our Town*, lived among the conservative titans of business at 516 Summit for a year. F. Scott Fitzgerald penned part of his first novel, *This Side of Paradise*, in the third-floor garret of his parents' rented home at 599 Summit, hoping to impress Zelda Sayers, the young woman he loved. He pressed his editor, Maxwell Perkins, to rush his book to print claiming "*I have so many things dependent on its success – including of course a girl.*" Scott's plan came to fruition when he married Zelda on March 30, 1920, a scant four days after *This Side of Paradise* was published.

Due to its adjacency to St. Paul, Breck School (just across the river) had many boys from the capitol city. They were a curiosity to us west-siders – like foreign-exchange students from an English-speaking country like Canada but without needing visas. There actually were some language differences. In Minneapolis we call shooting the puck off the ice "*lifting,*" while St. Paul hockey players call it "*raising.*"

Minneapolis residents listen to WDGY top-forty radio, St. Paul residents prefer KDWB. The formats are the same, but at least it gives the rival towns something to debate. Rival camps read the *Pioneer Press* or the *Tribune*. Sometimes, Minneapolis residents venture across the Mississippi to tour the state capitol or attend a play or concert.

■ ■ ■

For me at a young age, the enmity between the two cities had its roots in sports. In the 1890s, Minneapolis and St. Paul had baseball teams in the Western League. In 1902, the American Association was formed. Both towns had franchises until the Minnesota Twins brought Major League Baseball to the state in 1960.

Lexington Park in St. Paul and Nicollet Park in Minneapolis were separated by only seven miles but, if distance were dictated by animosity, they would have been half a world apart. There were accusations of ungentlemanly play as far back as the 1890s. The *Minneapolis Tribune* warned that Saints manager Charlie Comiskey would *"be served with a formal notice that the Minneapolis club will not play today's game unless guaranteed that there will be no spiking of Minneapolis players, no interference on the part of the crowd, no throwing of rocks, no throwing of dirt in the eyes of the Minneapolis players, and a few other tricks which the game yesterday was featured by."*

In 1929, on the Fourth of July, a brawl broke out that was described by one writer as *"the most vicious affair ever witnessed at Nicollet* [Field]*"* that *"required fully a dozen policemen to quell the disturbance."* Miller bench reserve player Sammy Bohne threw so many haymakers in the skirmish that *Tribune* reporter Halsey Hall's recap the next day began with the headline, *"Sammy Bohne Doesn't Play But Gets More Hits Than Those That Do."*

The players were not always combative. Sometimes romance was in the air. My Grandfather Edward *"Cleve"* Harrison took my mother, Leslie, to most Miller home games at Nicollet Park starting in the late 1920s. They sat in the front row right behind the Minneapolis dugout. When she matured into a young woman, players started sending her notes asking for a date by slipping a folded piece of paper through the cracks in the back wall of the dugout. Grandpa was a formidable chaperone, though. This was a man who called his daughter *"Babe"* until his dying day.

The quality of baseball was excellent, and the Twin Cities' squads produced twenty future Cooperstown Hall of Fame inductees. The Minneapolis fans were so distraught when the New York Giants called

St. Paul Saints celebrate a home run.
Photo courtesy of Minnesota Historical Society

up Willie Mays that the big-league club president Horace Stoneham paid for a full-page apology in the *Tribune* to explain the move.

"*Those were the days when everybody took their best dates to the Hip [hockey rink], rode a 10 cent fare, ate a beef dinner for a buck and saw Moose Goheen dump enemies into the fifth row for a 75-cent ticket.*" (*Dimensions Newsletter*)

Minnesota is a hockey-crazy state. The State High School Hockey Tournament usually sells out St. Paul's NHL arena, drawing upwards of 125,000 fans to the four-day event. The University of Minnesota venue, located on the Minneapolis campus and named for the Godfather of Minnesota hockey, John Mariucci, holds up to 10,000 spectators. This is a gargantuan arena by most college hockey standards. The University is the only institution to have separate arenas for the men and women pucksters.

Our family loved sports. Dad was a boxing, football and hockey devotee who found baseball too slow and boring and had no interest in the nuances and strategy that make the game fascinating. Mom, by contrast, was a tomboy influenced by her father and loved baseball and most other sports. She was the parent most likely to play catch with me in the yard.

We went to college hockey games, but the most exciting contests were the Minneapolis Millers and St. Paul Saints minor league tilts. The Minneapolis Arena on Dupont Avenue in the Uptown district was considered state-of-the-art when it was completed in 1924. It was known simply as "The Arena" and held up to 5,400 hockey fans. Admission in the early years was 40 cents for the cheap seats, and attendees were invited to skate after the games ended.

For me, the golden years of Twin City minor league hockey were between 1959 and 1965. I often went to games with my father, my friend Robbie Pearson and his dad Jim. It was like going to a circus with scarier mammals. Rob and I were in hockey heaven. The early-model Zamboni resurfaced the ice between periods with Bubble-Up pop (we did not call it soda) advertising emblazoned on each side.

The organ player performed in a cage to protect him from errant pucks. Between periods we cruised the corridor. A stop at the concession stand was a must. Rob and I bought a Coke and a Nut Goodie candy bar for a dime. We cheered, booed and ducked when projectiles were launched by surly fans. Then came the brawls.

Goalie Harry McQueston. Minneapolis Millers, 1948
Photo courtesy of Minnesota Historical Society

One Thanksgiving evening, we went to a Millers game after our afternoon meal. An epic brawl erupted while sister Martha visited the bathroom. I think she may have been secretly working for AAA as she always inspected rest rooms whenever we took a road trip. In her absence the benches emptied, and bottles and chairs were launched over the chicken wire while cops and fans wandered around the ice at their own risk. Martha returned to her seat crestfallen, just in time to witness the aftermath with players sorting out jerseys and equipment shed during the melee.

In those days, teams only carried one goalie on the roster. If he were injured during a game and unable to continue, the public address announcer asked the crowd if a net-minder was in attendance. Usually, a volunteer rushed down to the dressing room, suited up and took the ice. While I was way too young, my status as a fledgling goaltender made me dream of the day I could answer the call.

Once or twice a season we headed east to St. Paul to see the Millers play in enemy territory. An adult cheering for Minneapolis in the Saints lair did so at his or her own risk. They were kind to pre-teens, however, and teased Robbie and me mercilessly without malice.

Erected in the early 1930s, the Saint Paul Auditorium was more of a multi-purpose venue than a hockey arena. Sometimes we had to sit on a cement step when the crowd exceeded capacity. The Fire Marshall was nowhere to be found.

The Fruen family had a standing date in St. Paul every New Year's Day evening at Aunt Betty's Jefferson Avenue home. She married Uncle Charles O'Connor, and he was not about to leave his hometown for Minneapolis. The west-side Fruens forded the Father of Waters to celebrate Grandma's birthday. In 1962, my niece Tracy honored her great-grandmother when she was born on January 1.

■ ■ ■

"Minneapolis is at once considered one of the most livable cities in the country, and the one with some of the greatest racial disparities in housing and income and education. There's a dissonance, locals say, between its progressive rhetoric and the reality of how people of different races experience completely different cities." (Sarah Holder, *"Why This Started in Minneapolis"*)

The Twin Cities have had the reputation of municipalities that work with great neighborhoods, well-educated and liberal citizens, wonderful green spaces, dedication to the arts and racial tolerance. There is a dark side to this squeaky clean image, however – the Minnesota Paradox. Oddly, soon after statehood, very progressive laws and policies were in place. The opportunity for blacks to vote in the Gopher State came before the 15th Amendment was ratified. Segregated schools were excluded from state financial support. Blacks began to be seated as jurors. Then it all came to a grinding halt.

White activists were on cruise control, perhaps thinking their work was done: "[Minneapolis] *to a large extent, even though this is, for the most part, a progressive/liberal city. It's also a city in which the races live in parallel universes. It is possible for white people to have no contacts at all with blacks unless they have kids in the schools, or at my university, or they're in the military, or prison."* (William B. Green, history professor, Augsburg University, *"Why This Started in Minneapolis"*)

Rondo neighborhood, St. Paul truck accident draws a crowd.
Photo courtesy of Minnesota Historical Society

James J. Hill house, St. Paul
Photo courtesy of Minnesota Historical Society

In Minneapolis, real-estate covenants red-lined blacks by prohibiting sales to them, and other minorities, in certain neighborhoods. In 1910 the city was largely integrated, albeit few African Americans called Minnesota home then. The restrictive covenants came when the population grew by leaps and bounds.

Imagine my shock to discover that our house on 5232 Clinton Avenue South, built in 1928, was right in the middle of a south Minneapolis red-line zone. The Supreme Court struck down the covenants across the U.S. in 1948, but the effects live on. The populace may be enlightened, but change has not kept pace with expectations.

St. Paul had similar restrictions, but the city had a flourishing, proud black community, Rondo, in the Summit and University areas. There were integrated schools, businesses, churches, social clubs, culture, entertainment and affordable housing. Black-owned barber shops and beauty salons were social hubs. In 1950, Rondo was home to 80 percent of St. Paul's African Americans. Plentiful job opportunities existed in the railroad, meat processing and the service industries. Literacy and education were valued, upward mobility possible and home ownership achievable.

The effort to provide speedy access between the Twin City downtowns scattered Rondo's citizens and commerce to the wind. The path of Interstate 94 was more deferential to white businesses than black. The Federal Aid Highway Act of 1956 provided funds, and the city planners' finalized freeway path gutted Rondo. Its legacy lives on in the form of Rondo Days, an annual celebration held on the 3rd Saturday of July.

It should come as no surprise that St. Paul and Minneapolis face the same challenges encountered by all large U.S. cities. Do they live up to their squeaky-clean reputations? No. Am I still proud of the Mill City despite its faults and the hard work that remains? Yes. I am first in line to point out all the merits of Pig's Eye, too. I mean St. Paul.

The chalet with an updated color scheme of forest green and red orange, May, 2021
Photo by Ross Fruen

Fifty Years Down the Road

*"Cities are never random. No matter how chaotic they
might seem, everything about them grows out of a need
to solve a problem. In fact, a city is nothing more than a
solution to a problem that in turn creates more problems
that need more solutions, until towers rise, roads widen,
bridges are built, and millions of people are caught up in
a mad race to feed the problem-solving, problem-creating
frenzy."*

Neal Shusterman,
Downsiders

MAKE NO MISTAKE, MINNEAPOLIS is no fairytale oasis devoid
of the myriad issues challenging American cities. Economic, housing
and racial inequities have long existed and erupted in tragedy in front
of an international audience in 2020. The reality of policing approach-
es in different neighborhoods came in stark contrast to the Mill City's
squeaky-clean image. The Minnesota Paradox and its inconsistencies
persist in a city long heralded as one of the most livable in the United
States. The reality is this quality of life pertains only to certain pockets
and neighborhoods.

I come from privilege. A nice home in a neighborhood with all the
amenities: Pearl Park and Lake Nokomis to the east, the Parkway and
Minnehaha Creek to the north, Diamond Lake to the South and Lake
Harriet to the west. An excellent education, top-notch medical and
dental care, and a good diet. The family standard: We had everything
we needed but not everything we wanted. My privilege extended to our
family who provided support and affection. We lived in what was officially Southwest Minneapolis in the "Page" area.

So what exactly can be done to improve the quality of life for all

Minneapolitans? To address the seemingly insolvable problems? I am no Urban Studies expert, but I do know that we, as individuals, have two things to offer: time and money. I do not know the details of my family's financial donations to charities, but I am pleased to report that the Fruen family, following my grandparents' lead, volunteer and work countless hours to make Minneapolis a better city. Lake Minnetonka and Bassett's Creek have received the same attention.

My parents rarely said no when approached to participate in community projects. My father coached youth sports teams even when he had no child on the roster. He did it for the love of the game and the players. Dad supported and campaigned for candidates at the local and state level. He served coffee after church while my mother worked in the nursery so the parents could attend the service. Frequently, she invited me in to see an adorable toddler.

Mom was a master delegator, recruiter, and manager. Her pleasant manner drew people to her and before they knew it, they were deputized. Leslie chose to view the world as a wonderful place filled with people with unlimited potential. She wore many different hats from Camp Fire Girl leader to being a member of the Breck School Board of Trustees.

As a nod to the family's Minneapolis roots, Leslie was a guide at the Ard Godfrey House, the oldest remaining wood-frame structure in the city. Ard Godfrey came to the Mississippi in 1848 to build a lumber mill and a dam at St. Anthony Falls. Two years later logs began floating downstream.

■ ■ ■

Agri-business giant Conagra purchased the Fruen Milling Company in 1971 and, despite a commitment to expand many categories, the conglomerate was only interested in the racehorse feed and closed the Minneapolis operation soon after. There was excitement when Frich Development announced plans to turn the towers and elevators into upscale condominiums with stunning views of downtown and Theodore Wirth Park. Restaurants and retail would occupy the ground level.

Access is a big hurdle. To reach the property, one must cross two sets of railroad tracks, one used by Canadian Pacific and the other by Burlington Northern. CP granted permission but not BN, so the plan remains moribund. Others have tried to jumpstart the project including Fruen Mill Partners Inc. and Lippert and Associates. Access remains an issue, and other impediments like the soft commercial real-estate market, financial liquidity and back taxes further complicate matters.

The gray metal husk of the Mill still stands in the Glenwood hollow. It is dilapidated, dangerous and defaced to the point of ugliness with a Conagra sign still visible. Hopefully the historic site will someday be revitalized. Another plan is in the works. "*So it's perhaps proper that Fruen's mill still overlooks the creek and the park he and his family made possible with their innovation and largesse over the years. And when a developer does somehow manage to navigate all the obstacles necessary to rehabilitate Fruen's [William's] masterpiece, we'd hope that the resulting structure would make the old machinist proud.*" (Sharon Parker, "Down by the Old Fruen Mill," *Minneapolis Observer Quarterly*)

■ ■ ■

The family operated Glenwood Inglewood until 2004 when it was sold to Deep Rock Water of Denver to expand their distribution, mainly by buying the brand and then consolidating bottling to minimize the freight impact of the heavy product. Glenwood spring water is sold in the Upper Midwest to this day. The plant remained vacant for a few years until the 18,000-square-foot building was converted to Utepils Brewing Company using Great-grandfather's spring-water wells.

The original name was slated to be Bryn Mawr Brewing, but the owners were stymied by a trademark conflict and switched to Utepils, a Norwegian term for the initial beer quaffed on the first sunny spring day. During the current contest of who can brew the "*hoppiest*" beer, Utepils goes the traditional Bavarian route with malt balancing the hops. This is right in my swilling wheelhouse.

My great-grandfather and grandfather would likely disapprove, particularly since land the family donated to the Park Board was used to complete the project. I am not abstemious and am happy to have activity in the glen again. And they make great beer. The voluminous tap room is appointed in the German beer-hall style, and an outside beer garden hugs the banks of Bassett's Creek with a fire pit fashioned from some of the old mill's machinery. The wide-open space in the brewery is a nod to traditional German beer halls.

Ruins of the old Fruen Mill
Courtesy of Hennepin County Library

The Utepils Brewery uses the remodeled Glenwood
Inglewood facilities and water from William Fruen's spring.
Trademark issues forced the name change from Bryn Mawer
Brewing to Utepils. *Photo courtesy of Utepils*

■ ■ ■

Acute Myeloid Leukemia has plagued our family for generations. The pernicious blood-born disease claimed the lives of my father, cousin Libby O'Connor's pre-teen son Brian and my Dad's cousin Glory, a beautiful young woman and my mother's childhood friend, who introduced my parents. Brother Mike succumbed to the pernicious disease in December 2021. The genetic disposition of this form of Leukemia is prevalent in the Braden branch of the family passed on through Great-grandmother Henrietta "Nettie" Braden Watson Emerson.

Our Braden cousin from Oregon, David Frohnmayer, and his wife Lynn traveled to Minneapolis seeking a bone marrow match for their two daughters stricken with Fanconi Anemia, often a precursor to Acute Myeloid Leukemia. The Fruens turned out en masse for blood testing, 50 strong including some local Bradens, but the search yielded no matches.

Next stop was Musquodoboit, Nova Scotia, a Huguenot community where John Braden settled after fighting in the Revolutionary War. For England.

> *"Aunt Jen Braden*
> *Was born in Nova Scotia*
> *At Musquodoboit*
> *Near Shubincity*
> *And not a great way from Antigonish"*

Family Verse

"*The community responded so immediately, so genuinely, so personally that it made you feel as though you came to a family reunion just a little too late.*" (David Frohnmayer)

Once again, the Frohnmayers were met with open arms but without success. David's career as Oregon Attorney General and President of the University of Oregon prepared him for the benefits of persistence, networking and creative thinking. Lynn managed a branch of the Oregon Children Services Division and was a nationally recognized childcare consultant and a fierce advocate for all children. Fanconi Anemia was a fight Lynn and David would not win. At least not yet.

"Such a blow would have crushed most people, but Dave and Lynn responded with fists clenched. Two lay people, they took responsibility for the sorry state of medical knowledge. Scribbled notes, photocopied journal articles, and hasty phone calls grew into the Fanconi Anemia Research Fund with assets of $5 million, which sponsors research into the condition and funds support families it affects." (Garrett Epps, "The Man Who Battled Death to a Draw," *The Atlantic*)

A third Frohnmayer daughter, Amy, battled Fanconi into her late twenties while earning bachelor's and master's degrees from Stanford and another masters from Oregon State, but the disease eventually progressed to AML. Amy died at the age of twenty-nine. Her parents once again fought through their grief and continued their quest for a cure by founding the National Marrow Donor Program in Minneapolis.

■ ■ ■

Following in Great-grandfather Watson's footsteps as Hennepin County Superintendent of schools, many in the family became educators. Sister Martha taught elementary school in Florida and England while my cousin Marnie O'Connor spent her career teaching special education. Aunt Louise Fruen Barnett is a retired academician with a love of history and the written word who taught school in Santa Barbara.

Big Island neighbor, now family member Lois Granrud Fruen, is a nationally renowned author, Director of Curriculum, head of the Science Department as well as a chemistry and science educator at my alma mater Breck School. Now retired and working as a consultant, she is still a sought-after expert and honored scientist. Nominated by five of her high school students who attended the celebrated Massachusetts Institute of Technology, she received a MIT Inspirational Teacher award.

Lois is a contributor to and a board member of the *ChemMatters* magazine published four times a year by the American Chemistry Society, founded in 1876 with the purpose of illuminating the connections between everyday life and chemistry. She has received many grants that allow her to expand her expertise and give her students an extraordinary educational experience.

There are politicians in the family. Sister-in-law Lael Fruen served as President of the Minnesota Young Republicans, and cousin Galen

O'Connor ran for state legislator as a third-party candidate to offer an alternative.

■ ■ ■

Aunt Mona and Uncle Doug Fruen are devout Episcopalians and met at a teenage dance at St. Paul's Episcopal Church just off the northeastern shore of Lake of the Isles. After retirement they sold their family home and moved into an inner-city Minneapolis duplex to independently perform missionary work from volunteer activities to leading Bible-study groups.

Aunt Mona identified a need for shelter, sustenance and rejuvenation for single women often on probation or parole with the goal of reuniting them with their children. She presented her passion project to Metro Hope Ministries, who shared her aspirations and helped bring the Healing House, located near the Little Earth American Indian community in the Phillips neighborhood of South Minneapolis, to fruition.

The residence accommodates up to 20 women and 24 children and accepts those in need of recovery from addiction and abuse. At the age of ninety Mona Fruen recently stepped down from her position on the Metro Hope Ministries Board of Trustees. My aunt and uncle still live independently in a Northeast Minneapolis apartment.

"*Damascus Way is a halfway house program serving men with criminal histories. Assistance in finding employment, permanent housing, and a support community is offered. But more than that, we provide opportunities for our residents to consider the deeper issues of their lives. Those who come to Damascus Way are here because they have lost their freedom. The misuse of freedom results in being locked up in addictions, destructive behaviors, and ultimately, behind iron bars.*" (Damascus Way website)

Cousin Craig Fruen served as the executive director for the 18-bed facility. Damascus Way offers shelter, meals and recreation in a private woodland location in addition to meetings dealing with substance abuse, coaching sessions and the tools to aid in the transition to post incarceration life and avoid recidivism.

■ ■ ■

The Fruen Family has not forgotten its obligation to the waterways of the Minneapolis area from Lake Minnetonka to the Mississippi.

■ ■ ■

Minnehaha Creek Watershed District Appointment Whips up Waves of Anger

"[David] Cochrane, the mayor of Greenwood, was named...by the Hennepin County Board to replace Donald Fruen, Orono, who had been the district's chairman since its formation in 1967... The switch made Fruen angry. It made other members of the district's board of managers angry. And it made Hennepin County Board Chairman Robert James angry... The caustic Fruen called it the work of 'a couple of two-bit politicians' namely E.F. (Bud) Robb and Rep. Salisbury Adams, Orono Conservative. He said he antagonized them by urging in a legislative hearing that the Gray's Bay dam at the mouth of Lake Minnetonka be rebuilt six inches higher as a means of controlling floods on Minnehaha Creek... It is no secret, even to Fruen, that his outspoken manner contributed to his removal."

Charles Whiting,
Minneapolis Star

■ ■ ■

It was an incestuous triangle as Donald was my grandfather's cousin and Budd Robb was a friend of our branch of the Fruen family. Admittedly, Donald was an irascible old coot. However, as president of Glenwood Inglewood, he knew quite a bit about clean water, which was a major goal of the board. Like his grandfather William Henry, Donald was an inventor devising and patenting a cooler for bottled water. His other civic-minded activities included the presidency of the Minnesota Wildlife Federation and a member of the Upper Mississippi and St. Croix Commission. Donald Fruen was posthumously inducted into the Bottled Water Hall of Fame. Yes, there is such an organization.

The Bassett Creek Watershed Management Commission has a mission with many goals, but the succinct phrase at the bottom of the web page simply reads, *"cleaner, healthier water."* When Great-grandfather first visited the stream, it flowed through woodlands and prairies. As Minneapolis grew, cement and asphalt replaced much of the wetlands that held rainwater and storm run-off that then drained quickly into the creek, carrying unfiltered pollutants with it. Today the stream meanders twelve miles through nine different municipalities beginning with its Medicine Lake source in Plymouth to Minneapolis, where it empties into the Mississippi.

The Commission strives to minimize storm run-off and flooding as well as improve habitat for wildlife and the valley's natural beauty. Brother Mike Fruen was a commissioner in the organization until his death, giving back a bit of the largesse afforded the Fruen family by the waterways of its adopted city.

■ ■ ■

"'They went gangbusters in technical assistance,' [Duane] *Scribner* [Dayton Hudson Foundation] *said...'Our feedback from within Target was that the idea was wonderful. Retail fits Target. It has the industry contacts and lots of ideas.' Fruen and several Target volunteers planned the store layout, merchandise mix and equipment... Without Target, it's clear that the project probably would have failed because PPL knew nothing of the retail business. Target introduced PPL to vendors. Some agreed to donate surplus merchandise or sell at volume discounts to PPL. Target interviewed several candidates for the critical job of store manager, established a bookkeeping system and oversaw store design."* Neil St. Anthony, *Until All are Housed in Dignity*

Project for Pride in Living is a nonprofit organization dedicated to building, rehabbing and financing housing for low income, inner city Minneapolis residents in conjunction with job training for the unemployed and under-employed. Joe Selvaggio, a streetwise Chicago ex-priest with an edge and a penchant for social justice. He was the tireless driving force behind PPL who conceived the idea of a thrift store not only to provide career readiness for those in need but to provide low price merchandise for the Minneapolis Phillips neighborhood that was underserved by big-box discount retailers.

Selvaggio contacted the Dayton Hudson Foundation, and I was asked to determine the feasibility of the concept. Once the enterprise was green-lighted, my Target colleagues and I (from Real Estate to

Human Resources to Merchandising) volunteered to kickstart the store's operation. We were aided by a $60,000 grant from the foundation. A run-down storefront on the corner of Chicago and Franklin, located on major bus routes, provided access to those without other forms of transportation. PPL workers rehabbed the building, and a ribbon-cutting ceremony took place on November 4, 1985.

Tart-tongued Joe, emboldened by the successful roll-out, could not resist taking a shot at me. Assuming I was part of the Mill City suburban gentry, he asked, "*So where do you live, Edina?*"

I replied, "*No, Minneapolis.*"

On the steps leading to the Brick House
L to R: Amy Fruen Kenner, Kyle Fruen, Laura Fruen Fahey
Photo courtesy of Kristin Fruen

In the late spring of 2021, the inevitable came to pass when a portion of the Crown Point property was listed and quickly sold for over the asking price. The family's major stakeholders were absentee owners who visited the island infrequently, and the cost of upkeep was not insignificant. The purchasing couple was local, and I had a connection to Mark's family. He grew up on Christmas Lake, just a hop, skip and a jump from Minnetonka's St. Alban's Bay.

It was a bittersweet time with emotions all over the map. After time to digest, I believe that the Fruen family's Big Island heritage will be maintained and enhanced with the new ownership providing added energy and resources. The Latin word "Excelsior" seems appropriate: onward and upward.

The July 1987 super storm hovers over Lake Minnetonka. My parents navigated the open water between Big Island and Orono's Brown Bay in blinding rain.
Photo courtesy of Nate Anderson, KARE 11

Nature Bites Back

*"Nature, in her indifference, makes no
distinction between good and evil."*

Anatole France,
THE REVOLT OF THE ANGELS

DESPITE ITS BEAUTY AND bounty, Lake Minnetonka is not always
an idyllic retreat, and the Fruens were not immune when nature extracted some revenge. The 1930s drought welcomed the family to their
recently acquired property on Big Island. The lake level dropped sev-
en feet, and docks were extended many yards to reach navigable water.
Dad's generation made the best of it. A tiny island was exposed, and
the children had their own private picnic grounds. Huge boulders were
uncovered, and sandy peninsulas appeared.

The Upper Midwest was not as affected by the Dust Bowl years as
the south-central region of the country. It was merely an inconvenience
for the Crown Point Fruens compared to the devastation suffered by
the 3-1/2 million displaced Americans and the misery of those trying to
scratch a living from the earth. Topsoil turned to dust and blew away in
black blizzards. The dearth of precipitation sounded the death knell for
fruit growers around the Big Water. Labor and raw material shortages
caused by World War II planted the final stake in the lakeside industry.

■ ■ ■

A series of thunderstorms with significant displays of lightning struck
the western metro area of Minneapolis and Lake Minnetonka during
the Memorial Day Weekend of 1944. Three streetcars on the 4th and
Glenwood line, close to Glenwood Inglewood and the Fruen Mill, were
struck. One car contained 40 passengers, but no injuries were reported.

The Crown Point shoreline retreats during the 1930s drought
Fruen family photo

Fruen dock extended to reach water during the drought
Fruen family photo

Our Brick House was located on one of the lake's highest elevations, and a bolt of lightning burned the structure to the ground. Fortunately, the family had returned to Bryn Mawr before the inferno.

"*The Crown Point home of Alderman Arthur Fruen on Big Island, Minnetonka, set afire by lightning, burned down after Excelsior fireman, ferrying their equipment to the island, failed to halt the blaze.*" (*Minneapolis Evening Tribune*, May 31, 1944)

The outbreak of six tornados on May 6, 1965, is the most in Minnesota recorded history and did not spare Lake Minnetonka from its destructive swath. The meteorological event, now known as "*The Longest Night*," included two twisters that touched down on the lake. It was early for such violent weather but uncommonly warm temperatures – mixed with high dew points coupled with a colliding cold front – created the volatile system.

The first two of the six tornados struck Lake Minnetonka at dinner time, 6:08 and 6:27. The initial twister touched down near Lake Susan in Chanhassen and headed toward the northernmost part of the Lower Lake. It skirted the east end of Big Island and wreaked havoc on the Deephaven neighborhood. One hundred fifty homes were destroyed.

There were no deaths or injuries reported, which many credit to radio and television alerts and the first use of Civil Defense sirens. Moving and sounding like a locomotive, the funnel knocked down trees, uprooting and tossing at least two into the lake. The Peavey Lake Bridge on Ferndale Road was totally blocked. The tornado then hopped over my Uncle Ralph's home high on a Brown's Bay bluff.

My mother's brother was intelligent and a storied sportsman but entertained an unorthodox twister strategy. Ignoring the conventional wisdom of hiding in the basement, he pressed his shoulder against the front door as the maelstrom roared over his rambler-style home. The contrast in air pressure blew out the large picture windows but the rest of the house – and my uncle – were unharmed.

The second tornado, rated F4, touched ground in Carver County before dissipating in Minnetrista, killing three and injuring 175. The Upper Lake town of Navarre was hit hard. Many buildings were flattened including the Mobil Gas station and the drive-in movie theater, leaving only the marquee that soon read "*Gone with the Wind.*"

The awesome power and fury of the storm were undeniable. Witnesses watched as the funnel peeled water from the shoreline, raising the

Brick House struck by lightning on Memorial Day, 1944
Fruen family photo

The May 6, 1965 tornados sucked the water out of Christmas Lake and certain bays
of Lake Minnetonka. Boats at the Minnetonka Boat Works were picked
up by the twister and strewn like a box of toothpicks.
Photo by Earl Seubert, Minneapolis Star Tribune

levels of the bays as much as three feet. Docks were shredded into large toothpicks. Cars and boats were scattered with one vehicle deposited in the basement of a destroyed home. A Minnetonka Boat Works facility filled with watercraft still in dry dock was leveled; its contents strewn like a game of Pick Up Sticks. Someone's horse was found tangled high in the branches of a tree. Armed Army reservists were dispatched and guarded against looting and other mischief.

■ ■ ■

On the morning of July 23, 1987, my father was released from Abbott Hospital after his final chemotherapy treatment. Weakened but happy for some freedom, my mother and he made a beeline for Big Island. A few hours after their arrival, a night-black line of thunderstorms approached. Around six that evening, my parents saw the approaching tempest. They hurriedly left Crown Point after checking the radio for information and headed north to Brown's Bay where Dad's new fiberglass boat was moored when not in use.

Halfway there the winds and heavy rain arrived in earnest, greatly reducing visibility and churning the water. Upon finally reaching Brown's Bay, Dad entered the lagoon containing the boat slip, threading the needle of the narrow entrance while fighting the buffeting wind and the sheets of pelting rain. After quickly securing the boat, my parents hurried to the car and headed east on Highway 12 before exiting on to Highway 494.

The rain was torrential, eventually setting a record of ten inches at the Twin Cities Airport. The massive flooding damaged 7,000 homes and caused thousands to abandon their vehicles. The meteorological event, named the *Superstorm*, was deemed a one in one-thousand-year event by the Minnesota State Climatology Office.

As my mother and father approached the France Avenue exit, Dad could see submerged cars in the hollow below the bridge. They quickly left the interstate and took refuge in the lobby of Fairview Hospital. Eventually the storm relented, and they made the short drive home to Clinton Avenue. It was an inexorable, frightening, exhausting day.

Make no mistake: While Minnetonka is a wonderful body of water, it is not to be underestimated.

A summer day at the Excelsior Amusement Park.
The wooden "Cyclone" roller coaster is in the background.
Old postcard

Random Lake Minnetonka Summer Rhythms and Ruminations

"In the summer, the song sings itself."

William Carlos Williams

IT IS CURIOUS WHY some memories stick and others fade. Why are prosaic recollections significant when others, important at the time, disappear? The original lower-level Chalet wood screen door survived scores of years and thousands of slammings. It had the rigidity of a floppy disc as it bounced back and wobbled in reaction to its abrupt close. The screen was perpetually bulging outward from young children ignoring the wood push-bar right at their eye level.

Summer after summer, decade after decade, Fruen children tossed the small stones littering the lake bottom near the Crown Point shore into the larger boulders preceding the walkway. No matter how many hours were spent, progress was elusive. Still no sandy beach. Why do these images resonate? Perhaps the repetitions created Mental Muscle Memory.

Some memories are forged through fear. Towards the end of her life, Great-grandmother Emerson wandered into the Big Woods behind the Crown Point outbuildings and was missing for several terrifying hours. She was located and, despite some scratches and insect bites, was unharmed. My nephew Chris, not much more than a toddler, once fell or jumped from the dock into the lake and sank to the bottom. His mother was paralyzed by panic, but my wife Kristin's lifeguard instincts prevailed. She dove into the water and brought the sputtering boy to the surface.

Other incidents are top-of-mind because of mystery. One summer night a few friends spent the night in the Brick House. A high school crony of Jim Hurd's, known as Brother Worker, was secured in the top bunk of the downstairs bedroom to a fence that was designed to prevent potential falls onto the unforgiving linoleum.

A few hours later, a loud crash emanated from downstairs. Brother Worker had plowed through the safety barrier and bounced on the linoleum. We rushed down to find him sitting on the back steps, clearing the cobwebs after his inadvertent plunge. He was gone when the sun rose and was never seen again. How did he get off the island?

For many years we celebrated my birthday, June 6, on Crown Point. It was early in the season, and the weather was often brisk. My friends and I usually soldiered through with a standard-issue menu of activities including a quick dip in the lake and posing for the standard photo of shivering, goose-pimpled, hunched-shouldered boys huddled together on the dock for warmth. We played games on the hill, had lunch, opened presents and ate cake.

One celebration is memorable due to extreme embarrassment. My mother always worked hard to provide a fun experience, but she did not sweat the details. She trusted the baker and did not bother to inspect the cake. When I stepped up to blow out the candles, I was horrified to read the message in large script, *"Happy Birthday Rose."* I was mortified.

My thirteenth birthday celebration coincided with a sorrowful family milestone. I knew something was amiss when Mom did not join us for the Big Island party. After an afternoon of frivolity Martha, Dad and I returned home to Minneapolis to discover the pastor of our church talking with Leslie in the den. Grandpa Harrison had had a stroke that morning and died at the age of 77.

■ ■ ■

Some recollections are prominent through kismet. One summer vacation Marty Schuster, a classmate from second grade through college, spent the night in the Brick House. The next day at mid-morning, he asked to be ferried to his car as he had an appointment. I said I needed to get going, too. As I secured the *Queen Merrie* at the landing, he drove away. I headed downtown, parked in my usual Mar-Ten parking ramp and walked the short distance to the august Medical Arts Building.

The dermatologist's office was a few feet from the elevator and, when I opened the door, there was Marty reading a magazine. His appointment was right before mine.

Sometimes a smile can produce a memory. My mother was naturally cheerful, but Dad was a bigger challenge. One summer my friend Dean Nikitas visited from the Berkshires of Massachusetts. He was so excited to visit the "frontier." The New Englander arrived at the Minneapolis/St. Paul Airport wearing a Stetson cowboy hat and was thrilled to see a Native American in the concourse.

After a car tour of Minneapolis, we headed to Lake Minnetonka. Dean struggled to ski but persevered. Finally emerging from the lake, he remained upright and made the quick circle from Crown Point to the Recreation Bay end of Big Island and back. My father grinned broadly at his new protégé.

It took three generations for the inevitable: The proximity of Crown Point to Point Comfort worked its magic. Cousin Jimmy Fruen married the girl next door, Lois Granrud. Big Island's southernmost tip was the perfect setting for the ceremony. The expansive lawn on the hilltop was manicured, and the crowd of friends and family was dressed in colorful summer sartorial splendor.

The ceremony proceeded until a brush fire flared just below the top of Point Comfort. A cigarette butt ignited the grass trimmings, and the conflagration was substantial enough to draw the Excelsior Fire Department boat brigade. They pumped water from the lake and sent vast plumes arching skyward before landing on the blaze. Once the fire was extinguished the wedding continued, and we celebrated by sitting on the lawn and eating a delicious smorgasbord of Big Island picnic provisions. It was a notable island occasion featuring a surprise display of pyrotechnics.

A few years later in late autumn, my sister-in-law Lael's brother Rick and his newlywed wife Kathy needed a honeymoon destination. They had a limited budget, and Rick accepted the offer of a deserted Crown Point vacation. He told Kathy they were headed to a secluded island location. She packed for a Caribbean or Polynesian trip only to be ferried to a lake cabin close to home. Hopefully, sweaters were part of her trousseau.

Some recollections are less specific and more atmospheric. To its detriment, Lake Minnetonka has been spit-polished and shined, erasing

Fire breaks out at the wedding of Lois Granrud and Jim Fruen.
Fruen family photo

much of its old character. The Excelsior Amusement Park and its rickety rollercoaster are long gone as is Danceland, which hosted the Rolling Stones and the Beach Boys early in their careers as well as a few fights between rival gangs. Regional bands were still popular in the area and teens jammed the dance floor. The Underbeats had a hit song, "Foot Stompin," which featured a prominent drum beat. The dancers followed suit, jumping up and down causing the already sagging floor to groan and sink further.

■ ■ ■

Old-school fishermen in their small boats are at the mercy of their wave-producing big brothers. Access for shore fishing continues to dwindle, making it more difficult for those who come from the city to catch panfish and the occasional lunker. I recall crowds lining both sides of the pilings at the Narrows, buckets at the ready to store the day's catch.

One does not see so many ramshackle wood docks anymore (The kind that looks home made with old tires acting as boat bumpers rather than the store-bought prettier ones). I miss the old character of the Big Water. The thrill a teenage boy would experience while driving a boat at full throttle over the surface of a mirror-smooth, almost-empty southern Lower Lake. A wooded shoreline that was more in evidence before the onslaught of development.

I even miss the chance of a getting a splinter. Or maybe a bit dirty. The smell of an outboard motor's exhaust. They were not as efficient as today, but they did cover the stench of a wet dog. I miss the time when walking barefoot down Water Street in Excelsior was not uncommon. Or passing by Bacon Drug and waving to Jim Hurd's little sister Kathy if she were working. On a hot, humid day I sometimes stepped into the air-conditioned store and ordered a cherry phosphate – a fizzy concoction dating back to the 1870s that consisted of cherry syrup, phosphoric acid and soda water.

Across Water Street and a few yards closer to the lake, Tony's Barber Shop remains in operation and maintains its status as one of the vestiges of old Downtown Excelsior businesses. Many of the sixty-year-old fixtures remain, including the vintage barber chairs. Tony's son Ed, approaching 80 years of age, runs the shop now.

A few times every season I waited to get my "Heinie" haircut trimmed, usually on a rainy day when we were "in residence" on the island. The barber stopped just short of shaving my head. The style was inspired by and named for the look sported by German soldiers. As I waited, I leafed through the Archie and Superman comic books and looked around the shop. A poster was hung featuring a myriad of hairstyles and included Butch, Crew and Flat-Top. The more sophisticated looks required combs and hair oil such as the "A Little Dab Will Do Ya" Brylcreem.

The Zembrycki proprietors were baseball fans in addition to their barbering skills. As I sat still in the chair I studied the 1959 Chicago White Sox American League Champion team picture. I can still recite the names of many of the featured players: Pitching ace Early Wynn and the slugging catcher Sherm Lollar. The silk-smooth fielding middle infield tandem of Nellie Fox and Luis Aparacio were not enough to overcome the talent-laden Los Angeles Dodgers led by the future Hall of Fame pitching duo of Don Drysdale and Sandy Koufax. They may not have won the World Series, but the names and faces of the '59 Sox were immortalized on the wall of the Excelsior barber shop.

■ ■ ■

For decades the Excelsior Amusement Park dominated the shoreline of the town, and the rollercoaster was recognizable from Big Island. It was first called the Mountain Ride, then the Cyclone, although it was known simply as the Roller Coaster to most. The 65-foot high and 3,000-foot-long ride was built on marshy terrain in 1925. The most harrowing section was not the inclines and sudden dips – nor the hairpin curves – but a straight-away that seemed headed for Excelsior Bay until a counterclockwise switchback brought the rider back over terra firma.

It became such a valuable piece of real estate that by the time I became aware of the facility, it was destined for the wrecking ball. We went there infrequently as children, because we were told that we had our own water park minutes away on Crown Point. The first owner, Twin Cities Rapid Transit Company, created the attraction to augment streetcar ridership, particularly on Saturday and Sunday.

Fred W. Pearce Sr. purchased the amusement park early on but, by the 1960s, it was in decline. Picnicking families began to stay away when the park became a haunt of bored teenagers interested in slouching, smoking, glaring and fighting. Only stopgap repairs were undertaken, and it was a rare occasion when all the attractions were in working order. The Scrambler was the ride most likely to cause abdominal distress. Other rides included a Ferris wheel, kiddy boat rides, bumper cars and a carousel with beautiful Italian hand-carved horses.

The Fun House was a favorite with wooden slides and grain sacks to sit on to reduce the friction from denim blue jeans. A mammoth spinning barrel challenged those brave enough to try to run to the other end without wiping out. A speedily rotating disc created a human roulette wheel, and centrifugal force ejected many who failed to stay on board. The padded walls offered some protection. An unexpected series of air jets shot through the floor.

I have a photo of Grandmother Harrison and my glowering nine-year-old mother sitting outside the Fun House. She was indignant when the blasts of air lifted her dress. Leslie was a tomboy, but this offended her. The Park was demolished in 1973 and now the space is occupied by condos and a popular sports bar, Maynards, just east of the Excelsior Commons green space shielded from development by the founders of the town.

Dining out on the lake during my youth did not require a line of credit. Haut cuisine was preceded by moderately priced dinner clubs without liquor licenses that allowed its guests to bring their own bottle(s), adding to the noise and merriment. I vividly remember eating at one with my family when a table of sloppy bibulous men, wearing riotously colored sport coats and strategically seated by the women's bathroom chanted a singsong, "*We know where you're going,*" every time someone headed toward that door.

The ultimate in casual Big Water dining was the floating drive-in restaurant that appeared one summer in the 1960s serving hamburgers, hot dogs and soft drinks as it prowled the lake for customers.

■ ■ ■

Decade after decade, from the Roaring Twenties to the Reagan Administration, Hart's Café in Wayzata was as iconic a fixture in the northern Lower Lake as the Excelsior Amusement Park rollercoaster was in the south. It was a converted Lamb Brothers dry goods store with the ambience of a family restaurant or a diner. There were six bowling lanes in the rear. My mother had dined there as a child. Every now and then Dad pulled the *Queen Merrie* into one of the café's boat slips, and we had a burger or a sandwich.

Hart's may evoke memories of rippling sails and twirling parasols from old Wayzata before gentrification, but it was at the forefront of the repeal of Prohibition around Lake Minnetonka where the "wets" and "drys" clashed. The town council had voted 25-7 to prohibit alcoholic beverages decades earlier. The seven nays were cast by men who had financial interests in the big hotels and resorts.

One could procure alcohol around the Big Water during the contentious period at speakeasies, blind pigs, drinking clubs and bootleggers. At least one of the grand hotels chose to ignore Prohibition altogether. Some patent medicines contained as much as 70-percent alcohol. Around the turn of the century, a bare-bones groggery operated sporadically on the northern end of Big Island. The bleat of a tin horn, heard on the mainland, signaled availability of freshly brewed suds.

Many towns around the lake had been dry for 50 years. Hart's received one of the first licenses to sell 3.2 beer when the Cullen-Harrison Act went into effect on April 7, 1933. This Act sounded the death knell for Prohibition. The repeal of the 18th Amendment was ratified by the final state, Utah, in December.

Bacon Drug, Excelsior
Photo courtesy of Excelsior Lake Minnesota Historical Society

Early downtown Excelsior
Old postcard

Tony's Barber Shop. Excelsior
Photo courtesy of Excelsior Barbers

After Hart's ran its course, a more upscale eatery – Sunsets – occupied the location for many years. Now coV, a self-described "*Coastal American Eatery*," has taken the spot on the east end of the Wayzata strip and essays to borrow its ambience and fare from Martha's Vineyard, Nantucket and Jay Gatsby's Hampton haunts.

> "*It's where Minnesota Nice meets East Coast Spice…*"
> "*…this original coV location combines Midwest comfort and hospitality with the unmistakable allure and energy of Nantucket or the Hampton's. The coastal environment and water views transform the Minnesota lakeside into a unique East Coast getaway.*"

Wayzata cOV Website

■ ■ ■

The Land of 10,000 Lakes has always had an inferiority complex regarding its rustic heritage when compared to areas with a longer historical and cultural pedigree. One apologist for the Upper Midwest waxed poetically that good old Wayzata is now an "*upscale town with a new age vibe.*"

After Labor Day is always a special time on Minnetonka. Boats are put in storage; fishing equipment and golf clubs are banished to the garage. Traffic on the Big Water is greatly reduced, and the weather and foliage can be sublime into October.

■ ■ ■

I know there is no fool like an old fool, and I understand that time marches on. No one needs to tell me that old-school residents of Lake Minnetonka tend to see it through a prism of rose colored, nostalgia-tinged glasses. Certainly, there has been much progress regarding water quality and the further east one ventures, the clearer the water. The southern basin of the Lower Lake between Excelsior and Crown Point contains the best clarity on the Big Water.

Sewers are required around the lake, even on Big Island. Farm run-off has been virtually eliminated. Phosphorus and nitrogen levels

Margaret Harrison and
Leslie Harrison at the Excelsior
Amusement Park, early 1930s
Fruen family photo

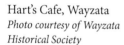

Hart's Cafe, Wayzata
*Photo courtesy of Wayzata
Historical Society*

The Fruen flag was
prominently displayed
on the Crown Point
flagpole right under
the stars and stripes.
Photo by Kelly Griffin

have plummeted. Invasive species such as Eurasian Milfoil and Zebra Mussels are being battled. Boaters are more closely monitored and are particularly watched for excessive alcohol consumption and dangerous watercraft operation. The struggle against residential development and recreational encroachment continues.

The latest threat to serenity and courtesy on the Big Water is the advent of Wave Boats, which range in cost from $80,000 to over $300,000. The expensive boats wreak havoc not only in the middle of the large bays but erode shorelines and foundations of the old boathouses perched on the waterline. The wake boaters ski and surf. The churning water makes it difficult to enjoy the lake. Speakers blast window-rattling music. Kayaks, canoes and small fishing boats are capsized by the inconsiderate pilots of many wake boats. "*Opponents...complain that the wakes, which rise several feet above the lake surface, ripple out and interfere with other water recreation... Last summer [2020], a woman suffered a broken vertebra when a wake boat tossed her motorized boat.*" (Katie Read, *Star Tribune*)

Images can be permanently imprinted. Our Crown Point flagpole was topped with the American flag and a navy-blue banner featuring Grandfather's signature in white positioned below the Stars and Stripes. It is reassuring to know that Uncle Dick's cremains are buried at the base of the flagpole. Our summer sentry in perpetuity.

Hiawatha Golf Course, the only public course in South Minneapolis
Courtesy of Steve Skaar

The Summer of 1969

*"We had the sky, up there, all speckled with stars and we
used to lay on our backs and look up to them, and discuss
whether they was made, or only just happened. Jim he
allowed they was made, but I allowed they happened; I
judged it would have took too long to make so many. Jim
said the moon could a laid them; well, that looked kind of
reasonable, so I didn't say nothing against it, because I've
seen a frog lay most as many, so of course it could be done.
We used to watch the stars that fell, too, and see them streak
down. Jim allowed they'd got spoiled and was hove out of
their nest."*

Mark Twain,

Huck Finn

IT WAS A CELESTIAL summer. A man on the moon. Comets and me-
teors traversed the sky as Fruens watched from the lookout on Crown
Point. We searched for the Northern Lights, craning our necks skyward
to watch the Sky Spirits perform their midnight dance. Staring straight
up at the night sky for a prolonged period played havoc with our equilibrium. Eventually, we staggered in an awkward, inadvertent dizzy ballet.
Our gymnastics were rewarded when we spotted the greenish glow in
the northern sky.

Summer came early that year. My parents gave me a trip to California for spring break as a graduation gift. I flew into LAX and took an
18-minute puddle jumper to Santa Barbara. The short flight offered a
view of the recently damaged Union Oil Platform A well and the massive three-million-gallon spill that resulted in a 35-mile-long oil slick
from Santa Barbara to Ventura. The disaster killed thousands of birds,
fish and sea mammals, began the country's environmental movement

Steve "Bones" Sondrall toying with the Hillovator
Photo courtesy of Steve Skaar

I am scolding Bones as he tinkers with the Hillovator, Annette is on my left.
Photo courtesy of Steve Skaar

and even provoked a visit from President Richard Nixon, not the nation's "greenist" President.

My elementary school friend Chris Briscoe had moved to California to live with his father six years prior, but we touched base annually when he visited Minneapolis and Lake Minnetonka in the summer. Even with our backs to the ocean, the view was striking. The narrow range of the Santa Ynez Mountains resembled the spiky spine of a Stegosaurus. (Fifty years later, Chris still remembers my reaction to the jaw-dropping beauty and his renewed appreciation of what had become familiar.) I will always value our friendship's ability to reveal insights and an epiphany or two through shared observations and adventures.

I spent a day at Santa Barbara High School with real live girls. The lunchroom was riotous, and I got to meet gung-ho gym teacher and tennis coach, Jack *"110-Percent-All-Out- Effort"* Teguera. Chris and I went to a party one night where I was cornered by a California Girl much more sophisticated than I who wanted to explore the nooks and crannies of my *raison d'etre*. At that point I had no personal philosophy other than getting out of high school and heading out into the Great Unknown. I knew that was not cosmic enough. I excused myself and walked away.

There was a very good band at the party, practicing more than performing. I was impressed by their name – Prufrock – a heady literary nod to T.S. Eliot's epic poem, "The Love Song of J. Edgar Prufrock," which included the line, *"Do I dare to eat a peach?"* They tried to recruit a bass player from the assembled to no avail and later launched into a fine rendition of the Beatles "Nowhere Man," which did not really require bass guitar.

Heading south, we stayed at an Anaheim hotel (for an hour or two before being evicted) the night before visiting Disneyland. Chris and I have always been interested in feats of athletic prowess. We had wrestling matches with the loser's watch being the grand prize. The battle was spirited and loud that night as nightstands went flying out from under the soon-to-be-broken lamps. After a few warnings, we were shown the door.

Unrepentant, we spent a few hours in the Magic Kingdom, continued south and crossed the Mexican border into Tijuana's infamous Zona Norte. We were accosted by countless scam artists and the denizens of dark bars like the San Souci and Bambi clubs that extolled the virtues of their shows and assorted depravities. I returned to Minnesota with a wealth of stories and an encyclopedic knowledge of surfer slang.

■ ■ ■

I had a summer job working at the city's Hiawatha Golf Course, a public version of the movie "Caddyshack." As the season progressed, the night sky darkened and, when lying on my back in the middle of a fairway, the immensity of the universe was humbling. I could locate a few constellations but except for the "Dippers," I did not know the names.

The youth of America were an economic force in 1969, and pop culture flourished. The anti-hero was king of the silver screen as "Easy Rider," "Midnight Cowboy" and "Butch Cassidy and the Sundance Kid" ruled at the box office. "Hogan's Heroes" and "The Dean Martin Show" were my favorite TV fare. Tommy James' "Crystal Blue Persuasion," Elvis Presley's "In the Ghetto" and Junior Walker's "What Does it Take?" seemed to be on every radio station. Somehow, I found the time to read Mario Puzo's *The Godfather* and Kurt Vonnegut's *Slaughterhouse Five*.

One afternoon I was driving and enjoying the 35-cents-per-gallon cost of gas and pulled behind a car at a stop light. When the light turned green, I peevishly laid on the horn when the vehicle in front did not move. A moment later and much to my horror, a fire truck raced through the intersection, horns screeching and red lights flashing. I sheepishly turned down the blaring Beach Boys song. Had my father known, it would have been no more "Fun, Fun, Fun" when Daddy took my ride away.

Never again would I feel so free, at ease, energized and confident. My 12-year run at a boy's school was complete, and I was giddy with excitement in anticipation of the next leg of my journey as the start of college loomed.

■ ■ ■

"I almost wish we were butterflies and liv'd but three summer days – three such days with you I could fill with more delight than fifty common years could ever contain." (John Keats, *Love Letters and Poems of John Keats to Fanny Brawne*)

It was the Summer of Annette. She was so lovely in every way. Impossibly, our relationship was chaste and passionate at the same time.

We rarely discussed our liaison. As if it was too delicate for the slightest verbalization or scrutiny. We spent every waking hour together when not plying our summer trades. Annette was a part-time telephone operator, and I would dial "0" until she picked up the call. I suffered from a case of temporal dislocation. The days were long and languid, but the weeks seemed to pass with warp speed.

Annette and I took advantage of an exquisite Minneapolis summer. One night when the heat and humidity had dissipated, we visited the rose garden adjacent to Lake Harriet – a place filled with a riot of color and fragrance. It was a gentle summer night. The kind poets substitute "zephyr" for "breeze." The bronze and marble fountain was purchased in Florence, Italy, and shipped to the 1-1/2-acre site after World War II. We sat on a tree stump and kissed. We were alone among thousands of roses representing hundreds of varieties.

We took advantage of some of the many cultural offerings of the Mill City, from the esteemed Guthrie Theatre to Dudley Riggs' Brave New Workshop, the longest running satirical, improvisational sketch comedy review in the United States. Shakespeare's *Julius Caesar* was not really my preferred type of play, and I was disappointed to discover the stoppage in the production was an intermission, not the conclusion.

Ironically, one of the goals of the Guthrie was to fill the void of classic theater left by the commercialization of Broadway. This appealed more to me than the Elizabethan era. I did not have access to complimentary Broadway tickets nor transportation to New York, but I would have rather seen *Hair*.

I had started visiting Dudley Riggs earlier in high school and loved the cynical lampooning of sacred cows and current events. The Vietnam War, President Nixon, the counterculture and other topical subjects provided ample fodder for the snarky, and sometimes dark, humor. The U.S. Army Chief of Staff in Southeast Asia was interviewed as if his forces were a football team and he was the head coach. General William Westmoreland was given a sports nickname, "Billy," and gave trite responses to the reporter's queries.

When asked, in a precursive ESPN style, about his "team's" prospects, the actor playing Westmoreland deflected with "coach speak," "*Well, we have a lot of rookies, a lot of vets….*" During intermission at the late Saturday show, Dudley Riggs himself purchased the early Sunday edition of the *Minneapolis Tribune* and put his comedic spin on the headlines while the performers prepared for the review's second act. Annette had an out-of-place smudge of rouge on her left cheek that night. I did not mention it. Our relationship had just begun, and I did not want to embarrass her. She seemed flawless to me.

■ ■ ■

Cast against my fairy-tale season was a summer of tumult. Four major historically significant events took place in less than thirty days spanning mid-July to mid-August. In addition to the lunar landing and Neil Armstrong's walk on the Moon were three other seismic occurrences, political, cultural and sociological, that resonate to this day.

On July 19, sketchy details began to flood world media outlets. U.S. Senator Ted Kennedy left the scene of an accident after the black Oldsmobile he was driving broke through the Dyke Bridge railing over Pucha Pond on Martha's Vineyard after attending a reunion for brother Bobby's 1968 female campaign staff members. Ted swam from the scene of the accident, leaving twenty-eight-year-old Mary Jo Kopechne to drown alone in the submerged vehicle. The tragedy, and the Senator's self-serving actions afterwards, effectively ended Kennedy's presidential aspirations. It also flickered the vestiges of the Kennedy Camelot legend.

The innocence and communal living experienced in the canyons of the Hollywood Hills gave way to paranoia and dread as mass murders, cults and celebrity trials entered the country's consciousness in early August 1969. Charles Manson was the master puppeteer directing his "Family" to carry out the gruesome murders of actress Sharon Tate and nine others.

While his motives remain cloudy, the 5-foot-2-inch, 125-pound Manson was a megalomaniac, albeit a cowardly one, who enticed others to carry out crimes to support him financially and to execute his grim, convoluted agenda. The murders, trial, and prosecutor Vincent Bugliosi's bestselling account, *Helter Skelter*, were not only seared into the nation's psyche but spawned a spate of true-crime non-fiction. Trust and idealism in the Southern California musical enclave suffered a severe jolt. Graham Nash of the supergroup CSN recounted, *"...up until then everybody's door was open, nobody gave a shit. Y'know, come on in, what the f&#@ - and then all of a sudden it was like: I gotta lock my car. I gotta lock my door. It was the beginning of the end....*" (Michael Walker, *Laurel Canyon: The Inside Story of Rock-and-Roll's Legendary Neighborhood*)

A few days later on the other side of the country, Nash performed in a much different kind of community, over 300,000 young people strong, in rural upstate New York. The Woodstock Music and Art Fair offered "Three Days of Peace and Music" and with a skeptical, wary world watching, the slogan delivered on its promise. The promoters had planned for a crowd of 50,000 but, when hundreds of thousands descended on Yasgur's Farm, the plans were useless.

Make no mistake: This was no bucolic garden party. Logistics were a nightmare. Roads to the festival were strewn with abandoned cars. Food supplies and bathroom facilities were overwhelmed, drug overdoses and acid trips gone wrong were an issue and – when the rain began – the dairy farm's pasture became a muddy quagmire. Hills of garbage were piled high. Amazingly the throngs, the townspeople, musicians and promoters faced the challenges together, not only averting disaster but creating a brief shining moment of solidarity amidst the chaos of the times and the doubters hoping the great event would fail.

"*...the Eden-like quality of the event had more to do with the idea of young people taking control over their lives, wresting their destinies away from the powers that were (parents, politicians, the draft board). It had to do with the still-relative newness of rock 'n' roll, the raw, naked power of an art form still struggling for recognition and respect. Music, at that time, was youth's lingua franca in the way that the Internet, cell phones and video games are today....*" (Reed Johnson, "What is Woodstock's Legacy?" *Chicago Tribune*)

Watching Woodstock from afar, the event was about the music. When the movie "Woodstock" was released, many epic performances were available for all the people who claimed to be there to finally see. The opening day turned into a salute to folk music due to issues of acts' inability to reach the site and the ease of setting up acoustic guitars and plugging them into amplifiers versus the heavy equipment needed to set up and power a full-blown rock band.

Richie Havens opened the festivities and energized the throngs with his open D tuning, percussive guitar-strumming style. The promoters encouraged Havens to extend his set to buy more time, and he mesmerized the crowd with what was to become his watershed, ad-libbed song, "Freedom."

"I don't know if you can, I don't know if, like how many people there are, man? Like I was rappin' to the fuzz, right, can you dig it? ...The New York Thruway is closed, man! That's far out, man!" (Arlo Guthrie, Woodstock, August 15, 1969)

Guthrie, John Sebastian and Joan Baez provided memorable performances that first evening. For the next two days set after set of outstanding music was delivered. In some instances, there were career-defining moments: Alvin Lee, Joe Cocker, Santana. The Who, Janis Joplin and Creedence Clearwater Revival rocked the crowd. Sly and the Family Stone made them dance. The Jefferson Airplane gave a Sunday morning greeting as Grace Slick advised, *"It's a new dawn!"*

Jimi Hendrix, part Cherokee, sported a jacket with fringe to match his moccasins and illustrated the counterculture's fascination with Native American customs. Hendrix was set to be the closing act of the festival on Sunday night but was pushed to Monday morning as most of the crowd had left, heading back to their daily routine. His performance was uneven, having jettisoned most of his band, The Experience, replacing them with poorly rehearsed musicians who muddled through many songs. Hendrix was also transitioning from San Francisco psychedelia to blues rock, which may have confused the band and audience alike.

The band caught up with its leader as the close was drawing near. A fiery thirteen-minute version of "Voodoo Chile (Slight Return)" was introduced by Jimi as the "new American anthem until we get another one." The song transitioned to his chaotic, definitive version of the Star Spangled Banner, bending strings to the limit and emitting a sonic display of improvisational virtuousity. The *New York Post*'s Al Aronowitz called it, *"the most electrifying moment of Woodstock, and it was probably the single greatest moment of the sixties."*

I had no desire to attend Woodstock. The idea of camping outside among tens of thousands (early estimate) of my peers did not appeal to me. I like sleeping on a nice clean pillow. But although I could not put my finger on it, something important had occurred. I was affected by the civil rights riots of North Minneapolis in 1967 and the Kennedy and King assassinations of 1968. Five cousins went to Vietnam and a sixth was advised to head to Canada.

Woodstock, in addition to being an aural *tour de force*, was about possibilities. For a moment, music was not about money as hundreds of thousands came together to enjoy brotherhood and sisterhood. Many attendees volunteered to help with the clean-up.

■ ■ ■

It was an exciting, confusing and frightening summer. I had one foot in the real world and the other planted in the comfort and familiarity of my hometown. Big Island was a constant when I was not working.

Hiawatha Golf Course was another Minneapolis Park Board reclamation project. Located in the south side of the city, Rice Lake, also called Mud Lake, was not much more than a marshy, mosquito breeding ground fit for cattails, frogs, turtles and not much else. The dredging of 1.2 million cubic yards of muck, however, created a fourteen-foot-deep lake renamed Lake Hiawatha. The displaced material was then used to fill the adjacent wetland to form the eighteen-hole golf course.

The project was originally completed in 1931 and, for decades, it was a money-maker for the city, catering to golfers from all over the demographic map including blacks, Native Americans, whites, kids, senior citizens, working class duffers, top-notch amateurs and suburbanites who returned to the old neighborhood to play.

During the summer of '69, I was a member of the Hiawatha "Crew," a tight-knit group of high school and college students who worked out of the golf course clubhouse. We collected greens fees, dispensed food, beverages, golf cart keys and the occasional dose of justice when disputes broke out on hot, muggy days when tempers were short, and gambling and cheating were involved.

Heavy dew decorated the grass as I left for a 5:30 A.M. shift. The rising sun shone with such intensity on the greenery along Minnehaha Parkway that it stung even with sunglasses. Bleary-eyed golfers subscribed to the *"hair of the dog"* remedy, and a few of my co-workers could have benefitted from an *"eye opener."*

There was a broad array of characters in the Crew and the other hangers-on that frequent golf courses. Nicknames proliferated: Wibby, Ma, Boobs, Beefo, Rhodie, Rose, Silent Frank, Nelly, Brumley, Gippy, Freddie, Season Ticket # 55, Bones, Big T, Nord Bottom, Bulldog, Nipper and Sprague. I was known as "Fru." We developed our own imitations and catchphrases, making light of the pandemonium that ensued during a typical day at Hiawatha.

The golfers provided endless entertainment. One ordered black coffee every weekend morning and, when the poured coffee neared the rim of the cup, he always stopped the process and advised, *"Leave a little for the Lord."* Joe meant Lord Calvert, the Canadian whiskey. His pint of spirits then appeared from thin air. Abe was a pull-cart guy and referred to himself as Season Ticket #55 when communicating with the staff. Abe always asked for *"a booklet of matches and an Eskimo Pie."*

One afternoon Al McGinnis, who could have been called "Slim," ordered a beer by name, "a Smitts." Steve "Bones" Sondrall, one of many "Crew" wise guys, quickly responded, *"Alvin, I can give you a Schmidt's, or I can give you a Schlitz, but I can't give you a Smitts."*

We sped around on golf carts, rooting out slow play and chasing kids who darted from their shrubbery and pine tree lairs to grab balls still rolling on the fairway. The kids then tried to sell the balls back to the original owners three holes later. Minnehaha Creek meanders through the back nine before entering and exiting Lake Hiawatha on the way to its final sprint over the Falls and into the Mississippi. Upon evicting young ones from the creek, the Crew played our own version of Volleyball with the net stretching over the streamlet anchored by a pole

Gallery at the Bronze Golf Tournament, Hiawatha Golf Course, 1971
Photo courtesy of Save Hiawatha

on each bank. The water softened our acrobatic dives and emboldened us to execute feats of daring.

We had a busy social calendar with parties on Big Island in parents' basements and on the golf course after hours. Blankets were strewn on the 16th fairway with snacks and beer provided courtesy of the Minneapolis Park Board. One night well after dark, two police vehicles raced toward us, fishtailing with lights flashing and sirens blaring.

A disembodied voice yelled, "*Anyone under 21 get out of here!*" I did not drink in high school, but I must have had a guilty conscience and ran to the bridge over the creek connecting the 13th and 16th fairways. I crawled under and hung upside down from the rafters like the troll from "Three Billy Goats Gruff."

Eventually, dizzy from my stint under the bridge, I staggered back to the party to a chorus of hoots, hollers and gales of laughter. I had been pranked. The squad cars were Park Police and they were in on the ruse. Marty Schuster also fell for it and climbed over the fence separating the golf course from the boulevard along Minnehaha Parkway. It was not the only occasion I was pranked that summer. In a time-honored tradition, I was asked to set the clock adorning the clubhouse fireplace chimney by sticking my hand up the flue. I never located the "dial," but my arm was black with soot and ash.

The most exciting event at Hiawatha was the annual Upper Midwest Bronze Golf Tournament. Originally called the Minnesota Negro Open Golf Tournament, the name was changed at the urging of the NAACP. The tourney started as an opportunity for black players who were not welcome at whites-only competitions unless they were caddies.

It was like a raucous family reunion with entrants from all over the Midwest: Chicago, Kansas City, Detroit, the Twin Cities and other locales. The celebration may have had its roots in golf, but the social aspect was just as important. The golfers displayed an astounding array of accessories including cars, jewelry and apparel. Hiawatha neighborhood residents grabbed lawn chairs to watch the cavalcade of vivid, colorful style in the middle of white-bread Minneapolis.

"'*Buba' Brown would have walked away with the grand prize for the loudest dressed golfer. He wore a blue-and-white polkadot shirt, tired worn-out jeans, a tri-colored tassle cap (green, red and yellow) and scuffed-up tan shoes that had seen better days. Green alligator golf shoes greeted the grass under the feet of Jimmie Slemmons, mayor of Bronzeville and one of the tournament promoters. His yellow and green combination was completed with pale yellow snickers, sox and striped shirt."* (Jane Brown, "Expert Golfers Walked Off with Prizes, but Colorful Attire Caught Eyes of Many," *Minneapolis Spokesman*)

Jimmie Slemmons was indefatigable. At the tournament's peak, it is estimated that 5,000 spectators crowded the roughs of the 18 holes. Not only the marketer, planner and gracious host, Jimmie worked tirelessly to accumulate gifts and prizes from his wide network of donors. Over the years, "The Bronze" attracted an array of celebrities including heavyweight boxing champ, and 1957 bronze winner, Joe Louis and Twins manager Billy Martin and his old Yankee teammate, Mickey Mantle. Everyone was welcome to play no matter their race. Hiawatha was the only municipal course in South Minneapolis and one of the few options for golfers of color in its first few decades. Tiger Woods visited in 1999 to kick off the First Tee Program, introducing the sport to city youth. He donated not only his time but money for improvements to the driving range.

■ ■ ■

The summer of 1969 was waning and, as I began to say my goodbyes, I knew I had been sublimating the conflicting emotions bubbling to the surface now that my departure for New England was imminent. The realization that my first love would be walking around the University of Minnesota campus among tens of thousands of young men began to register.

Annette and I went to Crown Point in late August to attend my father's 50th birthday party on the porch of the original cottage. For me, it served as a farewell to my family: parents, sister, brothers, sisters-in-law, nephews and niece, uncles and aunts. And a goodbye to Crown Point. I would return, but it would be different.

Post Script

*"Round a corner, turn a page, get born again, leave one
class for the next, trade in one school for another;
take one more step toward maturity.
You won't miss your past so much."*

J. Earp

I BEG TO DIFFER with Earp's quote. It just is not that simple. Lives, and places, have stages, transitions and rites of passage. Mid-August 1970 was such a time. My summer job was done, and I invited a group of college friends from our freshman year to spend a week on Big Island before heading back to school. Bill, Titus and Mike from New York, Rob from Vermont, Dan from California, and Scott from Ohio were the co-conspirators as well as Marty and Jim from Minnesota.

Although we were progressing to manhood, this was an opportunity to hold onto boyhood for a moment, reminiscent of Mark Twain's Tom and Huck. Our base of operation was the Chalet. Sleeping bags were strewn about both levels. I may have pulled rank and slept on the brown couch, contorting around the broken springs. I would like to say we were lulled to sleep by the lapping waves poetically kissing the shoreline, but we were too tired to appreciate the sounds and rhythms.

It seems cliché, but the weather was ideal. The temperatures were typical for an Upper Midwest August and created the perfect environment for swimming, skiing and playing touch football on the sands of Cruiser's Cove on the thin neck of Big Island.

My parents were staying in the Brick House and hosted the eight rising college sophomores downstairs, giving us our space while graciously feeding us and tolerating our antics. We had a turntable in the Chalet to prevent the LPs from melting in the sun; the speakers were strategically placed outside for optimal listening. I remember hearing

Led Zeppelin II blasting over the water at one point.

We ventured from Minnetonka for some sightseeing around the Minneapolis lakes and finished our tour at Minnehaha Falls. We attended a Twins baseball game where the out-of-towners acquired a taste for Grain Belt Premium beer and kept the vendors running. Jim's and Marty's parents hosted impressive outdoor dinners and, although the latter required a car trip, we arrived at Jim's house in Cottagewood by boat, five minutes from our Crown Point headquarters.

The Easterners were introduced to Minnesota sweet corn-on-the-cob and consumed voluminous amounts. Anytime we ventured from the island all eight of us squeezed into the battle-tested Alumacraft *Queen Merrie* and sped away. Except for the few planned events, we created the daily schedule as we went. It was easy to reach consensus.

We celebrated the waning summer before the demands of college intruded on our last gasps of childhood. It was a magical week fondly remembered by the participants – even though it is now 50-plus years in our rear-view mirrors. Still, there was something in the breeze. A terminus. It was as if those seven days were an epilogue to the golden years on Big Island.

Summer's End: Dan, Ross and Scott
Photo courtesy of Marty Schuster

Hurwitz Photography

With Thanks

It takes a village to create a book that people will buy and hopefully read. Well, I have some intelligent and creative neighbors.

The Talent

Editor, Nan Wisherd
Graphic Designer, Jackie Pechin
Cover Designer, Larry Verekyn
Sounding Board, Christopher Briscoe
Art, Anica Fruen
Marketing, Kate Crowley
Photography and Flagpoles, Kelly Griffin

Executive Storytellers

Louise Fruen Barnett

Douglas E. Fruen

Other Raconteurs

Paul Maravelas

Richard W. Fruen

Cheryl Fruen Broady

Craig Fruen

Todd Fruen

Tracy Fruen Bregman

Mike Melander

The Chronicler

David C. Smith

Keepers of the Flame

Carver County Historical Society

Minnesota History Center

Excelsior Lake Minnetonka Historical Society

Wayzata Historical Society

Special Thanks

To my wife, Kristin, who supports me, offers suggestions and puts
up with the colossal messes I make in multiple rooms

And Finally

To the countless people who shared my family's good fortune –
in Minneapolis and on Lake Minnetonka.

Ross Fruen
November 2022

Selected Bibliography

Alumacraft Corporation, Ad Copy

Belonsky, Andrew, "How the Log Cabin Became an American Symbol," *Mental Floss*

Benais, Eddie Benton, Ojibwe stories passed down from Grandfather

Boston Globe

Boston Herald

Brown, Allen, "Minneapolis vs. St. Paul"

Butterfield, Frank, "Recollections of the Battle of Shakopee"

Chicago Times

Christianson, Lydia, "Glimpses Into West Big Island," *Sun Sailor*

Cooper, Karen E., *When Minnehaha Flowed With Whiskey*

Crane, Stephen, "The Open Boat"

Damascus Way, website

Deephaven Historical Society Newsletter, Summer Report, 2004

Dimensions Newsletter

Dregni, Eric, *By the Waters of Minnetonka*

Elet, Elizabeth Fries, "Summer Rambles in the West"

Epps, Garrett, "The Man Who Battled Death to a Draw," *The Atlantic*

Etten, Richard, "At look at the Geologic History of the Wayzata Area," swnewsmedia.com

Fagerberg, Jerard, *Minnesota Monthly*

Fitzgerald, F. Scott, "The Ice Palace" and "A Night at the Fair"

Fruen, Henrietta Bergquist, "Recollections of a Pioneer"

Gray, Dick, "Icy Origin Determines Lake Minnetonka Character," Green, William, "Why This Started in Minneapolis"

Hallberg, Jane King, *Minnehaha Creek, Living Waters*

Hiemstra, Harlan, Minnesota DNR

Holder, Sarah, "Why Did This Start in Minneapolis"

Johnson, Frederick, *The Big Water: Lake Minnetonka and Its Place in Minnesota History*

Journalette, Minneapolis Rotary Newsletter

Krohn, Tim, "Grumpy Old Men on Ice," *The Free Press*

Lake Area Explorer

Larson, Paul Clifford, *A Place at the Lake*

Longfellow, Henry Wadsworth, "Song of Hiawatha"

Lynes, Russell, *Snobs*

Maravelas, Paul, conversations and presentations

McKenna, Dr.James, letter

Melvin, Karen and Bette Hamel, *Legendary Homes of Lake Minnetonka*

Meyer, Ellen Wilson, *Tales from Tonka* and *Happenings around Deephaven*

Michener, James, *Chesapeake*

Mihelich, Josephine, *Andrew Peterson and the Scandia Story*

Mill City Museum, website

Minneapolis Business Journal

Minneapolis Chronicle

Minneapolis Journal

Minneapolis Park and Recreation Board, "Pearl Park"

Minneapolis Star

Minneapolis Tribune

Moberg, Vilhelm, *The Emmigrants*

New York Times

Northwest Organizer

Parker, Sharon, *Minneapolis Observer Quarterly*

Peterson, Andrew, *Diaries of Andrew Peterson: Swedish-American Horticulturist*

Richards, Bergman, *The Early Background of Minnetonka Beach*

Riggs, Missionary Stephen, Dakota Observations

Roberts, Kate, *Minnesota 150*

St. Paul Express Editorial Board

St. Paul Globe

St. Paul Pioneer Press

Schwartz, Eddie, memoirs

Scribner, Duane, *Until All are Housed in Dignity*

Scriver Family, family memories

Shaw, Lois Griswold as told to John Mugford, "Legendary Boat to Remain on Lake"

Shefchik Rick, *From Fields to Fairway*

Smith, David C., *City of Parks: The Story of Minneapolis Parks,* "The Worst Idea Ever" and "The Mother of All Minneapolis Golf Courses, Bryn Mawr I"

Tesson, Sylvain, *The Consolations of the Forest*

Thoreau, Henry David, "A Lake is the Earth's Eye"

Twain, Mark, *Life on the Mississippi* and *Huck Finn*

Wayzata coV website

Westerman, Gwen and Bruce White, *Mni Sota Makoce*

Wingerd, Mary Lethert, *North Country*

Winstead, Lizz, *Lizz Free or Die*

Wood, David, *The Griswold-Nordin-Fruen House*

Index